THE BRIEFER PSYCHOTHERAPIES

"A flexible approach, based on sound general principles of psychodynamics and adjustable to the great variety of those in need is ... a pressing necessity of our day."

FRANZ ALEXANDER (4)

The Briefer Psychotherapies

by **LEONARD SMALL, Ph.D.**

*Chief Consulting Psychologist, Altro Health
and Rehabilitation Services, New York City*

*Adjunct Associate Professor, Department of
Psychology, Graduate School of Arts and
Sciences, New York University*

BRUNNER / MAZEL Publishers • New York

BUTTERWORTHS • London

To

VERNA
AND
DAVID

Introduction

In our unsure society mental health plays an even more crucial role than usual: there is less of a margin for irrationality in any sphere of functioning, without dire consequences for us all.

Speaking only statistically, emotional problems have attained epidemic proportions, by the accounts of the Midtown Study, the Stirling County Study and others. Community mental health perforce becomes an important part of community health in general. It is part of the economic situation ($20,000,000,000 a year for patient care) and part of the problems of the body politic, as it plays a role in every facet of daily community life.

Primary prevention and very early secondary prevention will have to play an increasing role in mental health care. The briefer psychotherapies are ideally suited to this need. They can do most of the job in these two areas, and some in the field of tertiary prevention—the minimizing of chronicity.

Doctor Small's volume provides an excellent guide to these crucial briefer therapies. While insisting on conceptual clarity and a sound theoretical foundation, he is very flexible in his approach: he is willing to adapt the method of treatment to the needs of the patient and to those of the existing situation. He is able to be therapeutically efficacious without compromising standards of soundness.

Brief psychotherapy has as much of a place in private practice as it does in community mental health clinics. If word of this fact gets around, many more people might be referred to us for treatment, many more in need of it might come. To be sure, nothing said in favor of brief psychotherapy should be construed as speaking against the proper place and function of longer therapies, including classical psychoanalysis.

The last statement was necessary because black and white thinking is so prevalent. This fact takes me back to my concerns with community mental health. So much energy and thinking went into planning mental health services as a delivery system, that the goods to be delivered have often become quite shoddy. Before we get to the point of having a splendid postal service with *nothing* to deliver, it will be useful for all concerned to steep themselves again in sound knowledge of what makes people tick and how to help them do it with less maladaptation.

This present volume would be a good way for many to start doing it.

LEOPOLD BELLAK, M.D.

Contents

TABLE OF CONTENTS *(Cont'd)*

TABLE OF CONTENTS *(Cont'd)*

TABLE OF CONTENTS *(Cont'd)*

TABLE OF CONTENTS *(Cont'd)*

Foreword

When, in 1965, Leopold Bellak and I published *Emergency Psychotherapy and Brief Psychotherapy*, we reported our personal efforts in both private and public practice to develop and apply a brief psychotherapy. We had evolved one based upon the psychoanalytic conceptualization of personality and employing every available therapeutic intervention we could justify by the most rigorous application of our theoretical grasp. Lewis R. Wolberg's collection of papers by lecturers at the Postgraduate Center was published in 1965 just before our book was released. And D. H. Malan's superb book, although appearing in America in 1965 simultaneously with its publication in England, was unheralded and not yet reviewed.

Why another? ("Few books today are forgivable," Laing wrote in 1967, giving pause to all authors.) This volume emerges because for four years I have included brief psychotherapy in my practice, and I have followed a trail of study acquainting me with the innovative and creative work of many dedicated psychotherapists. The pursuit was like a bird-dog at work, following an erratic, meandering scent, from journal to book to journal and back again, crisscrossing the same ground but always moving ahead. The need for an organized presentation of this valuable material became clear. But as reading and writing progressed, a monograph grew to a volume. With it I seek these ends:

I wish to make readily available in a cogently organized form the wisdom and the experience of the surprisingly large number of therapists who have penetrated the "time-barrier" in psychotherapy. Others, I believe, will benefit as I have from comprehension of the processes of time-condensed treatment and from the light it sheds upon related processes in longer-term therapy.

I seek to proseletyze, to call attention to the impressive record of directed, intentional short-term psychotherapy. I wish to foster its acceptance, to help make it ever more available to a society that is becoming increasingly insistent upon the dignity, the well-being and good health of all its citizens. We cannot afford to minimize, and there is no danger that we can exaggerate, the need for mental-health assistance at every level of our society, in every community, for all colors and conditions of man. The briefer psychotherapies are one effort to meet that need; they are an indispensable effort if we are not to rely solely upon mood-directing medications. My hope is that this book will contribute to an increased awareness in government officials and community leaders that these effective and parsimonious therapies exist, and that it will provoke interest among psychotherapists in developing their skills in brief methods and in using them for the welfare of larger numbers of people.

I seek also the attention of students, to whom a part of my life is dedicated. The student I have seen in recent years seems in some respects in the position of a moon, trapped by the equal and competing gravitational pull of two planets. His scientific and professional models —his teachers—once the very *avant garde* of daring in conceptualization of human behavior, are now the traditionalists. These teachers have themselves usually been trained under the psychoanalytic influence in which a therapist in the course of his professional life may assist in a significant change in the personal lives of one or two hundred people. This model is influential, and many students are reluctant to learn brief therapy because its practice violates the model.

But an opposing pull comes from the sense of responsibility for and the responsiveness to the needs of that larger portion of the population for whom there will be no psychotherapy if the only therapy is long-term. Many students now want their effectiveness to be more far-reaching and their lifetime responsibility to be more socially oriented than the traditional model allows. The briefer psychotherapies are one road they may take in developing their own model, in which the knowledge gained from their intensive study of the individual can also be used for the quicker benefit of the many.

Acknowledgment

This book, like most books, has many roots, and I am indebted to many people for either their implicit and indirect or their explicit and most direct help. One indirect source of guidance I acknowledge with fond memory is the influence of my teachers of thirty years ago —Robert Griggs, Ira Hansen and Edith Mortensen—in developing my respect for description and classification, for structure and function, for growth and change.

To have good friends who are also good colleagues is great good fortune, and I am thus fortunate. Leopold Bellak, with soft heart and tough mind, helped with comments on many sections of the manuscript and specifically with the technical sections on drug and ECT therapies, as did Irwin Greenberg. Colleagues gave me leads to papers and books, to techniques and approaches. For help in this way I am indebted to Celia Benney, Jack Chassan, Wilbur Morley, Marcia Pollock, Amy Vanesky and Allen Williams.

Ruth Lentz patiently produced copy from handwritten notes, scrawls on envelopes, erratically typed pages and numerous Ediphone discs of sometimes dubious audibleness. I am deeply grateful to her.

The best has been saved for last. This book has been a family affair. My son David grappled the bibliography into its present state, giving it a single, sensible organization. My wife Verna did yeoman library work, abstracting and codifying papers, suggesting emphases, structures, and approaches to organization of the material. Her rare combination of editorial skill and knowledge of the material is very much present in this book. She cheerfully accepted the requirement that the book be part of our vacation last summer, and made both the daily work and play times possible. And so it was a happy vacation and this a happy book.

LEONARD SMALL

New York.
June, 1970.

THE BRIEFER PSYCHOTHERAPIES

I

BACKGROUND

CHAPTER 1

Beginnings and Growth

Brief psychotherapy is at least as old as Freud's efforts to find a cure for the neuroses. As modern psychotherapy owes its origins to psychoanalytic theory, so too does the concept of a brief psychotherapy. Historically, it is clear that Freud first sought a quick cure; when he began he could not foresee the developments that would lengthen the psychoanalytic process. Freud believed that to know the cause of a neurosis would lead promptly to its solution and resolution; his early emphasis was upon a quick diagnosis of the psychodynamics involved and their undoing through active interpretation.

Ferenczi was not the first activist in Freudian circles; Freud himself was. Jones (110) describes Freud's quick and apparently permanently effective treatment of the composer Gustav Mahler. Bruno Walter (234) recounts his treatment by Freud in six sessions in 1906. Even before, in *Studies on Hysteria* (27), Freud described his venture into the emergency treatment of an hysterical girl whom he encountered while on a mountain vacation.

3

Fenichel (60) recommends that those interested in brief psychotherapy re-read *Studies on Hysteria,* for they will find there many of its problems either solved or at least identified and discussed, even before psychoanalysis had been developed.

In those early days of the development of psychoanalysis, length of time was not a major consideration. The contrasting concepts of brief and long-term therapies did not appear until after psychotherapy and psychoanalysis had evolved into the lengthy processes they now are. Concern about the length of treatment emerged as Freud's theoretical comprehension of personality development and neurotic formation enlarged. As he sought a solution for the problems of resistance, psychoanalytic therapy lengthened steadily. Then, over the years, trained psychoanalysts undertook relatively isolated and sporadic searches for psychotherapeutic procedures that, while derived from psychoanalytic comprehension of personality formation and development, would produce therapeutic change in shorter time. As early as 1941, the Chicago Institute for Psychonalysis sponsored a national meeting, a Council on Brief Psychotherapy. If there was a consensus among the papers given, it was that a brief therapy derived from psychoanalytic comprehension of personality is possible. Alexander's approach, based on rigorous application of theory mixed with humane sensitivity for a suffering person, was apparent and his influence strong. Proceedings (174) were issued; copies are hard to locate today.

The superlative book by Franz Alexander and Thomas French, *Psychoanalytic Therapy* (4), appeared in 1946 to throw a strong clear light on the path toward a briefer psychotherapy derived from psychoanalytic comprehension of both personality and the process of psychotherapy. Creative and dedicated men, they sought with the collaboration of their colleagues at the Chicago Institute for Psychoanalysis to "define those basic principles which make possible a shorter and more efficient means of psychotherapy . . ." The light they shed continues to illuminate the field; it has not been extinguished by attrition nor replaced by any radically new theory or approach. Almost all of the subsequent efforts at a briefer approach are indebted to their search among the "manifold intricacies of human behavior" for the most suitable and efficient treatment for each *individual.*

Little further was reported during the 40's except in military hospitals, or during the next decade, to reflect the actual fact that brief psychotherapy was a growing reality. Lindemann's (137) investigation of the survivors of the Coconut Grove nightclub fire in Boston, and his enunciation of immediate procedures for intervention, almost alone advanced the concepts of emergency psychotherapy evolved during the war and enunciated by Grinker (174) and Kardiner (114).

In recent years, intensification of interest in briefer psychotherapy is marked by the publication of perhaps a half dozen books, a large number of papers and the emergence not of *a* brief therapy but *the briefer therapies*—varieties of crisis intervention, of behavioral treatments, family therapies, and others in healthy number.

The effort in this book is a consolidated review of the several brief psychotherapies now reported in the literature. Beyond stated theories and described techniques, I have sought the common denominators, those statements of fact, theory, observation and outcome that occur often enough to be credited with reliability; upon these dependable brief procedures can be established to meet the growing need for them. In a field marked by great variety, to which each contributor brings distinctively individual qualities, the search has not been easy.

THE EXPANDING DEMAND

As early as 1919, Freud (66) foresaw the possibility that psychoanalytic techniques would not be adequate for the demands placed upon the mental-health community. He wrote then, "At present, we can do nothing in the crowded ranks of the people, who suffer exceedingly from neuroses." He went on, however, to warn that ". . . one may reasonably expect that at some time or other the conscience of the community will awake and admonish it that the poor man has just as much right to help for his mind as he now has to the surgeon's means of saving life; and that the neuroses menace the health of a people no less than tuberculosis and can be left as little as the latter to the feeble handling of individuals." He foresaw that clinics would be developed to which analytically-trained personnel would be appointed, so that men could be prevented from succumbing to alcoholism, women helped with their burdens of privations, and children given an alternative to running wild or to developing a neurosis. He foresaw that this treatment should be free—and he concluded, "The task will then arise for us to adapt our technique to the new condition." He warned that psychoanalysts would ". . . need to find the simplest and most natural expression for theoretical doctrines." He believed it likely that psychoanalysis would have to be combined with direct suggestion, that even hypnotic influence would again find a role in the armamentarium of psychotherapy. He saw this as an alloying of the "pure gold of analysis" with the "copper" of these other methods.

And in 1965, Avnet (7), reporting upon an insurance plan for short-term psychotherapy, stated baldly, "Long-term reconstructive psychoanalysis, irrespective of its merits . . . cannot seriously be considered in the search for a solution to the massive dilemma of mental illness."

The Deterrents

Many psychoanalysts have been loathe to assign much credence to the efficacy of a short-term therapeutic effort. They are joined in their reluctance by psychotherapists whose approach to behavioral comprehension and modification is psychoanalytic in its origin. They are, in short, resistant to briefer methods, even for different goals.

Coleman (47) in 1960 contends that interest in brief psychotherapy must overcome the greater interest among therapists in the more extensive forms of psychotherapy. These extensive forms enjoy a prestige and status of such a nature and degree that the therapist doing brief work will often not acknowledge it, nor will he give to the "brief" worker much recognition. Brief psychotherapy, especially emergency therapy, Coleman states, has manifest theoretical, technical and public-health importance, but has not enjoyed formal professional attention. The phenomenon in some respects is not understandable, since the literature indicates that emergency therapy particularly has long been a regular feature of both private and clinic practice. Coleman believes that the almost mythical status held by the longer-term forms are responsible for this denial, that therapists may be somewhat embarrassed by their own brief techniques, believing them to be less than understandable in psychoanalytic terms and considered unscientific by their peers.

Psychoanalytic practice and theory during the past several decades have expanded and complicated the criteria of improvement, moving from a rather limited focus on alleviation and amelioration of emotional distress into a broader concept that is philosophical in nature. Frank (65) observes "As a result, the boundaries of mental illness became more and more vague, as did the indication for psychotherapy. Eventually psychotherapy was considered to be applicable to all forms of human suffering in which a psychological component was involved." The goal of psychotherapy concomitantly was expanded from a relatively precise and limited one of complaint improvement to the more nebulous one of developing the individual's emotional maturity and/or personality integration.

Stierlin (216) calls attention to the paradox that recognized need for psychotherapy has increased as psychoanalysis has become longer and longer. Perhaps recollecting the biological theory of recapitulation, Stierlin also notes that as in its early days psychoanalysis was of short duration and produced dramatic results and since 1914 has gotten longer and longer, so each analyst in his own career recapitulates analytic history, often starting with quick and dramatic successes and later finding the very same disorders less reachable.

For brief psychotherapies to be developed by psychoanalytically-trained therapists, aims and goals had to be separated from those of the long-term therapies. More than that, recognition of the value and utility of short-term goals and procedures had to grow among these practitioners. Two recent papers reflect this development. The concept of parsimony is introduced by Gillman (76) who finds that brief psychotherapy is not in contradiction to psychoanalytic psychotherapy. He believes that for 10 percent of the patients he sees, a parsimonious approach is the treatment of choice. This, he adds, is about the same percentage as those who are suitable for classical psychoanalytic approaches. Psychoanalysis is a suitable therapy for only a small group of patients, states Burdon (29); other techniques must be devised to provide effective psychotherapy for the majority of patients.

The Impetus

The impetus for the search for effective briefer methods has come from two facts. Ever larger numbers of people, most of whom can afford neither the expense of psychoanalysis or long-term psychotherapy, nor the loss of their earning hours that these processes require, recognize a pressing need for psychological treatment. The already short supply of trained psychotherapists is thus increasingly insufficient.

In World War II, the war-generated need for psychotherapeutic services for the first time in history coincided with a level of development and knowledge in the psychotherapeutic community that made some response possible. Grinker (174) states that brief psychotherapy derived from psychoanalytic principles was the "only" new treatment in response to war demands. Socarides (211) reporting on the usefulness of brief psychoanalytic contacts observes that the increasing demands for analytic therapy would lead away from lengthy procedures toward brief therapy that might prove to be effective.

One general hospital in New Haven experienced an increase of 400 percent in the use of their psychiatric emergency room that was not related to an increase in the population served (44). This increased use probably may be attributed to increased perception in the community of the hospital's practical value, as well as improved services and methods for delivering them. The New Haven hospital identified significant numbers of problems requiring brief psychotherapy and responsive to it.

Great demands for therapeutic services are sometimes expressed in day-to-day pressure. Romano (174) reports on a short experience in a hospital where he felt compelled to formulate "empirical categories" of patients and approaches because of both the numbers of patients and the pressing need of many of them for immediate help.

Fenichel (60) spoke of brief psychotherapy as ". . . the child of bitter practical necessity. This eternal necessity is now—due to social conditions—rapidly increasing."

Wayne and Koegler (237) believe that psychotherapy is unavailable to most people because of the time-consuming problems, and that unless procedures are abbreviated, most people would go unaided. Phillips and Wiener (172) identify the needs of nearly 18 million people in the United States for some kind of psychotherapy as the "silent" need, one seldom verbalized though sensed by both sufferer and the public.

The plight of disturbed elderly people has enlisted the attention of Goldfarb and Turner (79). They believe that all such people merit a trial of brief psychotherapy, since in their experience many such individuals have been able to remain at home instead of requiring transfer to a mental hospital.

Wolberg (243) calls attention to the "great disparity" between the number of people in need of psychotherapy and the personnel available to provide this assistance." Wolf (247) highlights the role that prepaid health and insurance plans are playing in increasing the demand for psychotherapy.

Pearlman discussing Speer's (212) 1962 study of brief psychotherapy with college women calls attention to the population explosion in higher education. Thirty-one percent of the youth 18 to 21 years of age were then in college, a total of 3,450,000 young men and women. He cites Bureau of Census figures predicting that within less than a decade, 44 percent of the individuals in this age range, approximately 6,400,000, may be expected to be attending institutions of higher learning. Pearlman believes that this population explosion will be accompanied by a need for more vigorous attention to the emotional problems of late adolescent students.

The rediscovery in America of poverty is cited by Strean and Blatt (220) as responsible for dramatically bringing into focus the question of therapeutic need and appropriateness. They contend that conventional long-term "talking therapy" is repugnant to members of lower socio-economic classes, who tend to be less verbal and more action oriented.

Jacobson (105) comments further on the discernible gap between the intention to serve the entire population and the relative lack of service to patients from the lower socio-economic classes. He observes that at every stage of the out-patient treatment process, individuals from lower socio-economic groups are less likely to be accepted as patients than are persons higher on the socio-economic scale. They are less likely to persevere throughout the duration of treatment. He notes that these observations hold for both private practice and community-supported clinics both private and public.

The compelling necessity for mental-health professions to provide more adequate services for the poor is stressed by Normand et al. (163). They fear that emergency, trouble-shooting, walk-in clinics will tend to follow traditional patterns of treatment (i.e., long-term insight-oriented). They plead that clinics instead develop new, more flexible approaches, and observe that experience in working with the lower socio-economic population has lead to reformulation of goals and treatments so that psychotherapeutic intervention has now taken on broader meaning.

Bellak and Small (20) believe that the increasing public demand for psychotherapeutic services, stimulated by the successes of psychoanalysis, makes the development of an adequate brief psychotherapy based on psychoanalytic principles a necessity lest the valuable insights of psychoanalysis be lost through their replacement by drug-centered treatment emphases. They see the purpose as twofold: to meet the increasing need that cannot be met by the present supply of psychotherapists with long-term therapy, and to try to preserve the contributions of psychoanalytic theory in the face of developing reliance upon socially available psychotropic medication.

THE RESPONSE TO THE DEMAND

Freud's prediction appears to be coming to pass. The demand is indeed eliciting government expansion of community mental-health services, proliferation of prepaid health insurance programs at the insistence of both employees and employers, and manifest efforts in the professional community to devise methods to meet the challenge. The supply of trained personnel has not been and probably cannot be expanded to meet this need; one alternative is to search for an effective shortening of the therapeutic process.

Prevention

The preventive role of brief psychotherapy is increasingly recognized. In connection with theory and technique for the treatment of acute grief reactions, Lindemann (137) observed in 1944 that the responses to traumatic experiences have become of great importance in mental-health practice, whether they develop into clearcut neuroses or not. Bereavement, the sudden cessation of social interaction, is of special interest because it is often implicated as a psychogenic factor in psychosomatic disorders. The prolonged war situation in the world has brought a great increase in grief reactions; Lindemann's work stresses that distorted grief reactions can be transformed into a normal pattern of mourning that will lead to resolution.

Klein and Lindemann (118) extend the preventive hypothesis further, stating their belief that general clinical services which emphasize prevention and health promotion can in time be made widely available to the public. The most effective deployment of therapeutic mental-health resources would be upon specific subgroups at times of specific life challenges which predictably bring about heightened tensions. They are concerned with preventive interventions which they observe differ from ego therapies of brief duration which have been developed during the past decades. Preventive intervention as they see it extends assessment beyond the intrapsychic structure and dynamics to social roles and relationships. There is thus a shift of emphasis to "the individual enmeshed in a social network."

The importance of a brief therapy in permitting intervention without delay is a critical element in providing early access and preventing chronic developments, according to Jacobson *et al.* (106). They observe too that the brief approach permits the optimal use of available manpower.

The effectiveness of brief therapy in a preventive capacity is discussed further by Lindemann and Dawes (138) who discovered that examination of careful histories, accompanied by concomitant studies of a child and the child's parents, the home and the school, always revealed that the difficulties had started in pre-school years but had not been recognized.

Kris (125) found that brief psychotherapy prevented or decreased the need for re-hospitalization of schizophrenic patients, thus avoiding in many cases loss of income and the breakup of homes. Koegler (121) recommends brief psychotherapy as a method of preventing development of schizophrenia in neurotic children and adolescents. Bellak and Small (20) cite the use of brief psychotherapy during episodic crises in a person's life to prevent the development of more malignant or chronic processes.

Wayne and Koegler (237) note that most emergencies are preceded by an "urgent" phase during which the individual is accessible to help and when treatment, if provided, could avoid the development of an acute crisis. Bellak (21) describes three types of prevention influences to be exerted by brief emergency psychotherapy: primary prevention in preventing a minor, temporary problem from becoming a major, organized disability; secondary prevention in restricting and minimizing the effects of a full-fledged disorder; tertiary prevention in confining and limiting the effects of a chronic disability.

Coleman and Zwerling (45) find that in the United States the great progress in the development of facilities for the care of out-patients has lead to an enormous response to these facilities, with an early detrimental effect observed in the fact that waiting lists for the services soon extend to six and to twelve months. This lag curtails the clinic's power to deal with the onset of illness, so that they lose their preventive power to forestall the deep incorporation of illness into the personality. They see the emergency clinic particularly as a device for preventing the development of more severe or chronic illnesses.

Farberow (58) also emphasizes the preventive aspects of inter-vention in critical situations. His many years of experience in the crisis treatment of suicidal threats leads him to believe that suicide-prevention services will gradually broaden their interest toward the broad area of emergency mental health, encompassing all crises. He sees the effort directed toward prevention rather than primarily as a limited intervention.

More Direct Community Responsibility

Ross (192), discussing the Social Psychiatry Plan developed by Dr. Arie Querido for Amsterdam in the Netherlands, stresses the im-portance of brief therapy in keeping people within the community rather than isolating them in special-purpose hospitals. Ross agrees that society must learn to keep all kinds of people within its operating scope, that everyone can do some useful work and should remain in society as long as possible. The effect, of course, in addition to reducing the cost of isolating institutions, is to keep disturbed persons involved in the community and the community involved with all its own. Ad-vocates of the importance of keeping disturbed people within the community comment upon improved prognosis, as well as the pre-vention of the chronicity induced by "the insult upon injury" import of hospitalization. The effect of making the disturbed less disturbing to those around them seems to have two-way benefits.

Crises and Emergencies

The role of a brief psychotherapy in crisis or emergency situations —ever more widely accepted—is examined by a number of authors.

Glascote (77) advocates the emergency service as a way of helping society become accustomed to dealing intimately with disturbed individuals, even when the disturbance is severe. The emergency service demonstrates to society that these pople can be dealt with effectively and safely within the community and returned promptly to an active and productive life. He also sees the emergency service as cutting down the delays now experienced at most mental-health services, delays that contribute to the exacerbation of serious conditions. Bellak (17) wrote of emergency psychotherapy as a procedure for saving life in severe depressions. Hansen (95) finds that many medical situations carry with them a "second diagnosis" of a critical emotional disturbance which if treated as emergent will cease to exacerbate the medical disability.

Bellak and Small (20) observe that many people seek psychotherapy *only* in crisis, while the course of almost every life moves through situations which may lead to major psychological problems— birth, marriage, death, injury, children in trouble, parents in disagreement, financial stress.

Quick and effective help in such situations can result in a decrease in pain, a shortening of the disturbed period, and a greater realization in the individual's life. Lewin (135) finds the very prevalence of human stress to be indication of the need for brief therapy. A plea for a briefer psychotherapy was made by Flanders Dunbar (174) over two decades ago, in order to ameliorate "the inter-relationship of man and his life's realm." We must respond to the "cry for help" urges Resnick (182) and establish networks of communication whereby these cries may readily be heard and answered.

The American Psychiatric Association (63) directs attention to the consequences of disaster situations likely to produce extreme emotional disturbances requiring quick, effective and wide-scale therapeutic services. Meerloo (148) and Rosenthal (191) among others, have written about the treatment of traumatic reactions to disaster situations. Bellak and Small (20) comment that more narrowly confined disasters, such as an explosion within a building in New York City that undoubtedly traumatized many of the survivors, might well bring into play the services of emergency psychotherapeutic teams. The Beekman Downtown Hospital in New York City now has a mobile emergency psychiatric team which goes to the sites of disasters within its locality.

Recognition of Other Pressures

The orientation of the behavioral therapist (Phillips and Wiener, 171) is that he practices brief psychotherapy since brevity is inherent in behavioral psychotherapy, which he holds to be the most effective available approach.

Crabtree and Graller (51) cogently observe that the effective range of contact with a patient in a military setting is so short as to demand an effective brief therapy.

Most people presenting themselves to general-hospital emergency rooms with emotional problems are not accessible to psychoanalytically-oriented therapy, report Coleman and Errera (44). They observed that the tremendous increase in the public's use of general-hospital emergency rooms exceeds the increase in population. More than half of the people who presented themselves to the New Haven hospitals involved in their study came from the lowest social-economic class, according to Hollingshead's classification. These people are unable to accept the authority aspects of the therapist role, upon which the resident doctor implicitly depends for his own sense of security. While they do seek help for personal perplexities, they bring the problems to a medical facility, not to a psychiatric one. Their coming is often symptomatic of an effort to resolve conflict by some sort of substitute formation. Some of them come, too, as a gesture of reaching-out for human contact when they feel cut off from their ordinary sources of social support. For others it is the impersonal nature of the setting which makes it acceptable, since they do not welcome or cannot tolerate personal involvement. Many also have no comprehension or awareness of the length of time required by psychoanalysis or by psychotherapy; in short, they anticipate quick results.

The briefer psychotherapies are thus responses to a variety of pressures: (1) There is increased public demand for psychotherapeutic services that is not matched by a comparable increase of available personnel. This situation is augmented by increasing public awareness of the availability and effectiveness of psychotherapy, by government programs making such services available to larger numbers of people and by the increase of health insurance plans. (2) Brief procedures have a preventive or limiting role in minor, acute and chronic situations. (3) Crises and stresses attendant to most human lives bring an urgent demand for quick intervention. (4) Quick and effective intervention is required in disastrous events. (5) Brief psychotherapy is the only kind of therapy conceived of as effective by some practitioners. (6) Certain settings demand an effective brief therapy because they permit only a short period of contact with the patient. (7) For a variety of reasons, some people are able to accept help only in a setting associated with brief, emergency procedures similar to those of a medical clinic.

CHAPTER 2

Distinguishing Features

Garner (74) defines brief therapy as treatment in which the interview length, frequency and duration over time is at the minimum necessary for reaching the most feasible goal for the patient. A difficulty with this definition for brief psychotherapy is that it could be read to imply that long-term psychotherapy takes an unnecessarily long time to arrive at a feasible goal, or that long-term therapy is a minimal-length therapy with infeasible goals. Perhaps more illumination lies in differentiating brief from other psychotherapies rather than attempting definition.

Bellak and Small (20) differentiate brief psychotherapy from psychoanalysis particularly in terms of: (1) goals, (2) time factors and (3) methods. Each of these will be examined in turn.

GOALS

Emergency psychotherapy is identified by the same authors as a method of treatment for symptoms or maladaptations which demand the quickest possible relief because of their crippling or endangering nature. They see the goal of brief psychotherapy, in distinction, as limited to the removal or amelioration of specific symptoms. In their view, brief psychotherapy does not attempt reconstitution of personality, except that they see any dynamic intervention as secondarily leading to autonomous restructuration of the personality. But specifically, they see the goal as symptom-directed and seeking to improve the individual's psychodynamic situation sufficiently to permit him to continue functioning and "to allow nature to continue the healing process." Similar goals were set by Grinker and Spiegel (174) in response to wartime pressures: the release of tensions, strengthening of the ego, decreasing severity of the super-ego. They had no ambition beyond these limited goals, no effort at restructuring of the personality.

Rosenbaum (188), in a similar vein, also sees the goal of psychotherapy as the relief of symptomatology. Greenblatt et al. (86) emphasize the goals of relieving symptoms and strengthening existing defenses. Restoration of previously effective defensive structures is also identified as the goal by Coleman and Zwerling (45).

The possible goals (or fates?) of symptom-focused brief psychotherapy are presented by Rosenbaum (188). The symptom may persist but its importance may change. The symptom may disappear without insight or discharge of affect. Numerous symptoms may disappear when a common cause is found. Some insight and effective discharge may bring relief. The symptom may disappear only to return later "in a better perspective."

Clinic services for the lower socio-economic population has led to a reformulation of goals of treatment, say Normand et al. (163). Current goals are to provide immediate intervention in a problem where a psychological disturbance of some degree is involved, to ameliorate the symptoms—not to cure, but rather to reestablish a prior more effective state of equilibrium or perhaps achieve an improved state of equilibrium.

A cogent statement of the aims of brief psychotherapy with children is made by Lester (133): any form of treatment is "an organic unit of moves which are predetermined successively by a preconceived scheme of action and the central aim of this action;" in brief psychotherapy the aim is to eliminate or relieve symptoms. In children symptoms are exaggerations of what would otherwise be age-adequate behavorial patterns, aggressions, inhibitions, and complex structures of bound-together defense, impulse and external prohibitions into repetitive abnormal behavior.

Malamud (143) sets the goal as the development of some degree of operative relationship with the environment. Lewin (135) is even more specific; in his scheme brief psychotherapy is directed toward the achievement of two goals: (1) reversal of the process of regressive infantile expectation of gratifications, and (2) turning of the complex of anger away from its inward direction against the self.

Kris (125) is concerned with preventing rehospitalization by helping discharged hospital patients return to the level of job and social functioning they enjoyed prior to hospitalization, essentially a rehabilitation goal.

Wolberg (245) also stresses the need to accept limited goals. These he identifies as: (1) relief of symptoms, (2) restoration to the level of functioning that existed prior to the illness, (3) some understanding of the forces that precipitated the current upset, (4) recognition of some of the personality problems that interfere with a better life adjustment, (5) some partial understanding of the origin of these circumstances in past experiences, (6) some degree of awareness of the relationship between prevailing personality problems and the current illness and (7) comprehension of those measures that can remedy current environmental difficulties. Arresting decompensations and restoring the person to a previous level of functioning is Coleman's (47) goal for brief psychotherapy.

The efforts of some workers are directed toward the immediately troubling circumstances. Dr. Gerald F. Jacobson, executive director of the Benjamin Rush Clinic in Los Angeles, is cited in a newspaper article (173) as indicating that the goal of his clinic is the "definitive resolution of the current crisis." In the same newspaper account Dr. Edward Stainbrook of the University of Southern California relates the goals of brief psychotherapy, particularly in crisis intervention, to the recurrent and persistent critical periods in human existence, saying "the geneticist figures you're done for when you're born; the psychoanalyst figures you're done for when you're six, but the crisis intervener says you're not done for until you're dead."

Bellak (19) emphasizes the preventive goals of both emergency and brief psychotherapy. He urges that emergency psychotherapy situations not be strictly compared with medical emergency-room situations, in that the former are not limited only to urgent crises, "We want to teach our population (the citizens served by the hospital) that to deal with more or less minor disturbances is often the soundest way to avert potentially serious difficulties. In a later paper (21) he identifies the role of emergency psychotherapy: ". . . to still pain, make functioning possible and save life."

Emergency treatment, wrote Waltzer *et al.* (235), seeks modification of specific incapacitating psychopathology without of necessity altering basic psychic struture. It seeks to prevent progression of a psychotic process, to restore equilibrium.

Malan (144) identified in his search of the literature both "conservative" and "radical" points of view about goals in brief psychotherapy. These will be dealt with extensively in the chapter on prognosis, but their content is reflected in the degrees of breadth that different writers permit themselves.

Brief psychotherapy is not abbreviated psychoanalysis, warned Rado in 1942 (174): its objectives, points of attack and conditions of administration differ from the features of psychoanalysis. Standard treatment is a *radical* procedure; it aims to raise the patient's operational efficiency by readaptation on the largest possible scale. Brief therapy is palliative, instead of reforming from within, it supports from without. Two decades later Rado (179) is lecturing that motivation rather than length of therapy is the key; if motivation is high (and it can be induced to greater intensity if need be) significant results can be obtained with the use of learning techniques.

Brief psychotherapy is viewed as a push toward further problem solving by Burdon (29). This leads to genuine maturation, and involves a helpful identification with the therapist, combined with a strengthening of self-esteem and increased tolerance for some previously unacceptable impulses.

Establishment of the therapist as an omnipotent agent in the mind of the patient, an agent who will help him in future conflicts, is seen as the aim of brief psychotherapy and the point of its termination by Socarides (211). He thus contrasts brief psychotherapy with intensive psychotherapy. He sees the latter as a design to stimulate full growth whereby the patient becomes free of all authority figures. (To interpolate, his view of the goal of brief psychotherapy appears to be the creation of a kind of dependence.)

Expectation theory leads McGuire (145) to see brief psychotherapy as based upon understanding of only a few expectations and motivations of a patient before undertaking reordering of cognitive and emotional perceptions. In contrast, long-term therapy aims to understand thoroughly the patient's motivations. Nonetheless, McGuire observes a large percentage of satisfying change with useful insights in the area of conflict. Removal of a specific affective symptom is not the sole objective but often occurs. McGuire accepts the description of brief psychotherapy as manipulative if the word is understood to mean diverting the patient from conflicts or topics when the therapist decides this should be done.

The aim of crisis intervention, states Jacobson (105), is the "psychological resolution of the patient's crisis and the restoration of the patient through this means, at least to a level of functioning existing prior to the crisis."

The aim of short therapeutic efforts with adolescents is said by Miller (152) to abet and support the adolescent's effort to achieve integration. Most adolescent problems represent a crisis in his effort to maintain or to create an ego identity.

Most writers on the subject appear to adopt limited goals for brief psychotherapy, goals largely directed toward symptom removal or amelioration, the reversal of current distresses, or the prevention of more serious problems. They view such goals, while limited, to be significant. At the same time they cautiously keep the door open for infrequent, more dramatic, far-reaching and fundamental changes in personality structure sometimes observed as a result of the brief intervention.

TIME FACTORS

Obviously one expects brief psychotherapy to require considerably less time. For the most part this is so, but it is difficult if not impossible to put the case precisely. Phillips and Wiener (172) ask: "How short is short-term psychotherapy? An exact number of hours cannot be set; various figures are used in different studies, and any number is arbitrary."

I have found the range of session contacts defined as brief psychotherapy extending from one to 217 sessions. Even the simplest statistic on this factor is impossible. Imprecision is the order of the day in writing about the number of sessions comprising the brief psychotherapies offered: "Somewhere around ten as the average with a limit set at something less than 25" is one example.

However, five general time categories can be arbitrarily identified from the literature. The first comprises courses of psychotherapy reported to range from one to six sessions. (6, 20, 39, 45, 47, 55, 76, 86, 96, 102, 106, 122, 134, 142, 153, 186, 191, 195, 211, 212, 213, 223)

A second group reports ranges of sessions that average around 10 for the course of treatment. (1, 15, 25, 39, 53, 56, 76, 115, 212, 227)

The third group report courses of treatment running between 12 and 25 sessions (8, 12, 29, 39, 56, 76, 81, 104, 139, 146, 198, 201, 203, 217, 219, 224). Castelnuovo-Tedesco (35) describes a brief psychotherapy that averages "Somewhere around ten sessions" and something less than 25.

The next category is difficult to fit into an average since the range offered is irreducibly extensive or indeterminate. Haley (93) describes courses of treatment ranging from one to 20 sessions, Miller (150) three to 30 hours, Gillman (76) three to 36 hours, and Sifneos (207) eight to 50 sessions.

Wolpe (249), like all behavior therapists, identifies his treatment as specifically a short-term psychotherapy because of its "inherent efficiency." He discusses three studies of behavioral therapy in which the average number of sessions was ten. He also describes 39 cases in which the sessions range from four to 217. However, 34 of these required five or fewer sessions, while 20 of the cases required only between four and 10 sessions.

Finally, a few studies tell nothing about the number of sessions required. Walker and Kelley (232) indicate that sessions are held once weekly, but the full course of treatment is neither given as a range nor as an average. Koegler (121) discusses courses of treatment with children who were seen for a minimum of several sessions only, to those seen twice a week for up to two-and-one-half years. Meerloo (148) describes brief-contact therapy in emergency and first-aid situations but the period of time is indefinite. This is true for the account by Koegler (120) of the use of drugs along with brief-contact therapy in outpatient treatment.

Consideration of time factors must also include the interval between sessions; intervals of one week are the most frequently cited. Another aspect of time is the range required by the entire course of brief psychotherapy. With the trend for week-long intervals between sessions, a four-session course will take approximately a month, and so on.

Still another time consideration is the length of the individual session. At the low end of the continuum, authors speak of brief-contact psychotherapy (53, 120, 122) in which the sessions may last 10 to 20 minutes. Most authors refer to the so-called traditional psychotherapeutic hour of 45 to 60 minutes, with the mode about 50 minutes. Koegler (120) humorously refers to session length as PST (Psychiatrist Saving Time), a system of chronology in which one hour is equivalent to 50 minutes, a half hour to 25 minutes.

Short-term group therapy is reported by Keeler (115); his patients were seen between four and 16 sessions, over a one-month period. Cook (49) reports on group psychotherapy with hospitalized patients: more than 1,500 patients spent 27 days in the hospital during which time group therapy was conducted three times a week. Presumably these patients, on the average, received about 12 sessions of group therapy. Wolf (247) reports on experience in group therapy with patients covered by a health-insurance plan in which somewhat more than the 15 individual sessions were allocated; the number is not precisely stated.

Another variation affecting number and length of sessions and the span of time over which therapy takes place is provided by so-called intensive techniques. Terhune (224) describes a six-day program of residential treatment for industrial executives during which they received 12 hours of interviews with a treating psychiatrist. Goolishian (81) identifies a treatment for disturbed adolescents which he calls multiple-impact therapy: a psychiatrist, psychologist and social worker work intensively over a period of two or three days for six to eight hours each day with both individual patients and their families in all possible combinations. Variations include individual and group sessions, and multiple therapist session. Ritchie (186) describes a multiple-impact therapy of families that is condensed into two or two-and-a-half days, six to seven hours daily.

The marathon encounter provides intensity of concentration within the group experience. The group may meet without interruption except for sleep (although sometimes this too is forgone) for two or more days. Thus 30 hours of interaction and feedback may be encompassed in a weekend.

One model of the various time factors is furnished by the work of Levy (134) in maintaining a community-based crisis-oriented psychotherapy program. Patients are limited to a total of six sessions, which includes the admission interview. The first session lasts 45 minutes; subsequent interviews are 30 minutes or less. Intervals between visits are adjusted for each person at the end of each visit. The average interval between visits in one to two weeks, but some patients have been seen as often as three times in one week.

A somewhat similar approach is reported by Stein *et al.* (213) in the treatment of emotional reactions to physical illness among individuals attending an outpatient psychotherapy clinic. Their patients are seen from one to six times; a session may last from 15 to 50 minutes; visits are scheduled according to the needs of each patient, the usual pattern being at one-week intervals.

The time limits of brief psychotherapy are empirical, reasons McGuire (145, 146); they are evolved from clinical experience in which they have been found to be "approximately adequate" for achieving certain aims. Most significantly, in acknowledging the time dimensions, the aims and methods of the therapy are established.

METHODOLOGICAL DIFFERENCES

In Part II methods are discussed in detail; here general aspects of methodological differences noted in the literature are merely contrasted.

Alexander (174) views brief psychotherapy as freed from the investigative goals of psychoanalysis, hence an unfettered therapeutic enterprise. The implications of this for both goals and methods are direct and many. Thus, the rule of relative anonymity for the therapist as fostering an atmosphere of deprivation, considered essential for the development of a transference neurosis, is readily abandoned in brief-therapy methodology.

Wolberg (245) cites the lack of an adequate methodology for a brief psychotherapy: "The most pressing problem that confronts us today in short-term therapy is that we do not yet possess an adequate methodology." Wolberg sees us using the same tactics found useful in prolonged treatment; relaxed listening, allowing the relationship to build up into transference, waiting for the patient to acquire motivation, and working through resistance to reach the unconscious. From this he has developed the need for concentration upon "target symptoms."

Others have a more positive view. Dynamic psychotherapy of a brief duration is seen as a specific form of therapy by Lester (133), not as merely abbreviated therapy. Its main characteristics are that its aims are limited and well defined. The therapist while remaining non-evaluative undertakes an increasingly active role.

Bellak and Small (20) describe a brief psychotherapy that differs from traditional psychoanalysis in the limitations placed upon the use of free association, modifications in the use of interpretation, constraints imposed upon the development of a transference neurosis, the emphasis upon a positive transference in the working relationship, and the willingness to couple modified interpretation with other types of interventions (medical and environmental, for example).

Hoch (100) finds that the most important methodological difference is in the degree of activity on the part of the therapist. The therapist cannot be as passive as he might elect to be in long-term treatment; he will need to engage the patient's difficulties assertively and on occasion interfere with the patient's actions.

Therapists concerned with symptom change, removal or amelioration share one methodological dimension whether they be psycho-analytically oriented or adherents of behavioral-therapy schools: *the concentrated focus of the therapeutic effort upon the symptoms or relevant matters only.* Malan (144) differentiates his brief psycho-therapy from analysis in three ways: (1) the limited aim, (2) the limited number of sessions and (3) the "focal" technique. Wolberg (245) writes of "target symptoms," those aspects of the person's personality that are to be modified. Behavioral therapists concentrate upon manifest, observable behavior. Therapies with the economically and socially deprived elect to focus upon current real problems, the "here and now."

McGuire (145, 146) sees the methodology of brief psychotherapy as tightly structured into a process of selecting the emotional conflict to be treated, with the emphasis on active therapist participation, instruction in techniques, the sequential ordering of perceptions, and use of partial interpretations. Brief psychotherapy is not supportive therapy, argues McGuire; it selects and concentrates, and avoids those conflicts which involve character problems.

Gillman identifies basic methods of brief psychotherapy (76): (1) focusing on current reality; (2) face-to-face interviews of less frequency; (3) a "healthy" employment of free association; (4) regressive dependency and ambivalent transference are avoided; (5) the therapist is active.

The setting of time limits for the psychotherapy in advance appears to be an important methodological characteristic of many brief psychotherapies and has been the object of some study (171) which will be reported in the chapter discussing studies of outcome.

A recent review of brief psychotherapies by Barten (13) comments that despite the diversity of brief psychotherapies developed in the past decades, the various approaches reflect consensus on basic elements: (1) focus, the principle that a specific problem must be delineated quickly so that the patient is allowed little opportunity for exploration in other dimensions; (2) health orientation, promoting awareness and appraisal of ego resources rather than weaknesses; (3) time limitation, pre-setting the end of therapy.

An additional distinguishing feature of brief psychotherapy is its reliance upon a large armamentarium of interventions, skills and devices, rather than upon a single type of therapeutic effort. Stern (215) illustrates the need for a multiple approach in technique by citing the variety of situations that present themselves for quick intervention: depressions and suicidal attempts, excitements, panic states, deliriums and toxic states, threats, assaults, anti-social acts and drug-induced states. Waltzer *et al.* (231) define the brief therapy they offer in a large outpatient department as strengthening or modifying ego defenses, functioning and resources by interpretation, suggestion, environmental manipulation and somatic treatment.

CHAPTER 3
Supporting Theories

The theoretical propositions that practitioners have advanced in support of the feasibility of a brief therapeutic intervention are varied. Inevitably, theory is closely related to practice and in turn to prognosis, but in this chapter the effort is primarily to isolate the theories of personality and of change inherent in the brief psychotherapeutic venture.

The first are derivations of general psychoanalytic theory; then follow a variety of other theoretical and near-theoretical postulations. When, as in a few instances, the original author labeled his approach, I have used his title; when he did not, I sought for the word or phrase that seemed to communicate the essence of his statement. Accordingly, I am responsible for the appropriateness of most of the appellations.

GENERAL PSYCHOANALYTIC THEORY

Until the present time, psychoanalytic theory has been the theoretical base upon which brief intervention has rested, and for most writers it remains so. Menninger (149) reminds us that much has been learned from careful and long-continued psychoanalytic treatment that may be applied in the shorter treatment of other individuals. Alexander and French (4) demonstrated that the therapeutic principles of psychoanalysis could be consciously and flexibly adapted to the individual needs of each patient. Many workers express their debt to psychoanalytic theory of personality, neurosis formation and development, and to psychoanalytic technique for their brief methodologies. However, the distinction between a view of personality and neurosis based upon psychoanalytic theory and a highly specific psychotherapy known as psychoanalysis must be maintained.

Coleman (47) notes Hartmann's observation that analytic technique has lagged behind psychoanalytic theory; this comprehension underlies his working hypothesis in emergency psychotherapy: "We believe it is possible to make rapid evaluations of key dynamic issues by using data which comes not from the patient but from our theoretical knowledge about human functioning."

Most workers who owe their allegiance on matters of theory to psychoanalysis have made departures from psychoanalytic techniques or have sought to show that some *part* of the classical psychoanalytic procedure developed over decades of work may be applicable to a short-term intervention. Yet they stress that there is no short-term psychoanalysis.

Tannenbaum (223) in 1919 used the word "psychoanalysis" in the title of his paper, and even held out his treatment to be a "brief psychoanalysis," a claim that would be considered audacious or semantically erroneous today. Many others may be identified with psychoanalytic theory in a general or specific way. (5, 17, 20, 22, 52, 76, 90, 144, 150, 176, 193, 214, 245)

Bellak and Small (20) derive their brief psychotherapy from orthodox psychoanalytic theory. Without minimizing contributions from other theories, they believe that Freudian theory offers the most "systematic hypotheses available . . ." They select for particular attention the concept of psychic determinism, seeing causes and effects ". . . as events which one may expect to be linked with each other in a very high degree of probability." They find that determinism makes symptoms meaningful, and that the concept of over-determination permits a more sophisticated, more realistic view of an imbalanced situation. Continuity of the personality through time and levels of awareness is held to be a construct for a brief approach, permitting the psychodiagnostic linking of past events with contemporary ones, helping to find past causes for contemporary effects. Homeostasis is viewed by them also as a key analytic concept, though the specific terminology is not used by Freud; Freud wrote, however, of the constancy of organismic and psychic phenomena. They view the operation of the reality principle in opposition to the pleasure principle as a specific example of a homeostatic process, and in these terms view symptom formation as an "unstable compromise effort between drive gratification, on the one hand, and limitation of the drive by learned behavioral patterns on the other." They also point out that the structural aspects of the personality—id, ego and superego,—operate in a dynamic way to maintain homeostasis; disturbance in the balance between these aspects of the personality is disruptive. Therapeutic efforts directed toward correcting specific imbalances are able, they maintain, to be effective within short periods of time.

"SHALLOW" vs "DEPTH"

Frohman (70), supporting the feasibility of a brief therapeutic effort, points out that a neurosis may be acute without being deeply rooted in infantile or childhood traumas; therefore, long-term uncovering psychoanalytic processes are not necessary in all cases of neurosis, so that in some a brief effort may prove profitable. By way of corollary he states that an observed neurosis may be of long duration without being "deep." Each neurosis must be seen for what it is; if it is not "deep," even though it be acute and of long duration, it should hypothetically be susceptible to a brief intervention.

Alexander (174) as early as 1942 argued that treatment, when separated from research, can become effective in a shorter time than when the two are combined. It is wrong, he argues, to equate depth with length.

TRAUMA

Fenichel (60) supported a brief psychotherapy that could be approached systematically with the comprehension provided by psychoanalytic theory. Observations of trauma provided him with keys to the causes and possible quick resolution of a variety of difficulties.

Neurotic phenomena result from inadequacies of the normal control apparatus which result in "involuntary emergency discharges." These are induced by either: (1) an increase in stimulation to an unmanageable intensity, the traumatic experience; (2) an accumulation of internal tension—as the result of decreased discharge—so great that even a normal degree of stimulation may be traumatic (the previous blocking experience).

Conditions closest to traumatic phenomena are more likely to benefit from "external efforts" to help the person's autonomous and spontaneous efforts to re-establish equilibrium than are those induced by "previous blocking." These latter conditions require a dissolution of the defenses and hence are not likely to produce an "easy psychotherapeutic cure."

Fenichel notes two seemingly contradictory efforts at spontaneous recovery in traumatic neuroses; (1) to get distance, to rest, as if to store energy for the recuperative effort to master and control; (2) efforts to discharge tension evidenced in restlessness and other motor behavior, spells of emotionality, and in repetitive dreams and symptomatic behavior.

In cases of trauma, psychotherapy can facilitate both approaches to recovery by imitation. The therapist may suggest quieting procedures such as rest, he may offer reassurance, support, passivity, and dependency, or he may encourage discharge through catharsis, verbalization, and clarification of the conflicts, and through ventilation. The technical dictum derived from this theoretical statement is clear: the chief task in psychotherapy is "to find the relatively correct amount of catharsis and reassurance . . ."

While only a small percentage of difficulties are of a traumatic nature, Fenichel states that even the non-neurotic, the so-called normal individual, encounters conditions of acute upheaval in which the precipitating circumstances are comparable with trauma. A person in relative stability may encounter circumstances that disrupt his equilibrium: the experience of loss of a loved person, an episode damaging to self-esteem, alterations in living arrangements or circumstances. Any of these may require acceptance of a new and painful reality and the requirement to ward off tendencies to repression, dependency, passivity, or preoccupation with fantasies. If the person encountering these kinds of precipitating circumstances has latent conflicts of a defensive nature, a neurosis may emerge. Fenichel concludes that *both* the normal person and the latently conflictual one may be helped by similar means to re-establish equilibrium: rest, permission for limited regression, dependency, and "compensatory wish fulfillment" coupled with discharge techniques that through verbalization clarify the reality task required to reach stability, and ventilate irrational reactions.

While Fenichel states that ". . . acute difficulties of life present the first and foremost field of indication for brief psychotherapy . . ." he offers a theoretical rationale for its application to other conditions. Substitution for painful or alien symptoms may be offered through suggestion, incomplete or inexact interpretations, and be accepted by the patient provided ". . . the substitute offered is suited to the dynamic structure of the patient." The substitute in addition may be attractive to the patient in having either a sexual or reassuring significance—both secret. His case for successful brief psychotherapy is that psychoanalytic knowledge in general (personality theory and technical knowledge) and dynamic comprehension of the individual and his current discomfort may be combined to produce a relatively quick and favorable alteration in the dynamic balance of that person.

A somewhat different theoretical view of traumatic conditions is provided by Kardiner's (114) study of war-produced traumatic neuroses. The traumatic neurosis, according to Kardiner, is an abrupt disruption of or "injury" to adaptation, a failure of the organism to make a required abrupt change in adaptation. The traumatic neurosis itself is the new adaptation which makes up the symptomatology.

The major feature of the traumatic neurosis is an inhibitory process; this is the primary symptom, "all other things being secondary." The inhibition may be complete as in paralysis, or partial.

In traumatic neuroses with partial inhibition there are these features: (1) fixation upon the traumatic event; (2) the dream life is stereotyped; associations are very difficult to obtain; dilution and retardation rather than condensation and compactness are observable; (3) irritability to a variety of stimuli; (4) proneness to aggression and violence; (5) inhibition which is partial is in the form of fatigue, dizziness, and disinterest.

Kardiner acknowledges Freud's contribution to the theory of traumatic neurosis that when the normal defense against stimuli is broken, efforts (the symptoms) are made to master the overwhelming stimuli. However, Kardiner comments that Freud did not give indication of how this defense against stimuli was built up.

He then notes that instinct theory is useless in comprehending "modalities of activity" that constitute the "techniques of adaptation to the external environment." These techniques are learned, heterogeneous, and complex "action syndromes." They develop in relationship with experience, and, because of incomplete myelination at birth, the process is not completed for three or more years. When born the infant has no capacity for adaptation to the external world.

Internal activities governed by the sympathetic and parasympathetic nervous systems are synchronized and integral with the action pattern that adapts to the external world, but the internal activities cannot be controlled by inhibition in the same way as can be the adaptation activities. Inhibition in voluntary activities can thus cause disturbances in the autonomic activities.

The "effective ego" executive functions and those that coordinate perceptual processes are readily available for adaptation. Fatigue produces a state that replicates (with many differences, however) a traumatic neurosis: perceptual accuracy is decreased, irritability and outbursts of rage are noted, the person wishes to withdraw temporarily from the outer world. "The recuperative agent is sleep, a controlled and elastic inhibitory process." Hysterical inhibitions come about when the "utility function of an organ or limb yields to its erotic significance." These inhibitions are governed by the superego and in this way differ from the traumatic neurosis.

Action syndromes (body ego functions) are developed through all of the developmental tasks we are familiar with: sucking, swallowing, seeing, standing, walking, talking, reading, *etc.* The quality of developmental influences will determine inhibition or promotion of action syndromes, as in the character and timing of weaning, or parental reactions to masturbation, for example.

Traumatic symptoms intermingle with psychoneurotic ones and with character traits also.

With action syndromes (or symptoms) impaired, an impulse to action produces irritation and a desire for flight; self-confidence has disappeared, as have curiosity and avidity; the person feels helpless.

In the traumatic neurosis, repression and substitution are not possible as in transference neuroses, because of the adaptive requirements of the ego. The activity syndromes (ego aspects) have fixed functions and cannot be substituted for, nor can passivity be resorted to, since it has no value for adaptation to the outer world. Ego contraction is not here reinforced by the superego as in neuroses, but by the "discrepancy between the forces in the outer world and the resources of the ego."

Traumatic neuroses are no more repetitive than the behavior noted in psychoneurotic and normal individuals. It is only that whenever an action is started the same process is observed: inhibition and failure.

In the traumatic neuroses, the symptoms compel focus upon the executive ego functions that are impaired rather than upon the content (that is, narcissistic, pregenital, *etc.*). Treatment that facilitates the acquisition of mastery, the re-stabilization of activity syndromes, if swiftly applied, can prevent the "hardening" of inadequate ego states. Kardiner's theory contributes the concepts of "mastery"-oriented therapy and its speedy application as soon as possible after the traumatic experience.

Erich Lindemann and Gerald Caplan are often credited with promoting the current development of crisis-intervention efforts by delineating some of the basic theory, derived from their study of bereavement reactions among survivors and relatives of the many people killed in a disaster, the Coconut Grove nightclub fire in Boston in 1942. They observed that a crisis develops when a person's coping techniques are inadequate to deal with a new situation and that speedy intervention should be directed toward equipping the individual to do exactly that—deal with the situation. Their coping theory is similar to Kardiner's concept of "adaptation," and their recommendation for speedy measures to re-establish coping is similar to his therapeutic intent.

CONFLICT RESOLUTION

Fenichel (60) in supporting the development of a brief psychotherapy stresses that every psychoneurosis is the result of a conflict between impulses that are warded off and anxieties and feelings of guilt which are warding-off in their nature; only a change in the dynamic balance and relationship between these components of the conflict can change the neurosis. This he says can be done in one of two ways: (1) by an increase in defense, or (2) by a diminution of the defense. The first type of therapy is represented by authoritarian approaches in which the symptoms are forbidden by the therapist. This type of effect is temporary, and may also be brought about indirectly through procedures which arouse anxiety, thereby increasing repressions: "threats, maltreatments, symbolic castrations, and reproaches." The danger of the technique is the return or exacerbation of the symptom, or the development of new symptoms. The second type of treatment resolves the repression; it is represented by psychoanalysis. Undoing of repression permits infantile sexual drives to play a role in the development of the personality.

Yet Fenichel's claim for the removal of repression as an effort of psychoanalysis as such has not restrained those practicing brief psychotherapy from claiming that repression can be avoided, and certainly not increased, that conflict may be resolved in a brief venture without the danger of increasing resistance. Harris, Kalis and Freeman (96) are among those who find that therapy may be abbreviated if it is discovered that the patient suffers from a conflict produced in recent precipitating stresses.

Socarides (211) credits Alexander (174) and French (174) with providing an impetus for the development of brief psychotherapy. He reviews the conditions they postulate as necessary for an effective brief psychotherapy. A favorable combination of initial circumstances present must include the therapist's ability to see at once the precipitating difficulty in relationship to the total personality, the patient's capacity for insight, his ready confidence in the therapist, and the therapist's appearance of being particularly fitted to help a particular patient. Spotlighting of previously hidden conflicts sometimes produces an experience like a revelation. The therapist must have an immediate awareness of the kind of emotional climate in which a specific patient will have the self-revealing experience. Finally, the brief therapy is dependent upon the vividness of interpretations and the ability of the patient to understand them.

The traditional objection that brief psychotherapy does not resolve underlying conflicts is examined by Gillman (76). He reasons that there now are enough cases with established lasting improvement to suggest that reduction in anxiety through brief treatment can, in certain cases, permit growth and mastery. Conflicts, while unresolved, may be significantly decreased in their relative force; he likens this process to the normal increase in mastery in the development of children.

CATHARSIS

The roots of psychoanalysis in catharsis are observable in contemporary approaches to the handling and relief of traumatic neurosis. Bonime (25) describes a treatment of traumatic war neurosis using the repetition of significant past events of the patient's life in the current trauma and the achievement of catharsis provoked by this insight. His theoretical position links insight with ventilation in seeking the release of pent-up affects, which are held to produce disorganization within the individual. Miller (151) and Rosenthal (191) also strive in traumatic situations to achieve cathartic release and ventilation.

Specific cathartic expressions are sought in treating patients with dermatological symptoms. The dynamic meaning of the symptom—for example, the scratching of the excoriation—is made the basis of cognitive insight in order to produce a cathartic expression of repressed rage (198, 201).

AROUSAL

Specific statements may be made about certain aspects of psychoanalytic theory and psychoanalytic therapy that have been adapted in developing a brief intervention. Ferenczi (61) used the psychoanalytic comprehension of symptoms to advocate their exacerbation in order to stimulate the development of insight through the recall of repressed material. He reasoned that this kind of exacerbation would increase psychic tension, thereby facilitating the therapeutic work. Later (62) he was to be less sanguine and acknowledge that exacerbation might increase resistance. His earlier position finds allies today in what might be identified as the "arousal" theory. Sifneos (207) maintains that anxiety may be used to motivate a patient to understand the nature of his emotional conflicts, and the under-standing in turn used to assist the person in changing maladaptive behavior. As we will see later, he also evolved a short-term anxiety-suppressing therapy. Lewin (135) bases his brief therapeutic method upon the arousal of negative transference feelings via direct interpre-tation of defenses; resolution of the feelings thus aroused restores equilibrium.

Wolk (248) has developed a rationale for brief psychotherapy inherent in a technique he calls the "kernel interview." Each interview has a set of goals, just as it has an entire treatment plan. Anxiety is raised in each session and reduced before its end, so that the patient leaves feeling relieved and satisfied that he has accomplished some-thing tangible and meaningful. The rationale, while lacking the so-phistication and completeness of Fenichel's conceptualization of the traumatic neurosis, nonetheless can be seen as congruent with it in providing both discharge and rest.

"AVOIDANCE"

The development and analysis of a transference neurosis is stressed by Greenson (87) and other contemporary psychoanalysts as the process by which a psychoanalytic cure is fundamentally and ulti-mately brought about. The transference neurosis is the one aspect of the theory of therapeutic change that the therapist devoted to psy-choanalytic theory steers clear of in his efforts at a brief psycho-therapy.

Malan (144) identified transference as one of the major "lengthen-ing factors." Bellak and Small (20) warn of the need to avoid the development of the transference neurosis but argued that positive transference representing a favorable relationship of patient to thera-pist is "a prerequisite for the motivation to learn and re-learn in the short space of time available."

The essence of this position is that certain attitudes and expec-tations of and techniques employed by the therapist will lengthen predictably the therapeutic process. If psychotherapy is to be short-ened, these must be avoided through "skillful neglect" (Pumpian-Mindlin's (176) elegant phrase). These attitudes and techniques marked for avoidance are treated in Chapter 6 on techniques; here we may note that, in addition to transference, Malan cites repression as a patient-reaction to be avoided.

AUTONOMOUS DRIVE FOR HEALTH

Some authors are impressed by the autonomous drive for health observable in patients, and comment that the burden for improvement is placed directly upon this drive. Bos (26) and Koegler (120) believe that brief therapy merely accelerates a process that would occur anyway, that the brief psychotherapeutic endeavor is facilitating an autonomous process. The evidence cited for this by Koegler is improvement of individuals while waiting for therapy—"waiting-list" improvement. Forer (64) implicitly ascribes to autonomous striving the recovery function in those episodes of crisis which are part of the normal developmental process of life. Erlich and Phillips (55) may be describing this autonomous striving when they refer to "high motivation" as facilitating brief therapeutic ventures. Inevitably this leads to prognostic considerations, as does Visher's (227) observation that brief psychotherapy may be effective when the person is ready for a change or when the pressures of life demand a new orientation from him.

Knight (174) observes that brief psychotherapy can be effective as a turning point in an individual's life, as can any critical experience. The implication is that a short-term intervention coinciding with a period of set or readiness for change comprises the optimal circumstances for consequences extending beyond symptom change.

EXPECTATION AND HOPE

Expectation theory argues the power of the present and the future to mold, influence and modify behavior. It seeks to release causality from the past and imparts a markedly existential and teleological flavor absent from the psychoanalytic concept of determinism.

The direction of time as a force in behavior is the essence of expectation theory. It has excited considerable theoretical speculation. We will see that time-concept is a fundamental focus for accord between therapist and patient, that the influence of expectations derives from a wide variety of sources—intrapersonal, intrafamilial and cultural. Expectation theory is said to illuminate the resolution of conflict, to be inherent in the placebo effect and fundamentally to determine the outcome of therapy—a powerful force indeed.

A time-defined or time-limited approach is purported by some workers (160, 171, 203, 214) to compel movement on critical issues and shorten the time required for therapeutic results. The establishmen of a time-limitation, it is contended, creates the expectation in the person that a change will occur within the time allocated, and this *expectation* contributes to actual beneficial alterations.

The time sense and the expectations of the impoverished patient are examined by Chafetz (37) who studied the effect of an emergency psychiatric service on patients' motivation for further treatment. Success breeds success: he is able to state that if effectively helped in an emergency, the patients were likely to be motivated for further treatment. Successful crisis intervention has the effect of altering somewhat the expectations of these patients.

Hope is seen by Patterson (168) as a dynamic commonality in seemingly divergent therapeutic approaches. The problems that bring people into treatment are painful, undesirable states, conditions that warrant attempts to alter them. Man is capable of changing, he is not hopelessly predetermined, but at any stage may be pliable. Future hopes, anticipations, and expectations of the future influence present behavior. Behavior is not caused entirely by the past, but is influenced as well by expectations of future consequences. The expectation of change may vary, Patterson reasons, from the highly optimistic to the minimal, but it is always present.

The expectations of both patient and therapist are viewed as keys to success in brief psychotherapy by Baum and Felzer (16). The initial interview (in some cases the first few) is critical to success. They observed that patients with the most inaccurate or distorted expectations are the most likely to return.

The initial interview with the patient is also emphasized by Burdon (29). It creates a lasting impression, and its effectiveness is dependent upon the therapist's real interest in the human being as it is on the patient's need and willingness to trust a person. In many respects the patient's view of the prognosis will influence the outcome as much as the therapist's.

Aldrich (2) argues that the development of brief psychotherapeutic procedures may require exposure of some cherished traditions

of psychoanalytic theory. Seeking to encourage theoretical exploration
of adaptations of techniques that would permit short-term treatment,
Aldrich undertakes, himself, such an exploration. He addresses himself to the concepts of parental expectation and superego lacunae as
determinants of behavior disorders in children and adolescents of
upper- and middle-class families. His hypothesis is that behavior arises
from factors other than conflict, but that such explanation is often
insufficient, especially for delinquent behavior, which is not necessarily symbolic but may be a request for limiting acting out.

He cites the work of Johnson and Szurek (109) who found that
conflict did not explain delinquent behavior sufficiently, particularly
of children in customarily non-delinquent families. They identified
superego lacunae, which they saw as defects in behavior control sanc-
tioned unconsciously by the parents. He further cites the work of
Goldstein (80) in delineating the impact of expectations on the ego,
as for example the development of the school phobia in a child whose
mother has communicated her wish that the child will not be able to
get along without her. Aldrich believes that many other symptoms may
be found to depend on parental expectations, as for example hypo-
chondriasis, reaction formation, denial, conversion and other mechanisms which underline neurotic symptoms. The role of parental expectations in the double-bind genesis of schizophrenia is cited: the
child unable to respond because mutually exclusive expectations are
signalled to him. Aldrich goes beyond Johnson and Szurek in identifying sources other than parents as the sources of expectation that
determine symptoms, citing school teachers, camp counselors, golf
masters, among others. This makes it possible for expectations to be
in opposition to each other, so that parental expectations of control
or lack of control may be supported in some cases by cultural expectations and those of other individuals.

The extension to cultural determinants of superego lacunae has
implications for psychotherapy and for the role of the psychotherapist.
In treating delinquent patients, Johnson and Szurek recommend that
the superego defect be treated first, that the delinquent be converted
into a neurotic. In actual cases, however, it is seen that the treatment
of the superego defect is a prelude to further treatment. Aldrich
would place the emphasis upon *expecting* that the patient will be able
to use the ego strength he has gained in working out one problem in

the resolution of other problems, without the help of the therapist. To expect the contrary is to expect inadequacy, and would create an ego lacuna that would make the therapist's pessimism a self-fulfilling prophecy. The therapist practicing long-term therapy finds that his patients take a long time to respond, while good results are obtained quickly by the therapist who claims to be able to produce them in a short period of time.

Therapeutic repair of ego defense and superego lacunae both constitute improvement which is not accompanied by the resolution of the underlying conflict. He argues that treatment which is recommended past the relief of symptoms is only justifiable if in a definable way the longer treatment produces better results than the treatment which stops when the symptoms are relieved. Aldrich believes that evidence which would extend psychotherapy beyond symptomatic relief has not been forthcoming. This does not mean that symptom relief is all that a patient requires or that long-term treatment is always unnecessary. Many patients do not respond to treatment of symptoms despite the therapist's expectations. Long-term therapy is not useless, but it should not be expected to be the primary goal. Aldrich asks that the therapist be alert from the first interview for indications that the patient is willing and able to cope with residual problems. Therapeutic optimism or pessimism is one more expectation added to the accommodation of parental and cultural expectations.

McGuire (146) observes that patients assign a variety of meanings to their knowledge of brief therapy, and may anticipate a number of different happenings. Some patients believe their cure will require only a few visits. Therapy with such patients may progress well in the early phase, but bog down later on, since the patient may have expected a magical cure rather than one by his own participation. When patients believe that the "clinic does not care," they interpret shortness of therapy as indifference. In such cases, this belief must be recognized and worked with in order to insure success. When longer therapy is recommended, the patient's expectations of time must be made explicit. Long-term may mean the therapist will be relatively inactive, while in short-term work he will be directive. If the patient is receptive and flexible, such direction may be extremely helpful; if, however, he tends to feel resentful and subjected by his environment, he may feel manipulated and become ambivalent about suggestions the therapist makes. Guidance provided by the therapist supports the patient's ego and his expectations. The therapist suggests both that a problem exists and that it can be solved by the methods of psychotherapy. Brief psychotherapy according to McGuire affirms some expectations and supports certain ego functions in order to discover what expectations are causing the patient the greatest difficulty, and to help him to search for and benefit from insight. McGuire believes that the therapist creates the expectation in the patient that therapy is a task, and as a task it can be ordered and solved. "The clearest illustration of the patient's expectations that therapy is a task is his report of a sequence of happenings. He anticipates that the content of the sequence will be discussed and explained, *i.e.*, given meaning." The therapist's responsibility is to keep therapy a task for the patient, but to change the aim when necessary to avoid discussion of conflict and symptoms which may endanger the order process.

Therapy is unsuccessful when it supports expectations which the patient himself senses are unrealistic, not necessarily by supporting neurotic and unrealistic expectations in general. McGuire observes that a particular form of fantasy is induced by the individual patient's comprehension of briefness, and he identifies types of time-fantasies:

(1) Return of the past. The patient feels that unpleasant occurrences of the past are imminent in the immediate future. Feeling the same bad things happen repeatedly, the patient will be pessimistic about brief therapy as well: "This too will end up like everything else."

(2) Expected moment of realization. The patient feels that the immediate future holds the promise of change, happiness and fulfillment, not necessarily the distant future. False optimism is frequently observed. These patients are difficult to treat since a good deal of therapy must be spent stressing the reality of therapeutic possibilities.

(3) The present is alone. This patient isolates the present from both the past and the future. He feels petrified, unable to move, isolated and remote. The present lacks meaning and life; this is the dominant concern. McGuire finds these patients most difficult to treat since neither the present nor the future can be meaningfully brought into therapy.

(4) The present is the door to the future. This is unlike either "the expected moment of realization" (the future is seen to the exclusion of the present) or "the present is alone" (the present is viewed to the exclusion of past and future). In this fantasy the present is closely tied to the future, and the patient believes that both imminent and distant future will be determined by the present. The consequences of any commitment become exceedingly great, indicated in repetitive anxiety attacks during and preceding decision making. These patients usually respond to brief therapy with initial over-optimism and later with ambivalence or indecision as to its worth.

(5) The present is the inevitable result of the past. The patient believes that the present is the result, but not the cyclical reoccurrence, of preceding events. Life is sensed as a continuum and the patient believes he will continue to fail and to suffer. A lack of affect is common. These patients often respond to the offer of brief psychotherapy with feelings of humiliation and rejection.

McGuire inquires how the "timelessness of the unconscious" allows the apparent rapid resolution of conflicts, so often observed in brief therapy. His answer is that therapy begins with patients who are dissatisfied with their immediate situation, who are therefore motivated to attempt an alteration of their existing state, their environmental situation or both. Dissatisfied, they are motivated to change. Ability to use these conditions effectively in the patient depends on the therapist's ability to shift the responsibility for getting well from the therapy to the patient. He sees no conflict between the timelessness of the unconscious and rapid resolution of conflicts by short-term therapy. The conflict is resolved through explication of expectations and identification of related but previously unknown emotions. This method becomes the model for the patient's future resolutions of conflict.

Frank (65) comments that expectation influences every aspect of human functioning with its inclusion of the future into human consciousness. Indeed it is this aspect of the human creature that makes psychotherapy possible and influences the utilization of the positive hopeful expectations in the mental-health effort. Expectations are directly linked with degrees of confidence in the therapist. He cites the studies on the placebo response in relationship to hope as a prime example of its effectiveness in promoting health and fostering life when it is present, and interfering with the recovery and hastening death when it is absent. In evaluating the effects of hope and expectation on the outcome of psychotherapy, Frank argues that we should limit our evaluative criteria to those that are unambiguous operationally, ". . . rather than straining after those which may to be sure be more significant, but cannot be defined clearly enough to enable therapists using different methods to compare their findings." Individuals come into psychotherapy in periods of stress or when recovering from a crisis. Thus they will be more incapacitated and more distressed at the moment of entry into psychotherapy than they were a short time before or are likely to be a short time afterwards. They will show increasing improvement with the passage of time, thereby very likely obscuring the differences of short-term effectiveness from different types of psychotherapy. Some evidence indicates that when two groups of outpatients were compared on measures of social effectiveness, six months after one had received one hour a week of individual therapy contrasted with a half hour every two weeks with the other groups, initially very little change was noted for the group receiving minimal therapy whereas the other group moved rather significantly. At the end of three years, these differences had tended to disappear, so that the group which received minimal psychotherapy had gained significantly on the group which had received individual therapy. Whitehorn and Betz (238) note in working with schizophrenics that significant differences among results of different treatment doctors were eliminated gradually with the passage of time. These differences were reflected in the ratings of improvement of the patients.

From this, Frank concludes that if any aspect of psychotherapy produces even a short-term improvement by a clearly defined criterion it is worthy of consideration. The criteria that he has in mind include "global ratings of improvement by patient or therapist, diminished symptoms as determined by a symptom checklist, reduction in target complaint, improved social effectiveness as determined by interview, and scores on a variety of rating scales filled out either by the patient or by trained observers." Frank then reports on studies at the Henry Phipps Psychiatric Clinic at Johns Hopkins Hospital and concludes that the evidence is highly indicative that symptomatic improvement among psychiatric patients is positively related to the qualitative aspects of the psychotherapeutic setting that specifically arouse their hopes of receiving help. Part of the data is obtained from placebo studies which employed a symptom checklist, a mood scale, personality inventories and a test of automatic functioning to evaluate changes in symptoms. These measurements were taken prior to the administration of the placebo; afterwards patients were given the symptom checklist and mood scale. A half hour later these were re-administered and then they were seen again at one- and two-week intervals for remeasurements with the same instruments. Whatever the interval between initial and later measures, the improvement obtained was statistically significant. Considerably more patients reported improvement than reported worsening. The degree of such improvement was positively correlated with the initial intensity of distress. Anxiety and depressive symptoms were most markedly reduced. "The maximal response occurred immediately—from the beginning to the end of the initial interview. Three years later the measurements of average symptomatic discomfort remained considerably below the level these patients had initially indicated. At this time a placebo was given again to a group of the patients who had relapsed after an initial favorable response. No correlation was obtained between patients who responded on both occasions. Some who had shown a favorable response three years previously showed none, and vice-versa. Frank concludes that the placebo relieved anxiety and depression mainly, that the degree of relief is unrelated to personality and autonomic measures and that individuals who respond strongly to a placebo on one occasion may not do so on another. The extent of responsiveness therefore seems dependent on the interaction of the patient's state or condition at a specific time with certain aspects of the situation. The use of tests and questionnaires seem to have as much beneficial effect as the pill, suggesting that *any interaction which heightens expectation of help* will lead to symptom decrease and mood improvement.

Park and Covi (167) are cited by Frank as producing evidence that the placebo's effectiveness does not depend necessarily on the patient's belief of an active medication but more on what the administration of the placebo conveys to him of the therapist's attitude.

Fifteen patients were given deliberately confusing instructions along with the placebo, being told that it contained no medicine but was expected to help the patient as it had helped so many others. Of these 14 improved; the fifteenth refused to take the pill. Data obtained from interviews with these patients indicated that those who had firm convictions either that the pill was a placebo, or contrary to what they were told, believed that it was an active drug, experienced significantly greater improvement than those who were doubtful. The patients with these firm convictions were convinced that the doctor was "deliberately acting to help them." A very interesting example of the complexity inherent in individual hope and expectation was a mildly agitated depressive patient, unresponsive in prior medication programs, who showed a dramatic improvement. Whereas the doctor felt the improvement was the result of improved rapport, the patient insisted it was due to the pill which was not really a placebo but medicine; he even reported side effects. He believed the doctor told him it was inert so that the patient could believe that he had helped himself. Frank concludes: "Apparently the only way this man could improve was by disappointing the doctor's expectations."

Frank comments that the evidence for the placebo effect is somewhat confused, and that a more direct line of investigation is useful. He cites the work of Friedman (68) who investigated patient's expectations about improvement after a first interview at the clinic for evaluation. His populations are an American one and an English one, in large cities in both cases. Patients filled out a simple checklist *prior* to their evaluation interview. After completing it, they were asked to check it again according to how they hoped to feel six months after treatment. Then they had their evaluation interview; following this they were immediately asked again to fill out the symptom scale. Trends were comparable in both the English and American samples. Friedman reports a positive relationship between reported relief of symptoms following the interview and the expectation level prior to the interview.

Frank indicates his belief that the therapist is the most important ingredient of the therapeutic relationship and situation insofar as any aspect of this situation can stimulate a patient's expectation of relief. Frank supports this with data from a study which rated four therapists on aspects of their behavior during therapy. Their patients were rated on a number of measures of outcome. The most successful therapist contrasted with the least successful was demonstrated to have "greater expectations for his patients, greater experience, less anxiety about feeling that he was being evaluated, and less antagonism toward the research program."

The important ingredient in all this is the evidence that the outcome of therapy can be influenced significantly by what the patient is led to expect. Frank then reports the work of Shlien (203) on the effect of outcome of patients' expectation of how long treatment was to last. Shlien reported that an experimental group of patients improved as much as a result of 20 sessions as did a control group after 37 sessions. Shlien replicated this study in another clinic using another therapeutic approach but with the sessions again limited to 20 for the experimental group.

Frank then reports on the personal communication from M. T. Orne who observed that sluggish movement or a halt to movement in long-term treatment could be reversed if a few sessions were directed toward restimulating the patient's hopes and expectations by elucidating the goals and rationale of treatment. Following Orne's suggestion, Frank and his colleagues made a control test of the value of a similar stimulating interview prior to the start of a program of short-term psychotherapy—an interview they termed the "role induction" interview. Patients were interviewed by an intake psychiatrist who wrote an evaluation report for the therapist who would be treating the patient; he also made ratings of the patient which included judgments about his suitability for therapy. At this time the evaluating interviewer was given an indication by the research team as to whether the patient was to be a control or to receive the "role induction" interview. Control patients were called back and simply given an appointment with the therapist. Experimental group patients were seen again and given the role-induction interview, in the course of which it was communicated to the patient that he might expect improvement within four months, probably after some reversals. The role of the therapist was explained and also how he would conduct himself. The individual's role as a patient was delineated and he was led to expect that he would talk freely and describe fantasies, dreams, *etc*. The patients who received the interview showed more movement on five of seven measures than did the control group.

As Frank correctly observes, the interview not only raised expectations of improvement but also was a learning experience, introducing some clarity concerning the process of treatment. In short then, any quality or aspect of a therapeutic situation or relationship that can evoke or increase expectations of relief or improvement seem to be positively correlated with improvement over the short-term range in a significant portion of patients. This may be a placebo effect, but there is additional evidence that the essential quality is the ability of the "ingredient" to communicate the therapist's intention and ability to help the patient.

FOCUS AND CONCENTRATION

The concept of "focused" therapy is advanced by Stekel (214) and is inherent in the concept of sector therapy (52) and in Wolberg's (245) suggestion that short-term psychotherapy is feasible when symptoms can be identified as the target for concentrated therapeutic intervention. This concept is questioned by the research of Dreiblatt and Weatherly (53) who found that "when the patient's symptoms were made the focus of discussion in the brief contacts, they had no apparent beneficial effect." (Their findings are described at length in Chapter 12.)

Malan (144) defines the term "focality" "as the ability of patient and therapist together to find a focus quickly which is acceptable to both of them." His definition suggests an agreement between therapist and patient at the *beginning* of the therapy to concentrate selectively among the patient's problems.

EGO-FUNCTIONS

Bellak and Small (20) reason that since brief psychotherapy must direct itself to undoing specific impairments and every situation requiring psychotherapy involves an impairment of one or another ego function to varying degrees, the efficacy of a brief psychotherapy depends upon addressing interventions to the repair and restoration of damaged ego functions. This direction tends to bring about the selection of specifically oriented interventions which by virtue of their specificity are more quickly effective.

LEARNING THEORY

Learning theory also receives attention as the theoretical basis for a short psychotherapy. Bellak and Small (20) comment upon the relationship of a range of learning theories to the psychotherapeutic process and use learning theory in the development of techniques to facilitate learning through interpretation. They also call attention to the role of learning by identification, the process of introjection, and to learning by insight. Focusing upon a narrower segment of learning theory, behavioral therapists have been publishing forceful documentation of their position. Phillips and Wiener (172) advance a short term "structured therapy"; this means ". . . the purposeful selection, by the therapist and the client, of variables basic to behavior change." They ascribe therapeutic meaning to structure, stating that it is what results in satisfaction in human relationships and promotes problem solving. They turn to basic cybernetics for support of their structured approach: "in cybernetics the first and fundamental concept is control." The cybernetics concept of "feedback" is related by them to the "learning concepts of retroactive or proactive inhibition or facilitation . . ."

Wolpe and Lazarus (249), prominent in the development of behavioral therapy, state that it is ". . . evident that human neurotic reactions obey the principle of primary stimulus generalization." Behavior therapy seeks to change undesirable habits by the application of one or more of three categories of conditioning operations: counterconditioning, positive re-conditioning and experimental extinction. They, too, stress structure, the experience and control exercised by the therapist: ". . . the overcoming of a human neurosis is within the control of the therapist through techniques quite similar to those used in the laboratory." Wolpe and Lazarus consider abreaction in their theoretical review, but hold it to be an unpredictable resolution in that some patients may be worse off following the abreactive experience than they were before. An essential aspect of their theoretical approach to sexual problems is that ". . . sexual arousal is in itself reciprocally antagonistic to anxiety . . ."

COGNITION FACILITATION

A cognitive basis for psychotherapy is inherent in the use of insight as a remedial factor by therapists who indicate that insight may be achieved more rapidly by active interpretation coupled with support. (81, 217)

INCORPORATION

Rosenbaum (188) views the role of the therapist as the key to the feasibility of brief therapy: the role is designed to make it easier for the patient to identify more quickly with the therapist, and incorporate him, thereby diminishing the importance of the symptom.

AUTHORITARIANISM

Haley (93) and Howard (102) advocate an authoritative, controlling posture for the therapist, that he take charge of the symptomatology.

ENVIRONMENTAL FACTORS

The importance of environmental factors is stressed by Augenbraum, Reid, and Friedman, (6) particularly in the treatment of children. They found that children often are more effectively treated by working with the parents to affect those environmental forces playing upon the child.

FLEXIBILITY OF CHILDREN

The essential reversibility of childhood disorders is seen by Lester (133) as the basis for the effectiveness of a brief, timely and appropriate psychotherapy to correct these disorders and to open the way for further normal progress. Most childhood disturbances she finds are deviations from normal development caused by: (1) an absence of vital external supplies; (2) interference from the outside with the child's normal drive to adapt to and master his environment; (3) internal limitations of the child which oppose normal growth; (4) a combination of the preceding. Moreover, she concludes, there is sufficient fluidity and flexibility inherent in the ordinary developmental process to allow for a wide range of normality.

Limiting therapy with children to one session, or its reduplication or extension, is a logical decision when the environment is not a sick one, reasons Winnicott (241). A single consultative session may remove a block to the child's "normal maturational process" so that the "consequent forward movement can find environmental conditions that are ready and waiting to carry the child's emotional development forward."

CRISIS—THE PROPITIOUS MOMENT

Caplan (33) has identified phases in the crisis: a rise in tension, and of unpleasant affect, accompanied by some disorganization of behavior, following an impact with a hazardous situation that called for appropriate coping behavior; a lack of resolution continues the hazard, making tension worse; the tension increases to the point at which additional internal and external forces are mobilized (some resolution may occur at this time since emergency problem-solving methods may be used, the problem may be defined in a new way, certain goals may be given up); a major disorganization occurs when the problem continues and cannot be solved, avoided or freshly defined.

Reviewing Caplan's four crisis phases, Paul (170) derives some important corollaries for interventive action. A small influence can produce a great change quickly because of painful and precarious equilibrium, so that another person, a member of the family, a sensitive friend, can effect significant changes. The outcome is not determined by previous experiences, but by current realities, perhaps by unique psychotherapeutic and situational forces. A new equilibrium may be even more adaptive so that positive changes are possible and skills for coping with the future may be improved.

Klein and Lindemann (118) identify a situation they call the emotionally hazardous situation. They define it as any sudden alteration in the field of social forces within which the individual exists of such nature that the individual's expectations of himself and his relations with others change. Field alterations may arise from the loss or threatened loss of a significant relationship, the introduction of one or more new individuals into the person's social orbit, transitions in social status and role relationships brought on by maturation (*e.g.* adolescence) or by new social roles such as marriage or social mobility. In all instances "the hazardous circumstances are patterned by institutional and other socio-cultural forces." They differentiate the crisis from the hazardous situation. The crisis is an acute and often prolonged disturbance as the result of an emotional hazard. The individual crisis is often a manifestation of the group crisis; the group in turn may experience crisis because of the individual interpersonal crisis of a significant member. The term "emotional predicament" is used in a most generic sense to include both the crisis and the emotional hazard. Pain apparently is the force that pushes, that musters the energy to overcome inertia, to induce one to submit to another force, that of the therapist, and to initiate change. Pain must be sharp if change is to occur; one too easily bears a dull ache. Klein and Lindemann cite a personal letter from Caplan in which he likens the brief intervention in a predicament to giving a gentle push to a man standing on one leg, hoping thereby to restore him to his pre-crisis balance, and also to get results with less effort than might ordinarily be required.

Propitious moments for change in the human life cycle are reflected in the variety of crises discussed in Parad's (165) volume on crisis intervention: grief, parenthood, premature birth of a child, kindergarten entry, middle and later years, relocations, suicide, deaths of others. The process of "vocational commitment" is seen by Fast (59) as a critical stage when the proper intervention will not only prevent breakdown but also improve the person's functioning in other areas of life that otherwise would not be accessible to modification.

The role of crisis in delineating the responsiveness of individuals to brief psychotherapy is discussed by Mackey (141). He agrees with Rapoport that therapist activity does not have to be extensive in crisis because people are more susceptible to influence during these states. Rationally directed help, even of limited amount, purposively focused is often more effective than would be more extensive therapy given at a time when the person was less accessible.

Jacobson *et al.* (106) support the crisis theory of Caplan and Lindemann, the basic theoretic premise that a personal crisis results in a deficit in psychological functioning of significant proportions, that at such times both preventive and therapeutic opportunities exist if the patient is seen soon after the crisis erupts.

Multiple-impact therapy, described by Ritchie (186), is a brief encounter, usually of two days' duration, for intensive study and treatment of a family in crisis by a team of a guidance clinic. The intensity of the procedure is based on two assumptions: families and individuals in crisis are stimulated to mobilize and strengthen resources to meet the crisis, they are more receptive to interventions, more likely to be flexible than at other times; in any type of psychotherapy more dramatic and rapid changes are likely at earlier stages of the treatment, the change in the later phases of long-cerm treatment is the more gradual, strengthening the movement obtained initially during the first few sessions or weeks.

Stierlin (216) observes that seemingly casual and noncommittal relationships can have an intensive emotional impact, so that in brief therapy the therapist's emotional responsiveness and perceptual acuity are reinforced by the patient's willingness to reveal himself and let himself be moved. He comments too upon the propitiousness of certain life situations for change, as in a developmental crisis when the defenses are labile and the cathexes are fluid. Thus many adolescents are available to short, intensive encounters. Ongoing changes take place from these brief encounters, Stierlin argues; it is less well understood that moments of encounter may be ongoing, that inner dialogue may continue beyond the actual encounter. Because both patient and therapist know that the relationship will not last or continue, the tension of involvement is bearable because the end is in sight. This may permit the focusing of energy to such dimensions that it accounts for the enduring inner dialogue. The brevity of the contact also makes easier the endurance of the negative transference for both. Stierlin agrees with Malan that the capacity to mourn enables the patient to benefit from the brief encounter because he is able to tolerate the loss that termination brings.

The Crisis as Discretely Time-Limited

Miller (152) comments on the lack of personality theory that provides the therapist with guides for termination of short-term work. He favors a developmental theory visualizing life from birth to death as both a continuous and a discrete process. Disruptions occur, disruptions due sometimes to past events, but also on occasion to limitations of the individual for meeting the stresses of the present. Each crisis, therefore, may be seen in some measure as independent of other crises, so that Miller's goal in short-term therapy with adolescents is the formation of an identity that enables the youth to cope with the current crisis. "The practical solution appears to be one of terminating when there is satisfactory adaptation to the present, letting the future take care of itself." Rapoport (180) also observes that the crisis is self-limiting, that it does not continue indefinitely.

In a related development, the crisis theory of Lindemann and Caplan is expanded by Waldfogel and Gardner (231) to include the individual's contribution to the crisis. In their work with school phobias, they found often that external precipitating causes were minor compared to the child's regressive needs. Extant crisis theory also does not account for the well-known fact that some individuals are prone to repetitive crises because of internal compulsions—for example, work and marital problems, and problems of internal control. They find crisis theory strengthened by conceiving of a crisis occurring along an internal-external continuum. Some crises are entirely of external causation, and restitutional measures may be indicated to reduce the trauma, as with those infants observed by Spitz who have lost their mothers altogether. Some crises, however, result from less powerful external changes, they may be self-initiated and goal directed, as in the decision to immigrate or to change a job. In these instances the individual has some equipment to cope with the problem, and may be supported by his group, as in rites of passage. Often the intervention here need only be supportive. Some crises, in contrast, are due much more to intra-psychic factors; these are presumed to occur when the immediate problem is linked to an unresolved crisis or conflict of the past. Perceptions become distorted, the individual restricts or modifies present behavior, a compulsive recapitulation of maladaptive behavior of the past occurs. Here a corrective emotional experience is required to solve the problem. This can only be brought about when there is an unresolved crisis in the past and resolution at the present time can strengthen the patient for the future. The authors believe that a corrective intervention does not require a particular kind of setting but rather a particular kind of person, one skilled in and acquainted with psychodynamics—"a mental health specialist." The authors observed a striking relationship between remission of the acute symptom in school phobia and promptness of treatment. This is a surprising finding because of the weight usually given to psychogenesis as the primary cause in phobias; they believe that their findings justify the view that each critical stage in development is a choice point, upon which the past weighs heavily, but where new elements may be added that make restructuring possible.

The Crisis as Cross-Cultural

Jacobson (105) supports a crisis strategem for lower-class persons based on comprehension of and adaptation to their time sense. The strategem avoids an agreement to talk about self and experience over an extended period of time. Time perspective, values, attitudes toward the helping process and language difficulties may stand in the way of therapeutic success. These are not insurmountable; they may be dealt with under appropriate circumstances with appropriate techniques. The therapist must make an additional effort to understand and respect the specific cultural background of his patient. This leads to some modifications of approach to transference phenomenon (discussed in the chapter on techniques; see p. 153). Where psychosocial distance between therapist and patient is considerable, these differences must be minimized, while whatever is common to them is maximized. The crisis, however, is a universal experience, capable of unifying diverse individuals. Jacobson believes that a crisis at any age is rooted in some universally shared childhood experiences which precede the differentiation of individuals into cultural and social sub-groups. Therefore, there is a "congruity of motivation and process during crisis, regardless of individual and socio-cultural differences." Crisis creates a facilitating interaction between persons of divergent backgrounds that may counteract the separating effect of language, time expectancies and other cultural patterns. "The more acute the crisis, the less the sense of strangeness." The advantages to be gained from the crisis are maximized when the patient's crisis becomes the essential and deliberate focus of the treatment. The usual cost in therapeutic time of working through socio-cultural differences between patient and therapist is minimized in crisis therapy by: the brevity of the intervention, which limits and reduces the exposure of each participant to alien social-cultural forces; the circumscribed nature of the crisis intervention which limits the area of mutual interaction just as its brief nature limits it in time, and the focus on areas where the coping adaptive mechanism of the patient have failed, which assures the patient that other patterns of his behavior will not be scrutinized.

II

PROCESS AND TECHNIQUE

Psychotherapeutic processes and techniques, when born in theory, are tempered and modified through clinical experience; when they arise empirically in the course of clinical practice, they are scanned against theory. Practice and theory are in a reciprocal relationship, and the psychotherapist at work is the agent of that reciprocity. The agency makes many demands upon him: his cognitive equipment must be adequate to the task; he must be cautious, flexible, immediately responsive to the effects of an intervention, sensing or knowing when to modify, strengthen or weaken; he must be attentive, carefully scanning and scrutinizing the progress of the therapy, attending to small details while grasping a panoramic view of a human life. Finally, he must be endowed with enough humility to temper the quantum of therapeutic omnipotence or arrogance that his clinical experience has not yet had time to wither.

A psychotherapeutic technique seems easier to describe than the process. Apart from all the well known problems of the validity of one's inferences and the subtleties of timing, the complex aspects of the process always include some unstatable quality of the therapist. Given great gifts for communication, one might describe clearly the process and the technique of one therapist. Yet used by another they would not be quite the same, or even quite different. Our semantic shackles compel that we call the process in all cases by the same name, and the technique in all cases the same technique. Add to this the influence for variety brought by the patients and the settings, and the permutations for any process and any technique progress beyond our capacity for clear description.

But we must make the effort. Otherwise psychotherapy becomes a mystique, not teachable, not learnable, but given. Moreover, within all the countless variations are enough countable constants, enough dimensions, to be stated. Many are meaningful in some situations, some in most, perhaps one or two, or a few, in all situations. Given these, the therapist assimilates and integrates as he works; adjusting, tightening, loosening, altering—he makes them his own.

Thus this section of five chapters is an overview of experience with the process and techniques of brief psychotherapy. All of the fore-mentioned complexities are intensified by the number of different therapies—active, supportive, anxiety-arousing, anxiety-suppressing, behavioral, psychoanalytically-based, transference-engaging, transfer-ence-avoiding, reality-oriented, as well as the number of authors whose reports, varied in content and style, the review encompasses. Once more we are succored by the integrative capacity of the working psychotherapist.

The section begins with a chapter describing a variety of models, contextual frameworks, within which therapists practice brief psycho-therapy. These become the stages upon which techniques are deployed. Since consistently throughout the literature a comprehensive psycho-diagnosis is *de rigueur* before the initiation of intervention, a chapter on the psychodiagnostic process follows. Then follows a chapter on techniques—about seventy of them, alphabetically arranged, a chapter on termination, and a final chapter on research studies of process in brief therapy.

CHAPTER 4

Models of the Brief Process

The advocate of a brief psychotherapy displays more compulsion to describe details of treatment than does the current practitioner of longer treatment. The intensive therapies are established and amply described. Perhaps the worker using briefer processes, aware that his approach is still novel, feels the need to state his procedures in order to defend them. At best, the effort toward brevity has brought a clarity of view that becomes a natural impetus to communication. Whatever the cause or case, we are beneficiaries of a number of concise and fecund statements of models for the conduct or context of brief psychotherapies. They are indeed productive: we find both general guidelines and fingers pointed at specific techniques, both forest and trees.

GENERAL MODELS

Fenichel (60) has been a cogent commentator. He believed a brief psychotherapy based upon psychoanalytic knowledge can vitiate psychotherapies based on coercion and suggestion. He projects an approach of which the first stage is essentially psychodiagnostic: the therapist employs the patient's behavior, facts about his symptoms, data from his history and his utterances, to establish a "dynamic diagnosis about the patient's most important conflicts, the degree of pressure from repressed forces, the relative strength of the repressing and defensive system, the patient's qualities of rigidity, elasticity, and accessibility."

In the second stage, the dynamic diagnosis permits the therapist to predict the probability of the patient's response to various measures, and to select an intervention. Among those available, Fenichel lists limited interpretations or modified interpretations, encouragement, evocation of selected types of transference, outlets that provide substitutions, manipulations of the environment, suggestions and/or prohibitions of tempting situations or activities or those that may be reassuring, vocalization of the actual conflict or advice that is mental hygienic in nature. The third phase is the application of the selected interventions.

A flexible schematization of brief psychotherapy is described by Wolberg (245): (1) the early establishment of a working relationship which involves sympathetic listening, communication and understanding, confidence, reassurance that the patient can be helped, and particularly a structuring of the therapeutic situation; (2) the development of a tentative diagnosis; (3) development in conjunction with the patient of a hypothetical comprehension of the patient's psychodynamics; (4) focusing on an area for exploration, illuminating the neurotic behavior at work and encouraging the patient's recognition; (5) using dream interpretation (Wolberg warns that the therapist must be analytically trained for this); (6) resolving resistance as soon as possible, requiring that one be on the alert for its emergence; (7) preventing or avoiding the development of a transference neurosis by the quick management of transference manifestations; (8) recognizing destructive factors in the patient's environment and coping with them before they become harmful; (9) the quick coping with "target symptoms" such as extreme anxiety, depression, and tension; (10) instructing the patient in the use of insight as an ameliorating and modifying force in his life, teaching him the association between symptomatology and conflict, and making him aware of defensive behavior and mechanisms that are damaging to him; (11) developing with the patient a plan of action whereby the patient may bring his newfound insight to bear on the task of making changes in his life; (12) promoting the patient's ability to develop a "proper life philosophy"; (13) the termination process; (14) follow-up.

Bellak and Small (20) devote a chapter to basic procedures grouped under six rubrics:

(1) Identification of the present problem—initiating in the therapist a set of formulations and conceptual expectations which the history will either confirm, modify, or negate.

(2) Taking a history—seeking data to illuminate the personal experience of the patient and permit a diagnostic formulation, requiring most of the first session, and that the therapist be skilled in facilitating communication.

(3) The establishment of causal relations—considering the probability of overdetermination.

(4) The choice of intervention—having determined the cause of symptoms, proceeding to the task of undoing. The therapist must quickly identify those factors which either demand change or lend themselves most readily to it. Interventions may be verbal operations, or may be chosen from among adjunctive measures available to the therapist. Interventions based essentially upon oral communication between patient and therapist are considered primary, the others, secondary or adjunctive. The authors employ an assessment of ego functions to guide the choice of interventions, selecting approaches with a view toward achieving either the strengthening or the lessening of reliance upon a particular ego function.

(5) Working through the problem—the achievement of reinforcement of the learning of new behavior and the extinction of neurotic modes of adjustment.

(6) Ending of treatment—exercising care to leave the patient with a cultivated positive transference and a clear understanding that he is welcome to return.

Their model rests upon two basic assumptions. One has to do with three processes they find common to all dynamic psychoanalytically-oriented psychotherapy: communication, insight and working through. The second devolves upon the role of transference phenomena. This is discussed in the alphabetical section on techniques (see p. 153); suffice it to note here that they find a positive transference essential to brief psychotherapy, to permitting communication of sufficient data quickly enough to enable the therapist to achieve a psychodynamic formulation, and to select interventions. Negative factors are not ignored or left uninterpreted; they are, however, clarified immediately lest they impede the therapeutic progress.

McGuire (145, 146) in a rather philosophical survey of the "process" of short-term insight therapy offers the "phase model for guiding interventions," especially interpretations. The variables in his model are: (1) positive transference, in which the patient unrealistically loves his therapist and appears "to follow" him; (2) a transference neurosis, indicated by expansion of associations to include "infantile oedipal references," by sudden blocking or by a tendency to associate the therapist with the parent of sex opposite to the therapist's; (3) the "experience bias," that part of the character structure which is present throughout therapy as it is in all stress situations; (4) symptoms, which when increasing suggest unrecognized feelings toward the therapist and also that the previously encapsulated conflict is becoming more diffuse.

There are four phases in McGuire's model.

(1) Perceptual ordering. The therapist sets goals, notes experience biases, dissects out problems and the positive transference begins.

(2) Perceptual reordering. This is introduction of new perceptual relationships, reordering of conscious material, clarifying, some confrontation, and development of new and uncovered thoughts and emotions which are interpreted and woven into the patient's comprehension. During this phase, any adoption by the patient of the methods of introspection modelled on the therapist will take place. The end of the phase is marked by four characteristics: (a) an increase in symptoms, usually anxiety but often depression; (b) a decrease in positive transference with fears of antagonism; (c) the beginning of the transference neurosis; and (d) an increase in experience bias.

(3) Transference interpretation. This phase is often brief, sometimes of just a few minutes duration. The technical objective in this phase is to provide insights and understanding of conflicts, and to give perceptual reordering to an emotional and experiential existence through recognizing the patient's feeling toward the therapist.

(4) Termination and integration. If the interpretations have been correct, the patient will work with them. Symptoms, espe-

cially those therapeutically induced, will decrease. Time is often needed for review, for testing new perceptual modes.

A concisely ordered model is presented by Gillman (76): (1) select a crucial dynamic problem, (2) focus on current reality, (3) foster positive transference, but do not foster regression, (4) rely on spontaneous forces within the patient.

Socarides (211) offers a three-stage model for brief psychotherapy: the accurate appraisal and forceful interpretation of transference behavior at the first interview; the second interview even more active with explanations of dynamics by the therapist; the third stage a period of consolidation and working through.

Baker (9) offers six steps as the contextual approach to brief psychotherapy: (1) intellectual clarification of the problems; (2) advice; (3) catharsis; (4) interpretation of transference and resistance; (5) prolonged supportive techniques; and (6) the favorable attitude of the therapist.

Symptoms are emphasized as the focus of attention in the model drawn by Tompkins (225). The therapist is active, drugs are used more frequently, insight into dynamics is minimized, while the amelioration of "target" symptoms is stressed, goals are limited, visits are abbreviated and spaced according to need. These approaches, Tompkins avers, prevent excessive dependence.

The process of brief psychotherapy is seen by Burdon (29) to involve active mobilization and evocation of healthy aspects of the personality, while simultaneously negating, reversing or neutralizing negative and pathological aspects of feelings, attitudes and actions. The emphasis is upon health orientation and mastery: "The dynamics of cure are not the dynamics of illness; the patient does not benefit by a personally conducted case conference on his psychopathology."

MODELS OF CRISIS INTERVENTION

Levy (134) developed a six-session crisis-intervention psychotherapy using a team of professionals and aimed specifically at the prevention of hospitalization in acute episodes. Contact with the patient is limited to six sessions. The first session lasts 45 minutes, subsequent interviews 30 minutes. The interval between visits is adjusted for each patient.

At the first session, the goal of helping the patient avoid hospitalization is stated explicitly, with the announcement that this is to be accomplished within six sessions. The history is taken, with attention to precipitating factors in the current crisis as well as related past episodes. A supportive approach is actively launched: the patient's plight is empathized with, specifically his discomfort, his confusion, his chaos. The patient is enlisted into an alliance of effort toward resolution of the crisis. The availability of the therapist is emphasized, as is his intention to help the patient. Medication is often prescribed and adjunctive supporting services such as those of a homemaker or public-health nurse visit are arranged. Unique to Levy's model is that concurrent with the first session, the patient's family is simultaneously interviewed by the team social worker, who, while the patient is still with the therapist, telephones the therapist to relate important history or other current factors. The therapist in return informs the social worker of his planned treatment program, including any necessary manipulation of the environment, and sets the date for the patient's next visit. Thus the social worker is able to orient the family properly, and the therapist is in possession of any important corollary information. Continuity between sessions is assured by a brief staff conference at the beginning of each day. The social worker and the therapist cover all of their contacts with the patients and families who are to be seen that day; the clinic homemaker may relate her experiences of the past day in direct patient care. This keeps the staff abreast of potentially explosive situations.

In the second session, the therapist comments explicitly upon his observation of improvement in the patient, seeking thereby to reduce the patient's anxiety of mental deterioration, and also reinforcing the supporting role of the clinic. The patient's concept of "going crazy" is explored and tested in reality. Repeated differentiation between thought and action is found extremely useful. Any gaps in the history are filled. The current status is evaluated. Decisions about shifts in the home situation are based not upon the patient's report alone, but also upon the impression of the home situation obtained by the social worker in concurrent session with family members. A therapeutic program for the remaining sessions is derived from clarification of the history and the better understanding of the patient's environment. The therapist identifies for the patient his modes of response to people and events, as these are likely to initiate further acute episodes. He guides the patient both in a recognition of them and in suggested solutions. The patient is acquainted with his own signals of distress, the tightening of the stomach, increased heart rate, the feeling that the bottom has dropped out of things. The interview ends with repetition of the therapist's recognition of the patient's improvement and expression of optimism for continued improvement.

The third session begins with repetition of statements concerning the patient's improvement and increased ability to cope with his illness. This session concentrates upon clarifying causal dynamics of the illness and reinforcement of the patient's awareness of signals of distress. He is helped to express feelings. The emphasis may be shifted from precipitating factors to current life situations. He is helped to develop planned approaches to conflict situations, recognizing their destructive influence upon him and preparing him to learn alternative solutions for such difficulties. The therapist makes no effort to cover all the major problem areas, but instead focuses upon teaching the patient methods of coping with a particular situation. The approaching termination of the therapy is discussed in relationship to the patient's developing ability to master his problems.

The fourth and subsequent sessions also open with repetition of recognized improvement and increased mastery. The patient's efforts at practicing his new coping techniques are reviewed. If he has failed, the failure is explored. Stress situations are anticipated and the patient's approach to them rehearsed. This rehearsal is considered an extremely important procedure. Levy reports that the early life experiences of the majority of the patients he has seen at this clinic have predisposed them to defeat and potential mental disintegration. Therefore he concentrates upon teaching them mastery of their "comparatively simple family or life situation." In terminating, an ongoing relationship with the clinic is established by informing the patient of the clinic's availability should further crises arise. The central element in this model is the team approach to the short-term treatment of patients in acute distress. The treatment of the disturbed family by a social worker simultaneously with the treatment of the patient by the psychotherapist is an inherent feature.

The emotional crisis is approached in the following way by Sifneos (206): (1) determination of the patient's need and suitability for a specific therapeutic approach must be made quickly; (2) therapy is made a "joint venture" utilizing the patient's motivation to get better; (3) the development of the crisis is reviewed for the patient so that his understanding of its course is assured; (4) practical, realistic steps to resolve the crisis are encouraged; (5) "antitherapeutic" actions are challenged; (6) the patient is taught to predict the danger of emotional difficulties arising in situations similar to the current crisis; (7) the therapy is terminated early, a goal achieved by avoiding entanglement with the patient's characterological problems.

At the Benjamin Rush Center, Jacobson et al. (106) train from the following model, particularly for crisis intervention: (1) active exploration of the current situation in which the precipitating event is identified when it is not otherwise readily apparent; (2) analogous situations in the patient's past are identified; (3) the patient's problem is stated for him in concise language that he can understand; (4) support is lent to the patient's efforts at this point to deal with the problem as a result of his increased understanding; (5) discussions of chronic problems are avoided; (6) the therapist must be prepared to accept the patient's wish to discontinue further professional help after equilibrium is established.

Some of the philosophical attitudes inherent in the Rush Center approach are described by Morley (156). The therapist must be impressed with the effectiveness of limited goal treatment and not consider it a "second best" approach. Discharge as the goal is inherent from the moment of the patient's entry for treatment, in order to muster the full energies of both therapist and patient for the resolution of the crisis. The goal of the treatment is explicitly the patient's return to his pre-crisis status. Assessment is directed primarily toward the identification and understanding of the crisis, rather than to an exploration of the pre-crisis personality. The therapist must be willing and able to be active, and equally willing and able to assume a variety of roles in the employment of an array of techniques.

The Rush Center has been productive of a number of useful and cogent ideas about and approaches to the resolution of crises. Among these Jacobson et al. (107) have identified two fundamental approaches to crises—the generic and the individual—that pre-determine techniques of intervention. The generic approach holds that each type of crisis (loss, divorce, for example) produces specific, identifiable patterns of response, some of which are adaptive, others maladaptive. The concentration is upon the course which each kind of crisis follows. This identification permits the selection of the similarly specific interventions which have been designed for "this kind" of crisis. The approach is broadly the same to all individuals experiencing a generically similar crisis. The approach permits intervention by workers who are not specifically mental-health professionals with techniques encouraging adaptive, coping behavior. Public-health as well as psychiatric nurses have been trained in the approach (157).

The individual approach governs most of the treatment conducted at the Center. The approach stresses the unique "biopsychosocial events" in the life of the individual patient, interventions selected for the individual and treatment conducted by "mental-health professionals." It differs from longer therapies in not being as concerned with pre-crisis dynamics except as they may elucidate the present crisis and guide its resolution. Additionally, family members and other important figures are more frequently involved in the treatment process.

The "patterns of responses for an individual or family necessary for healthy crisis resolution," are listed by Rapoport (180): (1) accurate perception of the situation, which is fostered by a search for new knowledge and by retaining consciousness of the problem; (2) managing affect by being aware of feelings and by ventilation to achieve tension discharge and mastery; (3) developing patterns for seeking and using help from both individuals and from institutions.

Klein and Lindemann (118) delineate a model for preventive intervention in family and individual crisis situations which includes: (1) appraisal and prediction (this proceeds from development of a relationship; the client's ego resources are mobilized by enlisting his collaboration in examining the problem in terms of his own feelings and those of others); (2) planning the intervention (this includes determining whether the crisis is of recent origin, and how the emotional hazards bearing on a group affect all of the individuals); (3) altering the balance of forces (achieved by restoring equilibrium in a social group—perhaps removing obstacles to new relations and widening the range of object relations in general, the redistribution of the role relationships within the group, developing alternative means for satisfaction of needs that cannot be satisfied within the present social order, and by redefining the predicament which is usually implicit and which is especially important when the individual feels he is the passive victim); (4) resolving the crisis and anticipatory planning. A case is never considered closed; the patient and the family may always come back. The attempt is made to end on an optimistic note, the accomplishments are reviewed, and the implication for possible future emotional hazards are delineated. Followup contracts are arranged by visits or telephone calls.

THE SOCIALLY DEPRIVED

Wolk (247) has devised an approach to the treatment of socially deprived and economically underprivileged individuals which he calls the kernel-interview concept. This approach seeks to make each contact with the patient an entity of treatment separate and complete in itself. Each session is conceived of as having its own beginning, its own end, its own goals, very much in the way an entire treatment plan has goals and beginning, middle and end processes. The aim is to leave the patient at the end of each session eager for the next session; in each session anxiety is raised and then reduced prior to the ending of the session, so that he patient leaves comfortable, relieved, satisfied, feeling that he has accomplished something tangible and meaningful.

SPECIFIC SYNDROMES

Some therapists have sought to develop an individual model for a specific dagnosis or syndrome.

Grief

The "essential task" for the therapeutic management of acute grief is stated by Lindemann (137) as "sharing the patient's grief work" which encompasses the patient's effort to end his bondage to the deceased person and to find new ways or new outlets of "rewarding interaction."

Depression

The "tactical" approach to the brief psychotherapy of depression, advocated by Regan, (181) includes the following phases: (1) protection of the patient (treatment of the depressed patient requires that the therapist be highly astute and flexible in protecting his patient, therefore extremely sensitive to clues, cues and signals); (2) exploration, a means of arousing the patient into psychotherapeutic activity; (3) interruption of the ruminative cycle; (4) the use of physical therapy; (5) initiation of an attitudinal change; (6) effective collaboration with other resources. The crux, he argues, of a brief psychotherapy of depression is the flexibility and adaptability of the therapist, reflected in the care with which he reviews and plans the therapy of each patient.

In treating depression, Bellak and Small (20) suggest the following components: (1) raising lowered self esteem, often the first step in the psychotherapy of depression; (2) reassurance, if it can be derived realistically from the patient's tangible assets and ego strengths, to contribute to increase in self esteem; (3) reversal of intra-aggression; (4) where possible linking comprehension of dynamic features with both the precipitating situation and earlier genetic situations; (5) dealing with transference manifestations promptly and clearly; (6) offering support through the expressed availability of the therapist at any time, often an important feature; (7) guidance, particularly in cases of suicidal danger, may be crucial in avoiding situations which damage self esteem, or, where needed, guiding the patient into situations which may help channelize hostility through violent physical activity; (8) drug therapy may play a major role; (9) electroconvulsive therapy still has a definite place, especially if the suicidal danger is great. Where the suicidal danger is paramount, all of the above are especially pertinent, with emphasis given these additional features: (1) the suicidal attempt is generally accepted as equivalent to a call for help; (2) insight for work with the problem of aggression is especially important; (3) the acting-out features must be recognized, as often obtaining postponement of the suicidal attempt gains crucial time for other procedures; (4) a brief period of hospitalization may be indicated.

A model for supportive treatment of depression is described by Gross (89) as, (1) establishment of effective communication, and (2) mobilization of purposeful activity. From these guidelines he developed a rather precise regimen employing a wide variety of very active recommendations made to the patient by the therapist.

Panic States

For the treatment of both endogenous and exogenous panic states, Bellak and Small (20) present the following structure: (1) cathartic expressions of affects and ideations associated with the panic; (2) reassurance and support; (3) increasing the patient's competence; (4) interpretation of drives which are exciting the patient, along with their genetic antecedents; (5) vigorous interference with denial and repression; (6) simultaneous repression of one drive while encouraging another where indicated.

Depersonalization

The treatment of depersonalization described by Bellak and Small (20) involves the following procedures: (1) imparting intellectual awareness of the nature of the process of depersonalization, especially some of its physiological components; (2) use of appropriate drugs where depersonalization is primarily induced by anxiety-arousing experiences; (3) reversal of denial of aggressive impulses through interpretation.

Psychotic States

In the treatment of incipient and acute psychotic states, Bellak and Small (20) propose these guidelines: (1) regulation of the life of the patient; (2) active but cautious interpretation of the core conflict; (3) drug treatment; (4) brief hospitalization where necessary to safeguard during active interpretation; (5) support and reassurance.

Acting Out

Bellak and Small (20) are not sanguine about the effectiveness of brief psychotherapy with the acting-out patient, but call attention to Greenacre's (85) basic long-range goals of prohibition, interpretation and ego strengthening. They note that the diverse and complex nature of acting-out behavior indicates that the management of this problem will vary a great deal from one patient to another. Their model for an effort at brief therapy includes: (1) direct prohibition of certain relationships or behavior; (2) environmental manipulation to remove the patient from the situation which precipitates the acting-out; (3) direct cathartic interpretation of the drive expressed in the acting-out; (4) efforts to make the acting-out behavior ego alien; (5) intellectual outlining of the meaning of the patient's behavior; (6) predictive interpretations of consequences: (7) achievement of any delay possible; (8) strengthening the superego in certain cases; (9) increasing synthetic functioning; (10) use of appropriate drugs; (11) enlisting the help of others; (12) reassurance through availability of the therapist; (13) dissolution of inhibitions where the patient is inhibited in "success efforts."

Severe Somatic Conditions

For patients with severe somatic conditions Bellak and Small (20) use the following model: (1) the therapist assumes a realistic attitude toward the seriousness of the illness or disability and does not minimize; (2) the patient's distortions relative to his injury or illness are established, interpreted and corrected; (3) the specific meaning of the illness to the patient is identified and interpreted; (4) object relationships are improved; (5) any serviceable denial available is deployed; for example, helping the patient identify with prominent individuals who suffer the same disability.

A theoretically well-grounded approach to the treatment of emotional reactions to physical illness described by Stein *et al.* (213) emphasizes an irreplaceable target: an early diagnostic formulation of the clinical data. In this they are aided by three fundamental guidelines: (1) denial is the primary defense of these patients; (2) a narcissistic injury is usually suffered by the person who has experienced a severe illness or body trauma; (3) understanding of the actual facts of the illness or injury, its manifestations and implications is usually faulty because of cognitive blocks, which most likely follows as a consequence of denial. The authors find that familiarity with these guidelines enables an early formulation of the clinical data into a treatment plan that can be quickly initiated and effectively pursued.

Traumatic Neuroses of War

Grinker (174) delineated these steps in the treatment of war neuroses: (1) the development of positive transference; (2) the release of unconscious tensions, especially of earlier anxieties, using pentathol, repetition and reminders; (3) the gratification of dependent needs; (4) recognition of the temporal and spatial present, in other words the emphasis of the current reality; (5) the release of repressed hostility. The last step, Grinker notes, is the hardest task of all, one which often failed.

CHILDREN AND ADOLESCENTS

Guidelines in emotional first aid for children are provided by Green and Rothenberg (84): (1) prevent further emotional damage to the child; (2) inform responsible adults about the nature of the damage to personality to which the child may be exposed; (3) advise adults on positive steps to be taken; (4) advise adults on actions to be avoided; (5) reassure adults in contact with the children by offering understanding of the child's "language of behavior" in non-technical terms; (6) inform adults when it is desirable to secure professional help for the child. Some more specific suggestions are provided for the responsible adults: (1) maintain control of self in the child's presence; (2) hear the child out; (3) don't tell the child to forget his problem; (4) don't use ridicule, teasing or corporal punishment; (5) permit the child to repeat his account of his troubles as often as he wishes; (6) learn as much about the child's situation as possible before taking action; (7) don't compel the child into any situation to which he does not feel equal.

Brief psychotherapy in a private pediatric practice is described by Coddington (39); his basic technique is to encourage ventilation by the mother during the course of a regular office visit with the child. This requires rather rigid adherence to his appointment schedule in order to provide a relaxed and non-pressured atmosphere. The pediatrician must be sympathetic and interested in hearing the mother tell her story in her own words. He develops introductory comments to facilitate the mother's ability and freedom to communicate; these remarks are designed to show that the pediatrician not only understands the difficulty the mother is having with the rearing of her child but is sympathetic to them.

The process of short-term therapy with adolescents for Miller (152) consists of: (1) intelligent listening to the patient's communication, (2) encouragement of communication of relevant historical and current data, by (3) asking pertinent questions, (4) offering reassurance as needed, (5) encouraging and accepting emotional discharge and insight, (6) interpretation at the proper time, (7) guarding the patient's assimilation of recovered memory and of the emotional experiences that took place during treatment.

CHAPTER 5

The Psychodiagnostic Process

There would seem to be no room in a consideration of brief psychotherapy for the debate on whether diagnosis should precede, occur in the course of, or follow therapy. The authors who discuss the topic at all are in agreement: diagnosis is absolutely essential to the undertaking and progress of brief psychotherapy and must accompany every stage. The therapist working with crises may modify this statement somewhat, but only to obtain focus. He will urge, as does Morley (156), that the diagnostic assessment be the identification and explanation of the crisis rather than a description of the condition of the pre-crisis personality. The systematic formulation of the presenting problem is seen by Barten (13) as foreshadowing the process of treatment. A broad definition of psychodiagnosis is desired, one that goes beyond nosology, which is insufficient as a guide to brief psychotherapeutic treatment.

The laudable efforts to bring psychotherapy to all who need it have acquainted many clinicians for the first time with the colossally inhumane conditions of poverty. A recent panel discussion in New York heard a speaker argue that the poor were not sick; it was society that was diseased. Therefore, the first task of psychotherapy was to attack poverty. An example was offered. A black schoolgirl of 14 complained of going about in a daze. The mother of two illegitimate children, she slept with them in one bed in a small apartment crowded by some 10-15 persons. With understandable indignation, the therapist diagnosed her daze as exhaustion caused by these crowded circumstances, and set out to find appropriate housing for her. Perhaps he was right; but if so, he was merely lucky to have hit upon the one determinant among several possibly responsible for her complaint. Other clinicians suggested other possible causes for her dazed condition. Preoccupation, hallucinations, depression and cerebral lesions were among the determinants they reasoned needed to be differentially assessed, along with the effect of crowded conditions.

A hospital staff conference on brief psychotherapy reviewed the case of a young boy. A management problem at school, his unpredictable eruptions of anger were cited as his most disturbing behavior. Consideration was given to the harsh, physically punitive nature of his upbringing. But when the suggestion was made that a neurological basis for his anger be eliminated before a purely psychogenic one was given primary credence, objections were raised that this lengthened therapy, that it was not possible to hold poor people long enough to make this kind of differential diagnosis.

In the face of a very real problem—sustaining action-oriented people through a diagnostic process—the choice cannot be to abandon the diagnostic assessment. Therapy cannot be abbreviated by eliminating this important contribution to understanding and guide to intervention. Intervention cannot be made a matter of chance, hence more likely to lengthen rather than to shorten the process. The need is for more readily available, more rapidly responsive diagnostic services, coupled with action-oriented programs moving simultaneously upon crucial living problems about which something can be done.

Since brief psychotherapy is increasingly likely to be the psychotherapy of choice in extending mental-health services to the poor, we must understand that to abandon or drastically curtail diagnosis is to deprive the poor of that single element most likely to make the psychotherapeutic process helpful to them: guided therapeutic intention.

GENERAL APPROACHES

Bellak (21) is emphatic that "complete psychodynamic understanding of the patient and his presenting problem" is crucial. This must be achieved in light of the entire life framework and social context of the individual. From this comprehension, Bellak derives which interventions to use, in what areas of the patient's life, in what sequence the methods are to be applied, toward what goal, and what adjunctive procedures are to be used.

The problems of diagnosis were treated at a Council on Brief Psychotherapy (174) in Chicago in 1941 by Alexander, Kimberly, Levine, Grinker and Lewis. A clear positive relationship was seen by Alexander between the precision of a therapist's knowledge about the quantitative psychodynamic aspect of an individual and his ability to adapt interventions to individual patient's needs.

Semantic confusion in diagnostic statements, making them difficult to comprehend and nearly impossible to compare, was uncovered in a survey of 25 years of records at Austin Riggs by Kimberly (174). What, for example, he asks, is meant precisely by "ego strength"? He does not use the terms *ego, superego* or *id,* and diagnostically identifies only two groups of individuals: (1) well-built personalities who are only transiently off balance, and (2) less well put-together and much damaged individuals of long standing who must be put back together in better fashion. This will seem to many people to be an over-simplification of a very complex process and to offer little insight into the treatment process since it provides no guide to the selection of therapeutic interventions.

Levine (174) saw three levels in diagnostic thinking. Clinical diagnosis, the first level, has inevitable bearing upon the choice of technique: the suicidal manic-depressive requires psychotherapy in protected conditions along with very cautious use of interpretation; by contrast a depressive person with a need for suffering requires treatment that is not too reassuring, not giving or too friendly. Dynamic diagnosis, the second level, is a reading of the meaning and purpose of the symptom or behavior to the particular personality and its structure, and Levine includes both secondary and primary gains, the strength of the ego, the severity of the superego, the intensity of the id. Levine's third level is the genetic diagnosis which includes the life history of the individual as it may influence the therapy: for example, rejection in childhood calls for brief psychotherapy that is warm, consistent and accepting, and one not destroyed by provocations, aggression or repellent defenses of the patient.

Grinker (174) developed categories for a diagnostic formulation in approaching traumatic war neurosis: (1) the patient's history, including any record of previous neurosis; (2) evaluation of the degree to which exhaustion contributed to the soldier's break; (3) indication of previous but recent psychological traumata; (4) the severity of the precipitating traumata; (5) assessment of the quantity of anxiety; (6) assessment of the strength of the ego; (7) assessment of the capacity for psychological understanding; (8) evaluation of the degree of repressed hostility; (9) the type of clinical syndrome; and (10) the amount of time available for psychotherapy.

Lewis (174) summarized the necessary steps to be taken before the choice of a therapeutic approach. These include identification of the immediate precipitating factors, the type of onset, the intelligence of the patient, his temperament and characteristics, his physical health, and any evidence of personality changes which might suggest the possibility of schizophrenia, paranoid or deeply rooted hypochondriacal fixations.

A group of British psychoanalysts under the direction of Michael Balint in a workshop on focal therapy developed a series of diagnostic forms to facilitate an early diagnosis. Presenting each case in a number of forms is a burdensome task, and Courtenay (50) describes their modification in his application of brief psychotherapy to problems of sexual discord in marriage. The forms were seen as a way of reporting the content of an initial interview, or two or three interviews, so that all factors, positive and negative, pertinent to the patient's disturbance would emerge with clarity. The approach departs from the standard psychiatric examination, and is better viewed as a psychodynamic method in which the patient is permitted to relate his story in his own way. A minimum number of questions are used to induce him to provide the material he thinks relevant to his situation. The danger is that the diagnosis is possible only after a prolonged period, so that psychotherapy would occur only as a "chance phenomenon." The aim in the psychodynamic diagnostic interview is actually to achieve some change in the patient. This happens when the patient is helped to see his problem in a manner that allows him to make a move that is therapeutic.

The form as modified by Courtenay's group is intended to enable the patient to express himself freely, while simultaneously enabling the therapist to understand the patient's expression. The form guides recording of basic facts about the patient (in this case couples coming for marriage counseling), their families, information about the referring agency, data relevant to the patient's appearance and manner of presenting his story and material relevant to the diagnosis. Other sections permit recording of the development of the relationship between patient and therapist, the main themes developed in the interview and a summary of the therapist's impression of the real problem and of the patient's personality. The form was subsequently again modified with the addition of a section for recording the course of the interview, and any moments in it considered of special importance, and expansion of the summary to include assessments of the psychodynamics involved. The summary begins with a listing of all the ways in which the disturbance was manifested in the patient's life; from this the decisions about focal brief psychotherapy are established. The form identifies an area of the patient's psychic life in which, if an adjustment can be made, his symptomatology should be influenced for the better.

Malan (144), who participated with Balint in the development of this focal approach, describes the process in four steps: (1) the patient produces material, (2) this equips the therapist to discern and formulate a focus, which (3) he then offers to the patient, who (4) accepts, it is hoped, and works with the focus offered.

Malan also traces the similarities and dissimilarities between a medical and a psychodynamic diagnosis. The first step in both is to identify symptoms. The diagnosis itself consists of an explanatory hypothesis which relates symptoms to identifiable pathological processes. Here the parallel breaks down: in medicine most pathological process are at least pragmatically understood, while a psychological symptom implies almost nothing that is generally accepted as underlying pathology, nor can the future course be predicted with any degree of certainty. Despite these difficulties, Malan recommends the following model to be followed: the observer, the therapist, lists the disturbances; psychodynamic theory is brought to bear to formulate a hypothesis that links the disturbances with each other and to an underlying psychological pathology. He conceives that even more than sufferers from physical or physiological illnesses, each psychological patient requires his own separate hypothesis, being more dissimilar to each other than medical patients. Parsimony is desirable; the minimum number of hypotheses and the minimum amount of theory are used to link the various disturbances within a given patient to each other and to causal pathology.

Bellak and Small (20) follow a similar line of thinking which they present in considerable detail. They observe that current knowledge enables more descriptive diagnosis, permitting determination of a relationship between the patient today and both past and contemporary events in his life. Psychodynamic knowledge requires consideration of the stage of development at which the patient had a given experience. The therapist must remain mindful of the organismic equipment of the individual in as much detail as it is discernible. The task of a dynamic diagnosis is made more difficult because we are no longer permitted rigid determinism, but can think only in terms of the most probable causes. Since a diagnosis must be cast in terms of probability, they prefer to speak of a diagnostic formulation rather than a diagnosis, thereby extending exploration beyond the purely descriptive aspects of nosology. Care is required so that the necessarily rapid intervention is not haphazard, but rather is rooted in and guided by an understanding ascribing the patient's complaints to the dynamics of the precipitating circumstances and in turn to relevant historical factors. Such a diagnostic formulation must also enable the therapist to identify factors most susceptible to change and to select and apply methods for effecting the change. Treatment is carefully wedded to diagnosis in this approach. They comment that the first task in diagnosis is to understand the symptom, a process that proceeds from the most general to the most specific meaning of the symptoms concerned. Their comprehensive approach to the appraisal of disturbances further requires assessment of the strengths and weaknesses of the ego functions.

Wolberg (245) employs a diagnostic survey encompassing four factors: degree of disruption to homeostasis indicated by the level of anxiety or anxiety-equivalents; kinds of defenses employed; degree of independence, self-esteem and nature of relationships; potential for disintegration. He finds helpful a hypothetical formulation of dynamics in each patient as a guide to therapy, selecting "target" symptoms to be worked with.

McGuire (146) finds that the diagnostic-evaluation process serves an important prognostic function: "Of those patients who eventually gain insight, nearly all begin their own mental ordering and analysis of conflicts in the period between the evaluation and the start of therapy."

SOME SPECIFIC DIMENSIONS OF THE PSYCHODIAGNOSTIC PROCESS

Some writers have paid special attention to specific determinations to be made in the diagnostic process, or have concentrated upon developing skill and knowledge in such specific determinations.

Achieving Focus

The advocacy by Malan (144) particularly and by Wolberg (245) of concentrating and limiting one's effort from the outset has already been related. The use of a diagnostic consultant or a joint diagnostic effort has been found helpful in achieving focus. Normand *et al.* (163), seeking to use the diagnostic procedure to limit goals, found that the participation of a social worker helped the therapist to exclude the unrealizable and to limit goals in working with patients from lower socio-economic groups.

Joint diagnostic evaluation is recommended by McGuire (146) with the patient seen by a psychiatrist and then by a social worker. These two review the case and arrive at a recommendation. More than history taking is involved: motivations are assessed, problems are defined, and other related structuring occurs.

The Patient's Ecological Group

A concept of the person's ecological group is introduced into the diagnostic process by Miller (153). This group is important in emergency or crisis intervention, as any person in it may be critical to the progress of the patient. Identification and discussion of the constituents of his ecological group with the patient often enables him to muster his resources under conditions of diminished anxiety.

Expectations as Determinants of Symptoms

Aldrich (2) expands a dimension of the diagnostic formulation; he cites the work of Johnson and Szurek (109) who identified parents as the source of expectations which become determinants of symptoms, but adds other agents of influence in this process—teachers, counselors, scout masters, the culture. And so a further line of inquiry in the diagnostic process asks: What are the effects of expectations, from what sources, in the creation of the symptoms?

Assessment of Defenses

Working with college women students, Speers (212) sees symptoms arising as failures of defenses against the basic drives of hostility, sexuality and dependency, finding the drives in this group directed usually toward boyfriends or classmates as well as parents. One part of the diagnostic process is to delineate the nature of the drive and the object toward whom it is directed. He classified the defenses arising from various drive conflicts. Conflicts around dependency, for example, tend to breed the following: over-independence, frequently seen in the mothering of classmates, marriage or even pregnancy as the denial of one's dependency needs; denial of loss, or threat of loss, of the object upon whom the person is dependent; regression to a helpless little girl who is in conflict with growing independent wishes; direct demand for mothering on the part of those who feel cheated.

Among the defenses emerging in conflicts around sexual drives he reports: avoidance of sexual situations with an emphasis on intellectual activity; a search for an external superego, which may parallel regression to a little-girl stage in order to obscure one's own wishes and to make the girl's boyfriend "incapable of taking advantage of her"; rationalization, by idealizing the father, thereby depreciating boys as immature, avoiding interest in boys and the necessity to cope with the problem of sexuality; antisocial action in order to be restricted so as not to be tempted into sexuality; failure in school necessitating return to the parents' protections; a series of devices to indicate one is circumscribed or spoken for—such as marriage to a service man, engagement to a boy who is far away or to a known homosexual; rushing into the feared situation by indiscriminate and thoughtless sexual behavior; or assuming a religious posture. Another defense is to become deliberately involved in sexual situations but not go "all the way"—petting within well-defined limits or operating on the perimeter of a beat-group as if to get one's toes wet but never jumping into the water. Another maneuver moves into homosexuality, either in an impulsive, explosive manner, or in a deliberate, overt action with no desire to change. Finally, he lists deliberate heterosexual activity.

Conflicts involving hostility presented these defenses: conscious superego control in those aware of their hostility but unable to express it because of their situation; denial, or reaction formation of ingratiation and submission; displacement from parents to teachers; in-turning of the hostility, often producing academic failure and depression; reversal of affect; development of obsessive-compulsive symptoms; projection.

Assessment of Suicidal and Homicidal Potentiality

The necessity to guard against suicidal action is offered by some writers as the justification, essentially the requirement, of a thorough assessment. Stern (215) offers a number of guidelines in the assessment of suicidal risk. He observes that the affect of depression in itself is not always paramount in suicidal dangers; impulsivity may have to be reckoned with, or the presence of hallucinations which urge the person to kill himself. Physical signs are extremely important in the evaluation of suicide danger: insomnia (very frequent), weight loss, appetite loss, constipation (especially significant), menstrual irregularities, fatiguability, and diminished potency and sexual desire. Thought content provides extremely important clues:

The more self-depreciating the content the more danger there is of suicide. Profound depression with psychomotor retardation is not usually at first a suicidal danger, Stern finds; the greatest danger arises when improvement sets in. Particularly dangerous are sudden changes in relationships to important figures in the person's life;

these are of great significance when they involve a feeling of coldness and remoteness.

The assessment of suicidal or homocidal potentiality is regarded very seriously by therapists on emergency services. Waltzer, *et al.* (231) find that rumination in both cases is more serious than transitory thoughts. They find Kielholz' (117) signs of suicidal risk useful: (1) family history of suicide; (2) earlier suicidal attempts; (3) structural notions on how attempt will be made, *or* preparatory actions such as purchase of a weapon or drugs, reconnoitering the site, tidying-up affairs, writing a farewell letter; (4) lack of religious faith or loss of faith in higher values; (5) financial worries of serious nature; (6) severe physical illness, with prolonged sleep disturbances, alcoholism and drug addiction.

Yamamoto *et al.* (250) found no difference in frequency of diagnoses of psychosis or in history of psychiatric hospitalization between people who committed suicide and a control group. Significantly, they found that a greater proportion of the suicide group had manifested suicidal ideation *and* had been hospitalized. Alcoholism in individuals over 30, and loss (person, job) were frequent precipitating events.

Assessment of Crisis

Reference to the "biopsychosocial field" is necessary in the characterization of all crises, state Jacobson *et al.* (107), and must include statements relevant to the "social, intrapsychic and somatic" condition of the individual. The crisis may be precipitated by events in one of these areas and the effect spread to the others. Role changes and shifts in interpersonal relations are among the social factors assessed; intrapsychic shifts are seen as imbalances arising in a formerly stable system and involve both conscious and unconscious processes. Somatic alterations may be significant both in the emergence of a crisis (*e.g.,* as a response to a serious physical illness) and its subsequent development (*e.g.,* chronic psychosomatic complaints resulting from a pathological grief state).

Morley (156) finds that traditional diagnostic assessment is inappropriate for crisis situations; the assessment is of the crisis, its identification and explanation, rather than of the pre-crisis personality.

Assessment of Ego Functions

The need to utilize the available ego strengths in brief psychotherapy, reasons Burdon (29), makes for the importance of a careful history in identifying precisely what the patient's adaptive abilities have been in the past. He notes the common mistake of emphasizing pathological aspects, while neglecting strengths and healthy resources.

A most systematic presentation of the assessment of ego functions is made by Bellak and Small (20). They utilize Bellak's earlier (18) compilation and definition of ego functions, and descriptions of pathology and health in each function, or as is the more usual expression, strengths and weaknesses. Some function of the ego, they point out, is affected in every emotional disturbance. Determination of the functions disrupted or weakened guides the course and goals of treatment and supports the selection of specific interventions. They describe nine ego functions.

Adaptation to reality, best viewed as adaptation to the cultural matrix, the appropriateness of one's role-playing.

Reality testing, an integral part of role-playing, involving perceptions and judgment, the primary function being the differentiation of external (objective) data from internal (subjective) determinants.

Sense of reality, the differentiation of self from the rest of the world of objects, places and time. When the function is strong there is an absence of conscious awareness of self.

Drive control, the regulation of instinctual drives. Genetic endowments may vary here, as environmental factors also may influence the intensity of the drive. The strength of the superego affects drive intensity also, as the drives run counter to superego demands.

Object relations, including both the quality and intensity of one's relationship with people. Manifest aspects of such relationships should be supplemented by projective productions of the patient, his dreams and fantasies.

Thought process, dependent upon the maturation of an infant's perceptual ability, progressing from initial differences to increasing clarity and differentiation in all sensory modalities.

Defensive functions, the personality's barriers against both internal and external stimuli of threatening intensity or meaning. Repression was the first defense identified; many others have since been elaborated.

Autonomous functions, those activities—perception, intention, language, productivity, motor development—assumed to be independent of conflict. Closer examination finds that they are indeed likely to be involved, perhaps in a secondary way. They are, of course, susceptible to developmental deprivation and to organic damage.

The synthetic function, which tends to overlap most with the other functions since it involves the ego's ability to form *Gestalten,* to maintain the necessary functions of life, of adaptation.

Identification of the intact, healthy portion of the ego is of paramount value in emergency psychotherapy or crisis intervention, providing the therapist with a needed ally, so to speak.

Examination of a number of patients labeled with the same nosological title shows that in each different ego functions will be impaired or remain strong, and that these differences may be critical to outcome.

The Psychodiagnostic Formulation

For some time I have been developing a series of guides to the psychodiagnostic formulation (209). They consist of a series of implicit quesions which the therapist keeps in mind and uses as a sieve through which the data he obtains from the patient are constantly being sifted. They must be seen as separate from the explicit questions the therapist addresses to the patient in pursuing a history.

The implicit questions: (1) What is the complaint? (2) What is the precipitating cause of the complaint? (3) What are the antecedent analogues of the present situation? (4) What are the meanings of the symptoms? Their generic dynamics and their individual dynamics? Their possible other origins in determinants of physiology, endocrinology, neurology, genetics, culture? (5) What is the state of the ego system? The strength and weaknesses of the various functions? (6) What dynamic shifts are needed to restore homeostasis? (7) What interventions are most likely to produce the required shift? (8) What therapeutic allies are available? (9) What shall be the general procedure of this therapy? (10) What is the prognosis? (11) If the determinants of the symptoms include organismic and/or cultural factors, how do these affect the ego? the treatment? the prognosis?

THE DIAGNOSTIC PROCESS AS TREATMENT

In the treatment of depressions, Regan (181) divides the early period into an anamnestic and preparatory-exploratory phase. The uniform hopelessness in depression creates apathy and negativism and compels the therapist to arouse the patient into psychotherapeutic activity. The best means is through a preparatory exploration following one or two information-gathering interviews. As he describes it, the phase is actually an extension of the anamnestic interview. The therapist aggressively pursues ultimate details: "the patient's method of brushing his teeth, urinating and defecating, dressing, *etc.*" Every possible action, feeling and thought of the patient is sought out by aggressive, direct questioning. The therapist obtains a much richer picture of the severity of the patient's depression than he would otherwise be able to. The activity leads the patient into associations about events and provides a road to more dynamic exploration. A bond of empathy is created between patient and therapist and persuades the patient that his predicament is truly understood by another. Moreover, the demands are so limited in these inquiries that the patient is able to achieve success in responding; even this small achievement can interrupt the pattern of pessimism and futility.

In active supportive treatment of depressed college students, Gross (89) reports that the early stages consist often of inseparable treatment and diagnosis, a joint process that leads to decisions about further treatment. A student's ability to cooperate with and use the anti-depressive therapy serves a diagnostic function in itself, pointing either to the necessity for withdrawing from school, or for a longer-term intensive therapy of another nature if he is unable to respond.

Jacobson *et al.* (106) discovered that among patients who received only diagnostic services at a clinic, many considered that their problems had been sufficiently alleviated; they had themselves used the diagnostic procedure as treatment, however limited or inadequate it was for that purpose. The authors recommend, therefore, that every hour be considered "as if it may be the last treatment opportunity"; even the first diagnostic session is so considered.

The potency of a single session in removing blocks to the normal development of children is utilized by Winnicott (241). Exchanges between child and therapist based upon drawings and "squiggles" which are turned into something give the child the feeling of being discovered without being exploited. Very deep material indicative of stresses becomes available. These need not be interpreted. Changes come not from verbalized insight, but from the child's awareness that what before seemed "chaotic, mad or inaccessible" now is sensible. The child becomes optimistic and able to use people and "life itself" to find answers.

These reports counteract the view that diagnosis as a specific procedure is inimical to the therapeutic process, diverting it from the goals which the patient brings to therapy. In part this view may evolve from the position of some psychoanalysts of Freudian identification that because of resistance the diagnosis is complete only when the analysis is over. Some analysts object to a diagnostic procedure for fear that the nature of the inquiry and the activity of the therapist in pursuing it contaminates the development of a transference neurosis. And the view may arise too from the influence of existentialism upon the technique of practicing therapists.

Bellak and Small (20) note that the history-taking need not be a traumatic procedure, that even persistent questioning, done tactfully, will provide some narcissistic gratifications to the patient, enhance his sense of rapport, and even may be cathartic for the patient who has now the opportunity to unburden himself. The therapist, they urge, should not refrain from providing some therapeutic help once the history, a meaningful one, is obtained. The patient may be assured that his problem and its sources are understood, that he can be helped. A modest venture into insight may be made through a partial interpretation. Or the patient may be reminded that the history indicates he had had a similar problem before, or even a different one, and had worked out of it—all as part of the psychodiagnostic step in brief therapy.

CHAPTER 6

Techniques and Interventions: An Alphabetical Compendium

For the convenience of the practitioner, techniques are presented alphabetically in this chapter—independent of their numerous contextual models and their theoretical origins, described in previous chapters. The widespread tendency to confuse theory with technique leads me to embark upon this separate reiteration of the details of method. To discover in the course of study that our comprehension of human behavior is best illuminated by, say, psychoanalytic theory does not require that we use only psychoanalytic therapeutic techniques. As another example, behavioral techniques are not the property of the behavioral therapist or theorist alone. Relaxation techniques were practiced and recommended decades ago by Stekel and Ferenczi, and a recent paper (240) dsecribes the use of free association in establishing hierarchies in a behavioral-therapy program. Many psychoanalytically-trained therapists over the years have used their theoretical grounding to invent, select and apply interventions that depart markedly from classical analytical procedures.

The traumatized patient, the patient severely depressed, unable to cope, to exercise mastery, is not a suitable candidate at that time for psychoanalysis, although his condition may be precisely explicable by psychoanalytic theory.

Confusion of technique with theory has led also to the frequent misuse of the term eclecticism. Eclecticism properly applies in theoretical system-building where it is ". . . the selection and orderly combination of compatible features from diverse sources. . . ." (54) One easily could identify both formalistic and eclectic theoreticians who as psychotherapists use a wide range of therapeutic interventions.

Full use of the armamentarium is the keynote to successful technique in brief, emergency and crisis therapies; ". . . the appropriate and well-tailored selection of components . . . psychotherapy remains the cornerstone of treatment, but it is supplemented and sometimes preceded by any and all other modalities . . ." writes Wayne (236). Brief psychotherapy, reasons Stern (215), must rely upon a multiplicity of therapeutic interventions in order to meet the variety of needs that arise in crisis and emergency situations, which include depressions, suicide attempts, excitements, panic states, deliriums, toxic states, threats, assaults, anti-social acts, and drug-induced states.

The need is tersely expressed by Errera *et al.* (56): ". . . we encounter a diversity of patients whose varied pathology, interests and motivations require a wide spectrum of possible psychotherapeutic interventions." A similar sentiment is voiced by Strean and Blatt (220) who urge that no therapy in itself be considered a treatment of choice.

Speed of application is another essential in many brief treatment situations, especially of traumata and crises. Kardiner (114) observes that the goal in treating traumatic situations is to prevent the stabilizations of new, inadequate ego states. Hence the need for speed and also the explanations for the more favorable prognosis in situations of recent origin.

Some techniques must be stated negatively as the *don'ts*. Among these a prime example is the therapist's attitude of anonymity. Malan (144) has identified "lengthening factors" that lead to longer therapeutic courses. Some of these factors may be considered techniques; for the most part they are aspects of the patient's and the therapist's personalities, or general qualities observed in many neuroses. Awareness of them influences the choice of technique when the goal is a brief course of treatment. The lengthening factors are resistance, over-determination, necessity for working through, neurosis rooted in early childhood, transference, dependence, negative transference associated with termination, the transference neurosis, a tendency in a therapist toward passivity and willingness to follow the patient's lead, the sense of timelessness conveyed by the therapist to the patient, perfectionism in the therapist, and increasing preoccupation with deeper and earlier experiences. Malan concludes that a "rationally based technique of brief psychotherapy must be based on a conscious opposition to one or more of these factors, particularly those in the therapist." After careful study he advises that correct and active interpretation can deflect the effects of or avoid the development of resistance, transference, dependence, negative transference, anger over termination, and the roots of neurosis in early childhood. Discussion at the start of treatment, formulation of a planned, limited therapeutic aim, and the application of "focal technique" in the pursuit of this aim can avoid or mitigate the effects of passivity and therapeutic perfectionism in the therapist, the sense of timelessness, over-determination, and the development of a transference neurosis. Working through is necessary, but can be achieved within the time limits of a brief therapy. The most difficult element to counteract, he writes, is the waning enthusiasm of the therapist.

The "right person" is more important than the "right method," claimed Nolan Lewis (174), stretching somewhat his argument that the personality of the therapist, particularly his capacity for empathy, is an important technical factor in success in brief psychotherapy.

Querido (178) urges succinctly that techniques in brief psychotherapy should be prompt, total and warm.

Let us remember, too, that as early as 1946 Alexander and French (4) enunciated technical principles to shorten psychotherapy that stressed focus upon the real life problems the patient brings into treatment and the flexibility of the therapist in adapting interventions to meet the particular requirements of the individual patient.

There follows a listing of techniques and interventions employed in various brief psychotherapies. The more than 70 techniques listed are in themselves the most eloquent advocates of the need for the practitioner to adapt his approach flexibly from a large and varied armamentarium.

The nomenclature is not always consistent. Sometimes it seemed more reasonable to begin the title with a modifier rather than a noun (*e.g.*, Oral gifts). Always the effort was to use the title judged to be most meaningful to the psychotherapist reader. Thus, all interventions designed to work with the transference have been grouped under the heading, *Transference, management of*; all of the various modifications of transference are in the text, without separate heading. The titles used by the authors have not always been used here; in some instances I have followed my understanding of an author's intention in categorizing the technique.

Abreaction

Defined in the psychological dictionary (54) as "eliminating or weakening a complex or lessening the emotional tension caused by conflict and repression, a reliving—in feeling, action or imagination—the situation that originally caused the conflict," abreaction might be listed under Catharsis, since that is the method employed, while abreaction is the result. The technique is used by all varieties of theoretically allied psychologists (5, 202, 249). Wolpe (249) uses abreaction in situations in which the patient has been conditioned to circumstances that cannot be replaced adequately by stimuli extracted from the present. Coleman (47), on the contrary, comments that abreaction is not a desirable technique in brief psychoherapy because there are few opportunities in civilian life for discharge of emotion in the way sponsored by the abreaction technique.

Activity of therapist

Described (83, 236) essentially as a qualitative aspect of the therapy, this emphasis presumably is intended to distinguish the active participation of the psychotherapist with an immediate goal from the relatively remote and neutral demeanor of the psychoanalyst. One author (83) believes that therapist activity tends to counteract repression in crisis situations, and the therapist is admonished to do something for the patient.

Therapist activity is seen by Baum and Felzer (16) as a flexible and meaningful engagement in the initial interview in order to establish a therapeutic relationship. It should include open discussion of the patient's expectations. Patients of lower socio-economic groups are often found to be most literal in their expectations.

A superlative account of therapist activity is given by Gross (89), describing its employment in the treatment of depressed college students. The procedure, following Hollon, consists of discussions of the patient's illness in simple terms, reassuring him that he is not responsible, where guilt is exaggerated, prescribing a compulsive schedule and a maximum activity regimen, requesting a daily log and prodding him to furnish a detailed, concrete history. This may go on through a number of sessions. He may be required to perform a number of simple tasks that demand vigorous exertion, and ordered to eat a minimal amount of food. The regimen is intended to help the patient divert his attention from his depressive affect onto specific activities, thereby relieving tension at a concrete, primitive level. Gross suggests that the anti-depressive regimen is required by the patient's loss of ego autonomy, his diminished ability to initiate actions, a partial loss of identity and of the sense of certainty about the self, a subjective loss of the sense of time continuity, a decreased capacity for abstract thought and reflection, a decrease or loss of capacity for motor activity to produce tension discharge, a disruption in object relations and feelings of emptiness and helplessness.

The approach seeks to mobilize the patient into constructive movement in order to counteract feelings of impotence and powerlessness. The student's general situation is explored; then the interview may be limited to the specific areas of school and the depression itself. The depression is identified as the cause of the student's difficulty. The relief of the depression is made the first task of the therapy, while other problems are postponed. This narrows the field, provides focus on the work to be done, and relieves the patient of some guilt. The patient's first decision is whether or not to work with the therapist in combating the depression. Usually the decision is implicit, but on occasion, making it explicit, obtaining a verbal commitment from the patient, may be therapeutically advisable. Once this is obtained, the therapist may outline a series of specific assignments; sometimes it will be helpful, even necessary, to write these out for the patient.

Usually, the first assignment is to have the patient contact instructors to see whether his work can be made up, or whether he is so hopelessly behind that he should withdraw. When the situation is not as bad as he feared, the student gains hope. If the situation is hopeless and the student decides to withdraw, the pressure is relieved, the student has taken direct action with one problem, and now is better able to divert his energy to the resolution of his depression. Other assignments may require the student to clean his room as a physical, concrete, visible productive effort, or set up a compulsive daily schedule, prescribing vigorous daily exercise, or insist upon regular food intake, and finally reduce his sleeping time while insisting on scheduled work activities. "Depression is usually worse after periods of inactivity, especially when nothing constructive has been done about one's problems." The therapist may help the student organize his studies and in some cases ask for a daily log or a written detailed autobiography.

Frequent contacts are important, since the therapist is functioning as the patient's substitute ego until autonomy is restored. Access by telephone is of extreme importance because of the danger of suicide, but also because the patient will need quick access to support whenever the depression tends to bog him down into inactivity and misery. The theoretical basis of the active-therapist program is that in the depressed student the dynamics begin with a strong oral fixation, self-esteem that is overly dependent upon satisfaction of the patient's narcissistic needs by another person, and inwardly deflected aggression whenever faced with deprivation resulting in further loss of self esteem. Hollon comments that, as important as these dynamics may be, they are of little value to the depressed patient while he is depressed. Supportive therapy of this kind is aptly described as "lend-lease" therapy in which ego is loaned to the patient until his own is restored to operation.

Therapist activity, especially in the first session, is effective in obtaining greater utilization of short term therapy by blue-collar families, reports Avnet (7). Demonstration that the therapist "cares" appears to be an important element in determining response or non-response to treatment. (See also for related procedures: *Availability of therapist; Control by therapist; Dependency; Directiveness of therapist; Focus; Prodding; Self-esteem reconstruction;* and *Support.*)

Advice-giving

This implies the direct, unmitigated offering of a course of action to a patient. As such it is a special version of activity on the part of the therapist; on a continuum of directiveness, it could also be considered authoritarian. The technique finds a number of modes of expressions among authors (9, 12, 142, 227); one author advises the patient directly concerning the handling of symptoms (195).

Bellak and Small (20) note that the acting-out patient may require flat direct statements of desired action from the therapist, and in some cases compulsory adherence to the recommendations may be a necessary concomitant of the therapist's willingness to proceed with therapeutic responsibility.

Anxiety arousal or provocation

The technique described by Ferenczi (61) is designed to increase tension, on the presumption that this will facilitate both the perception and the resolution of the conflict situation.

Sifneos (207) describes the technique as dynamic and uncovering, centering upon the imparting of insight into the nature of emotional conflicts.

Anxiety suppression

Where the personality is considered too fragile to cope with the intensification of anxiety, this technique is advocated by Sifneos (207) for the restoration of equilibrium. It calls upon other techniques for its execution. (See also: *Reassurance; Support; Guidance and counseling; Drugs;* and *Carbon dioxide-oxygen.*)

Assertive training

Wolpe (249) trains the patient in the expression of "socially acceptable expressions of personal rights and feelings." The technique involves the counter-conditioning of anxiety along with the operant conditioning of the instrumental response.

Availability of therapist

This technique may be cross-referenced to Support and to Transference, but it merits a separate section.

Bartholomew and Kelley (14) report on the use of the telephone to extend the availability of the psychotherapist to distressed people. They note that such practice began as a suicide-prevention service in Halmgsborg, Sweden, in London, Berlin and Vienna; it has been extended in Frankfurt, Zurich, Birmingham, Paris, Seattle, New York City, Los Angeles, San Francisco, and Brooklyn. Their current report is from Sydney, Australia, where a telephone and correspondence service is available to distressed individuals who do not know where to turn for help or guidance. The staff is composed of volunteers, trained but unpaid, available 24 hours a day, seven days a week. The emphasis is on advice, not action. Patients are encouraged to talk at length. This opportunity is seen as often the greatest gift possible to give to these individuals. Appointments are then made if appropriate. Police are rarely informed, but may be when necessary. The service is listed with the Fire Department and the Police Department on a front page of the telepohne book. Two hundred volunteers took a course of twelve weeks duration, half a day a week, consisting of lectures, visits, group work, and role playing.

Cameron (31) uses a similar technique of extending psychotherapeutic assistance on a team model through a telephone answering service, and is establishing a county emergency service. The answering service takes the messages, team members respond with visits to the home, sometimes taking sheriff personnel if the report indicates that the patient is menacing. The doctor talks to the patient, the nurse works with the family, medication or direct hospitalization is provided. This effort was aimed to avoid an old practice of jailing disturbed persons awaiting other care.

Gwartney *et al.* (92) note that the mere presence of a therapeutic personality is a stabilizing factor in most acute and critical emotional episodes. One of their colleagues, Dr. Nelken, gives sensitive expression to the way in which the presence of a therapist may help to combat a patient's despair in an emergency. The emergency, he notes, isolates a person from the fellowship of other men. ". . . Imagine what it is like to have your most valued relationships . . . collapsing, a gulf of helpless misunderstanding widening between you and others, and even your esteem for yourself turning to abhorrence." It is this fearsome damage to self-esteem, the sense of loneliness and lack of mastery, that the availability and presence of the therapist directly combat.

The importance of the ready availability of a therapist, even at unusual hours of the night or weekends, is noted by Bellak and Small (20) as essential in forestalling suicidal ventures.

Avoidance, selective

A technique that might be identified as selective avoidance is proposed by McGuire (145). It is the active avoidance of efforts to resolve deeper issues. If they must become major issues in therapy, short-term goals are to be abandoned. Brief psychotherapy he sees as limited to mild ego reorganization, which is completed with the unconscious make-up remaining essentially the same as it was at the beginning of therapy. McGuire believes that one of the most difficult technical problems in psychotherapy is the separation of the treatable emotional conflict from its deeper, more extensive connections in an individual who suffers from a number of interrelated conflicts existing at a number of psychic levels. The dynamic inferences of most of the data available are not given to the patient in brief psychotherapy. The task of avoiding is often difficult, especially if the patient lacks conceptual organization, or has multiple real or unconscious conflicts, or offers a rich and suggestive set of associational sequences.

Banter

Banter is advocated by Coleman (43) as a therapeutic intervention for modification and mastery of sadomasochistic drives. It is a form of teasing, done in a friendly way and with warm tones. When used in response to a masochistic expression, banter appears to reflect the patient's self-depreciation (Oh, who could like you anyway?) but actually addresses itself to the patient's aggression. It is also, however, a form of affectionate interchange.

Carbon dioxide-oxygen

Wolpe (249) discusses the use of this gas taken one breath at a time for the reduction of anxiety (see *Anxiety Suppression*). He acknowledges that some patients are alarmed by the process. Bellak and Small (20) would interpret the patient's alarm as a perception or awareness of changes which threaten the ego. Wolpe offers this rationale: the gas effects the reciprocal inhibition of anxiety by direct effects of the gas, by the state of relaxation produced, or by both.

Case work, adjunctive

Wolberg (242) describes the use of the social worker in the manipulation of the environment of the patient to create a "corrective social environment." Bellak and Small (20) also discuss the use of the social worker. (See also: *Environmental manipulation; Activity of therapist; Support;* and *Guidance and counseling.*)

Catharsis

Classically, catharsis is the process in which an individual transposes an unconscious drive or thought into consciousness (9, 20, 147, 154, 191). The aim is a shift in the energetic balance, the opening of a hitherto dammed-up affect system, with the resulting release of tension and restoration of equilibrium. Bellak and Small (20) caution that careful assessment of ego strength is important before catharsis is provoked. With a reasonably strong personality "suffering a neurotic disturbance, the therapist may go directly to the core of the symbolic content (aggressive, sexual, exhibitionistic, *etc.*) of the disturbing sentiment." In intensive therapy, the opportunity for and the appropriateness of making cathartic interpretations increases with time as the patient gains increased insight and greater ego strength. In brief psychotherapy, this slow strengthening process is not available; attempts at catharsis must thus be geared to the circumstances at the time of the brief therapy. There is a tendency to believe that in a traumatic situation, catharsis is the technique of choice. The reader will keep in mind Fenichel's description of the need of some traumatized patients for withdrawal and rest rather than for unburdening before they become strong enough to face the troubling affect.

To avoid the danger of overwhelming a patient with the intensity of affect produced by a cathartic approach, Bellak and Small (20) advocate the technique of "mediate catharsis" to provide protection of the patient from the full impact of the repressed affects, drives and ideas. The technique is a modification of the cathartic interpretation: (1) it tempers uncovering potential by substituting more moderate words than might be used in a cathartic interpretation; (2) it reassures the patient at the same time that the uncovering goes on; (3) it provides an acceptable outlet for the drive or affect, so that even though the drive or affect is not confronted fully, it will not be dammed up; (4) it alienates the patient somewhat from the drive at the same time it is made more acceptable to the personality, usually accomplished by expression of recognition and acceptance for the drive, even identification with it by the therapist, then counter-poised with an expression of the general recognition of the need to curb the drive in certain areas of life activity; (5) it lends the therapist's ego strength to the patient in order to help him combat his own more punitive superego.

Fenichel (60) cautions against the use of cathartic hypnosis to obliterate repressions. Any recovery through this technique, he argues, devolves from the patient's dependent attitude upon the doctor. The patient may become able to remember forgotten events and so furnish material, but "the therapeutic value of this knowledge is not very great." The resistances thus overcome by authoritarian methods, instead of being resolved, tend to return.

Catharsis is discussed by Burdon (29) as emotional exposure that must be linked in the patient's mind with both his present difficulties and past traumatic events. Catharsis is not to be confused with indulgence and/or hysterical storms.

Clarification

At the Brief Psychotherapy Council (174) in Chicago, Dr. Maurice Levine noted that intellectual clarification was especially useful with both mature individuals and narcissistic persons. Coleman (47) comments that clarification by the use of a diagnostic word or title is often a great relief to the patient, contributing to defense by isolation. When the therapist says, "You are anxious" or "You are depressed," the patient, particularly if somewhat obsessional, is able to divert considerable energy of concern away from himself through the diagnosis.

Coleman develops the technique rather carefully. He defines clarification as an explanation of the patient's situation in which material which is generally conscious, sometimes preconscious, is brought together in what is for the patient a novel arrangement. This clarification may take one of two forms. It may be causal, linking precipitating events to their sequelae: "You feel the way you do because of your coming marriage." Or the form may be descriptive, in which the situation is defined: "So you felt left out of this relationship between your wife and your child."

Greenblatt *et al.* (86) use clarification of problems as a technique in preventing hospitalization.

Clarification of problems that led to the request for help is seen by Rapoport (180) as strengthening cognitive grasp and structuring. The factors which have contributed to the disruption of functioning are often preconscious, therefore identification which leads to a formulation of the problem facilitates cognitive restructuring and integration. Usually the individual is not fully aware of the precipitating stresses and their consequences, so that clarification of the precipitating event and the contributing stresses often facilitates the reestablishment of emotional equilibrium.

Community attitudes, modification of

Maxwell Jones (111) finds it conceivable that some patients—for example, those with character disorders—might be treated more economically by modifying community attitudes than by treating the individual. This would become an aspect of social psychiatry and psychology for which there is at present no truly adequate training. Inherent in this suggestion is the intention to convince the community to be more tolerant of behavioral deviations and thereby to avoid imposition of a traumatic hospitalization upon the individual.

Concept control

This is a rubric under which Wolpe (249) has gathered a number of techniques aimed at enabling the patient to control either the for-

mation or the frequency of occurrence of certain ideas. Wolpe uses:
(1) exaggerated role training in which patients are encouraged to
adopt roles antithetical to their usual behavior; (2) hypnosis employing suggestion and relaxation in order to increase the vividness of
images; (3) thought-stopping, in which the therapist encourages the
patient to indulge in obsessive rumination, then interrupts by yelling
"stop" during a "futile thought sequence" (apparently this technique
may be accompanied also by an electrical shock); (4) imparting rational beliefs; (5) imparting rational values; (6) correcting misconc-
ception by providing factual information. (See also: *Reality testing;*
Intellectualization; and *Guidance and counseling.*)

Conference by treating team

A crisis unit conducted by Dr. Richard A. Levy in Portland,
Maine, (134) starts the working day with a team conference in which
social worker and psychotherapist cover all of the agency and family
contacts concerning patients to be seen that day. A staff homemaker
may relate her experiences of the previous day in visits to patient's
homes. The staff reports that this practice helps keep them in touch
with potentially difficult or dangerous situations and avoids treating
their patients in a vacuum.

Confrontation

This is a form of active technique. Gelb and Ullman (75) reporting on "instant psychotherapy" at the Maimonides Center state:
"Immediate, active, empathic and accurate confrontation of the patient with examples of his neurotic functioning is more effective than
passive working through." In one respect this is a mirroring technique:
the patient is confronted with his actual behavior; it is held up to
him on the basis that we are all more or less unaware of what we
actually do or say. Some authors confront the patient with his defective behavior and the secondary gains he gets from his symptoms
as a method for dealing with psychosomatic emergencies (230). Bellak and Small (20) warn that one must consider the depth of the
uncovering sought directly or obtained inadvertently by the confrontation process. They indicate that among the dangers of confrontation
are increased denial and repression; more serious possibilities are the

eruptions of panic, deep depressions, serious acting out and possible suicide. (See also: *Interpretation; Catharsis.*)

Conjoint consultation

Bellak and Small (20) advocate a modification of conjoint family therapy for incorporation in some brief psychotherapies. The technique is used when the dynamics of the patient and his situation are well understood by the therapist, who may predict that the desired changes will come about more rapidly if the patient and therapist together face the figure or figures with whom he is most in conflict. The procedure requires that the therapist have a specific idea of what he wishes to accomplish. He determines his purpose in advance, based upon an understanding of the problems obtained from the history. His comprehension must include what goes on between the two or more people, so that when he brings them together the goals of the interview are clear in his mind, and he is able to steer it in that direcion. Usually the therapist is seeking by this device to enable the patient to solve a conflict or alter a relationship with a conflictual figure. Following the meeting, the patient usually should be seen alone for a review and analysis of what took place during the conjoint consultation.

Contact brevity

The rationale for reducing sessions to 15 to 30 minutes is based (120) upon the suggestion that the greatest benefit to the patient derives from the first minutes of the session and that extension of the session diminishes the benefits already established.

The College of Medicine at the University of Cincinnati reports sessions ranging from 15 to 50 minutes each, but gives no indication that the shorter or the longer end of the continuum is found more effective.

Dreiblatt and Weatherly (53) have studied the effect of therapy with hospitalized patients in which conversations were kept to five to ten minutes. Conversations were initiated by the therapist but were not directive in nature. They usually were begun with an open-ended question, but any discussion of symptoms was avoided. Their approach is based on the assumption that the impact content of discussions with patients lies in the "nature of the meta-communication associated with that content." The fact that the professional worker repeatedly though briefly takes time to converse in a friendly and formal manner with the patient communicates to the patient that he is accepted as a likeable worthy person. Conversely, focusing the content of conversations upon symptoms stresses the message that the patient is a patient and tends to reinforce his perception of himself as ill, thereby lowering his self-esteem. Koegler (120) also observes that brief-contact therapy may communicate a great deal more to the patient than is actually said and, therefore, is useful with persons of limited verbal communication ability. (See also *Non-verbal communication*.)

The use of weekly sessions of 15 to 20 minutes with patients of low economic status is reported by Cattell *et al.* (36). One resident psychiatrist can see 12 to 16 patients in a three-hour period. Schmale, discussing this arrangement, criticizes it as too high-pressure, forcing the therapist to resort to bad "treatment habits."

Contact frequency

Green and Rothenberg (84) advocate seeing the patient as often as necessary and as often as possible when the patient is in a crisis situation. Bellak and Small (20) observe that the frequency of contact may be modified by the therapist's judgment of transference needs, increasing the frequency in genuine crises, decreasing frequency where there is danger of dependent clinging.

Contract approach

The device of establishing an agreement, or contract, applied by Rabkin* in family treatment, establishes rules for behavior within the family around a point of conflict when insight fails to resolve the conflict. Members of the family agree to conduct themselves according to the rules mutually established. A similar, more focused device is used in behaviorally-oriented casework treatment. Client and worker contract for the therapeutic work to be done; problems for which help is sought are defined, changes desired are specified, and roles are clarified. A formal document is drawn up and signed by both parties.**

---

* Personal Communication from Marcia Pollack
** Personal Communication from Amy Vanesky

Control by therapist

Haley (93) refers to a variation of what might be considered an active, authoritarian or directive technique. The effort of the therapist is to control the patient's resistance by encouraging the patient to withhold information, or to control the symptoms by encouraging the patient to engage in the symptom behavior. The rationale, however questionable, is that in complying with the therapist's demand for this type of behavior the patient gives up control of the resistance and the symptom to the therapist.

Control of symptoms by isolation

Greenblatt *et al.* (86) found that helping the patient to isolate, identify and label his problem distinguishes it from reality and tends also to enable him to see his problem as non-pervasive and within his verbal control.

Counter-conditioning

Wolpe (249) describes this as one of the basic techniques of behavioral therapy, predicated upon the premise that a neurosis is a persistent, unadaptive, learned habit reaction, that neurotic anxiety cannot be overcome solely by insight or logical argument, and that it must be eliminated by or inhibited by the competing response.

Dependency

The patient from a disadvantaged segment of society is angry because he is deprived, because he feels without help. Because of his need for society he is unable to express his anger, but when he does, his behavior is likely to be asocial and cause punishment or rejection. "He is angry because he is dependent, but he cannot tolerate being dependent." With this hypothesis, Wolk (248) believes that dependency may be used advantageously as part of the treatment of patients from underprivileged sectors. In his technique, which he calls the "kernel interview," he strives to help the patient "to establish an operationally effective 'parent-child' relationship with the therapist." He believes that such people will only attend sessions regularly and punctually when they view the therapist as a parent surrogate,

friendly but powerful, able to provide the assistance the patient requires, and strong enough to make him attend. The therapist must
be prepared to undertake activities often considered extracurricular
to the psychotherapeutic process. He must be willing to accompany
the patient in a search for employment, to a government department,
to a court, or even to help a youngster explain some of his behavior
to his parents, to serve as an intermediary in the tasks of life. The
therapist must be prepared to leave his office to help the patient
"where he really has his problems, in the community." Wolk reasons
that this activity eases the pressure upon the patient and establishes
a relationship that has a real meaning for the patient rather than an
artificial one. (See also: *Support,* where the therapist is urged to be
an advocate for the patient bewildered by a crisis.)

Desensitization, systematic

This technique described by Wolpe (249) employs a physiological
state that is incompatible with the existence of anxiety, in order, first,
to inhibit a weak anxiety response to a stimulus. The stimulus is repeated until the weak anxiety response is eliminated completely.
Following this, stimuli of increasingly stronger degrees are introduced
and progressively eliminated. Relaxation is usually the anxiety-inhibiting state employed: "the autonomic effects that accompany relaxation are diametrically opposed to those characteristics of anxiety."
The essential steps are: (1) training in deep-muscle relaxation; (2)
construction of intensity-hierarchies of anxiety-producing stimuli;
(3) opposition of relaxation-arousing and anxiety-arousing stimuli
from the hierarchies.

Wolpe has devised variants of the systematic desensitization procedure, perhaps to be considered facilitating devices. Among them is
in vivo desensitization, in which the procedure is induced in real-life
situations rather than through imagery. One might want here to consult Ferenczi and Stekel on the use of real-life situations to heighten
emotional tension, with the object of increasing insight. In group
desensitization, people with the same phobia work together. The emo-
tive-imagery technique trains the patient to produce anxiety-inhibiting
images—a feeling of pride, of amusement, of love, of peacefulness, of
excitement, of adventure. These suggestions are reported to be

especially effective with children. Feeding responses are frequently employed as anxiety-inhibiting states. The reader may here recall the well-known practice, based upon psychoanalytic theory, of providing oral gratification to depressed patients. Additional techniques include the inhibition of anxiety by a conditioned motor response, the use of galvanic shock to interfere with the anxiety state, and the conditioning of anxiety-relief responses. In the latter, the patient is first made uncomfortable, then the discomforting stimulus is withdrawn with the expectation that the patient will become conditioned to the anticipation of relief.

Directiveness, therapist

This approach appears under several headings in the literature of psychotherapy with depressed and suicidal patients (154). In almost all instances, the therapist is advised to adopt an authoritarian attitude in scheduling events in the patient's life. Directiveness is used to maintain the focus of the therapy, as upon contemporary events (198). Ferenczi (61, 62) urged pushing the patient into dreaded activities in order to heighten tension. He also advised that the therapist induce the patient to renounce certain pleasurable activities which constituted defenses for the neurosis. Sifneos (207) recommends that the therapist make decisions for the patient, particularly when employing supportive techniques. (See also: *Activity of therapist;* for a converse but corollary position see *Avoidance, selective.*)

Drive repression and restraint

The technique of suppression is advocated by Bellak and Small (20) where an estimate of the ego strength of the individual indicates that the uncovering of drives and affects would be disruptive rather than consolidating, where it might increase anxiety or induce a psychotic regression. Among the devices used in this intervention are the prediction of consequences of continued behavior upon the individual and the people who are important to him, the appeal to reason and judgment and the suggestion of delay of gratification. Dreams must be carefully handled when drive repression is the device elected. Often a dream cannot be ignored and must be dealt with. The therapist is advised to work only with the manifest content, and to relate it only to contemporaneous events in the patient's life, or to deal with the fear of the counter-drive rather than with the wish for gratification of the drive actually exerting pressure.

Encouragement of the use of defenses against the eruption of a drive are pertinent here. The history may indicate that formerly, for example, an obsessive-compulsive defense was present and the therapist may encourage its return by praising this kind of behavior, or by pointing out specific areas in the patient's life where the defense may be applied. Finally, the authors discuss the use of substitute affects to provide sublimation.

Drugs, adjunctive use of*

All drugs useful in the treatment of emotional illness are basically of value in brief therapy, Bellak observes.** Some drugs, because of their prompter action, may be more useful in short term treatments than in other forms of psychotherapy. Also, the manner of utilization of any drug in brief therapy may be different than in other approaches.

As illustration, Bellak notes that the cautious use of a mixture of amphetamines and barbiturates may more often have value in brief therapy than the more recently developed mood lifters, energizers and antidepressants. The newer drugs, despite their advantages, generally require several days at least, and often two or more weeks, before becoming effective. The amphetamine-barbiturate combination, while possibly lending itself to habituation and having a less sustained effect, is immediately effective. In brief therapy, this immediate effect may be employed to mobilize a patient into activity, thus cutting through the secondary gains of apathy and reacquainting him, as it were, with the pleasures of functioning well. Prompt psychotherapy, following immediately after the drug effect has been obtained, may make possible the discontinuation of these medications within a few days after their administration had been started.

Bellak and Small (20) discuss drugs as an adjunct to brief psychotherapy, specifically to provide for the conditions which enable the person to embark upon psychotherapy, to facilitate communication with a person who is blocked, to decrease the pressure of impulses, to

---

* I am most grateful to Leopold Bellak, M.D. and Irwin Greenberg, M.D. for reviewing this section and the section on Electroconvulsive Therapy.

** Personal communication from Leopold Bellak, M.D.

promote a tightening of thought processes, to interfere with secondary gains and to assist in the management of depressions, as well as for their oral significance as a variety of placebo. They emphasize necessary precautions, since drugs may in some individuals induce changes in self-awareness that could cause panic rather than bring about a sought for relief.

An overview of the use of psychotropic drugs in "breaks and breakdowns" has recently been presented by Rosenthal (190). Under three rubrics—major tranquilizers, minor tranquilizers and anti-depressants—he lists generic and trade names, indications, one-day dosages, and contra-indications for about 25 drugs. The indications for the group of major tranquilizers (rauwolfia, phenothiazine and butyrophenone families) include anxiety, tension, psychosomatic complaints, schizophrenia, involutional psychosis, DT's, somatic complaints, depression and explosiveness. The group of minor tranquilizers are indicated in his list for anxiety, tension, stress, DT's, mild depression, depression with anxiety and rumination, mild anxiety among children, psychosomatic disorders, behavior disorders, agitation, and as adjuncts in convulsive disorders. The anti-depressant group (monamine oxidase inhibitors and tricyclic anti-depressants) is indicated, writes Rosenthal, for chronic fatigue, reactive depression, involutional depression, psychotic depression, severe depression with psychosomatic complaints and chronic debilitating disorders with depressed psychomotor activity.

Rosenthal finds the psychotropic chemicals useful in acute situations if: (1) they are directed toward amelioration of specific symptoms, and (2) the use of a particular drug and its dosage are scrutinized at intervals in relationship to concomitant evaluations of the individual's condition.

Among the major tranquilizers, he cites the use of the rauwolfia drugs in chronic psychotic conditions where anxiety is found in conjunction with hyperactivity, somatic disorders and aggression. This group of drugs, he notes, has only a minor role in the therapy of outpatients. He also stresses the danger of severe depression as a side effect of rauwolfia therapy.

The phenothiazine family is sedative, "hypnotic, anesthetic, anti-emetic, anti-pruritic, and anti-Parkinsonian" in action. Possible side effects are allergic and extra-pyramidal symptoms. The latter usually may be counteracted by other drugs so that the phenothiazines may be continued.

The sedative effect of certain phenothiazines (*e.g.*, chlorpromazine) is usually desirable in the early stages of "breaks and breakdowns," enabling rest and recuperation to interrupt the tiring insomnia and restlessness so usual in these episodes. But as more activity becomes desirable, others of the phenothiazine group may be substituted for daytime use, and anti-depressants in combination with phenothiazines may be in order.

The third family in the major tranquilizing group—a butyrophenone derivative (only one product was available when Rosenthal published)—is reported useful with hypotensive individuals, agitated and aggressive patients, and where the physician elects to practice deception with patients unwilling to take medication. The chemical is available as a tasteless, colorless liquid that may be added to food and drink.

Rosenthal would not separate drug therapy from psychotherapy. He views the drugs as enhancing the conditions for psychotherapy and urges that the patient's understanding be extended to the actions of the drugs used and his responses to them.

A study of the decisions made concerning the treatment of acutely disturbed patients by Brodsky *et al.* (28) provides another overview of the applicability of psychotropic medications. Treatment at their facility is guided by these principles: (1) target symptoms are to be eliminated as quickly as possible; (2) the social rehabilitation of the patient within the shortest possible time is sought; and (3) diagnosis is not a primary determinant of treatment method. The psychotropic drugs (and/or ECT) facilitate the process, the authors find, in that they suppress symptoms to the point where severely disturbed people are able to resume relatively normal activities. The drugs permit focus on an attainable goal: the elimination of disruptive symptoms.

The study of 100 consecutive patients admitted to their service identified seven "treatment types" of patients.

(1) "Action-proneness, disorganization of behavior, and interference with interpersonal communication" characterized this type. These patients may be assaultive, suicidal, delusional or hallucinating. They may grimace, posture and be over-active. Their range of affect included silliness, labileness, melancholy or

little affect. Primarily, phenothiazines were used with this group; degree of symptomatology determined the initial selection of drug from this family. An anti-depressant might be added, or methane-sulfonate prescribed for the control of extra-pyramidal effects.

Changes in treatment might be the addition of another of the phenothiazine group to cover a wider spectrum of symptoms, or the discontinuation of a drug when symptom remission was obtained, when no benefits were observed, or when serious side effects were produced.

(2) This group of patients exhibited "action-inhibition and withdrawal from interpersonal exchanges." Trifluoperazine or fluphenazine were used, with the aim of mobilizing energy and suppressing unrealistic thinking. Few changes in treatment regimen were required. As affect increased, depression might appear (see following reference to Ostow), so that an anti-depressant might be added to the phenothiazine therapy.

(3) Depression, accompanied by either agitation or psychomotor retardation, is the characteristic of this third group. Usually agitated, rarely deluded, their clinical condition permitted the use of slower acting anti-depressants (amitriptyline or nortriptyline). A phenothiazine—usually trifluoperazine—would be added if a paranoid feature appeared. Marked suffering or suicide risk might dictate the use of ECT.

(4) High mood, hyperactivity, irritability, distractibility and a tendency toward grandiosity are the features of this fourth type. They are seldom assaultive. "Chlorpromazine was the treatment of choice." Lithium* would be considered for them today, the authors note. The symptoms of these patients were viewed as the by-products of an "accelerated energy flow" that could be slowed by the application of chlorpromazine in "titered doses" to hold the patient between excessive drowsiness and hyperactivity. If depression appeared, anti-depressants might be added.

(5) The patients in this group exhibited "clear consciousness associated with a wide range of personally vexing symptoms." While not grossly delusional or frankly hallucinating, some patients concealed delusions. Suicidal dangers might exist in some in the absence of frank depressive symptoms. In others "pan-neurotic" symptoms prevailed: persistent intense anxiety, obsessive-compulsive features, conversion symptoms, and phobic aver-

---

* In a personal communication Leopold Bellak, M.D. observes that lithium salts, especially lithium carbonate, have been found to be almost specifics for and more effective than any previously known means in the prompt treatment of simple manic states. After several years of intensive research, it is just being made available as a prescription drug.

sions. Treatment was aimed at symptoms. The first order with some patients was a period of observation so that the clinical picture could be clarified and symptoms identified. Depressive moods resulted in prescribing of amtriptyline or nortriptyline. Pan-neurotic symptoms were treated with trifluoperazine on the assumption of a covert thought disorder.

(6) These patients presented clear consciousness with an absence of severe symptoms. Those receiving medication at the time of admission were continued on the same regimen. Others were admitted for observation without medication. Subsequently, those who had histories of behavioral disorganization usually required phenothiazines before discharge, while those with a history of prior depression usually remained free of symptoms and were soon discharged.

(7) In this last group the patients manifested symptoms judged untreatable by psychotropic medication or somatic therapies: adolescents with limited, "unverifiable" somatic complaints; weeping with unreasonable demandingness; alcoholism; habituation to sedatives or stimulants with evidence of toxicity. Hospitalization benefited these patients by separating them temporarily from stressful situations.

In addition to drugs and ECT, Brodsky, *et al.*, introduced group therapy into the daily program of patients. Individual psychotherapy was most intensively used when consciousness was clear and the patient motivated.

Mortimer Ostow is well-known for his efforts to understand the actions of and utilize psychotropic medications in accordance with a psychoanalytic rationale. While no studies of the application of his ideas to brief or crisis treatment as such are available to me, his recent paper, "The Consequences of Ambivalence," (164) demonstrates the sophistication of his approach. Ambivalence, he states, precipitates two frequently observed mental states, each accompanied by major behavioral changes. Ambivalence is equated with the feeling of entrapment in an overbearing situation in which manifest anger and aggression are not acceptable. The individual responds to the sense of entrapment with "detachment" (indifference, depersonalization, cynicism, retreat, denial, dissociation) or with "depletion" (the loss of libidinal energy leading to perhaps desperate acting out, search for substitute objects and melancholia.)

Ordinarily, these states balance each other to maintain some equilibrium. The onset of depletion terminates detachment. Failure of depletion to occur results in detachment. When this psychologic balancing fails to operate—when either detachment or depletion prevails —Ostow reasons that drugs restore the equilibrium since each psychologic state is associated with a somatic state which is responsive to drugs. Tranquilizing drugs induce depletion in the detached person, he holds, while the energizing drugs combat depletion and allow detachment.

Educative techniques

Teaching the patient a skill or mastery which the therapist perceives as important to affecting stabilization is considered a method of brief psychotherapy. Wolpe (249) educates patients to the origins of neurotic fears and elucidates behavioral therapy as a means of dissipating fantasies concerning the unknown. Wolberg (245) makes an effort to instruct the patient in the use of insight as a corrective force in the patient's life and helps him apply the insight to real-life situations; in this respect the educative technique is adjunctive to the insight-imparting process. Wayne (236) uses educative processes to identify the stabilizing elements in the patient's life, in an effort to counteract the fear of weaknesses. Sifneous (207) teaches the patient problem-solving techniques. Hansen (95), an internist interested in the emotional problems of medical emergencies, uses educative techniques concerning the medical emergency to help set reality limits and curb fantasies. Bellak and Small (20) find educational techniques adjunctively useful in making clear the nature of both physiological and perceptual processes, particularly as these processes contribute to feelings of anxiety and depersonalization. They explain, for example, that dizziness produced by hyperventilation in anxious individuals accelerates the anxiety. In a similar way, they advocate teaching the relationship between muscle tension and muscle aches, between depersonalization and perceptual processes to facilitate overcoming the anxiety of these circumstances. Gillman (76) also advocates educative techniques to enable patients to reach new solutions, with the educative techniques being based upon psychoanalytic precepts.

Electro-convulsive therapy (ECT)

Many authors report the use of this technique in severe depressions, with suicidal risks, or in cases of acute schizophrenia where the patient fails to respond to tranquilizing drugs. (20, 47, 70, 113, 219, 236)

Miller (150) advocates the use of ECT as effective in achieving 70 to 80 per cent remissions in suicidal dangers. Stern (215) believes that in suicidal dangers "the most immediately effective (technique) is ECT," this despite the many contrary voices. He holds that insulin has no advantages over ECT and offers several hypothetical postulates to explain why ECT works in suicidal danger: as punishment, it serves the need of a punitive superego; the amnesia is useful; there may be some changes in the endocrine balance, particularly in the adrenalin-pituitary axis.

Lindemann (137) in the management of grief on occasion found ECT necessary with agitated-depressive reactions which resisted all psychotherapeutic efforts.

Encouragement

Schoenberg and Carr (198) use encouragement specifically in helping patients achieve the expression of anger and hostility toward conflict figures. (See also: *Ventilation;* and *Catharsis;* encouragement is a special order of these.)

Environmental manipulation

Two basic efforts in therapy were identified by French (4) to ease a patient's situation: (1) the patient's environment is adapted to better meet his needs, (2) more radically, the patient's personality is modified to make him more compatible with his environment. He cites separating the patient from an exacerbating situation as one tactic of environmental manipulation, and placing the patient in an atmosphere more suitable to his needs as another. Alexander (5) recommends manipulation of a patient's life situation if the situation is a hopelessly chronic one. He includes this among brief supportive measures.

Bellak and Small (20) discuss a variety of such manipulations: the use of family and friends, particularly where the patient's life is in danger; recommendation of job training and proper job placement to increase self esteem and permit either the direct or sublimative expression of drives; the employment of rehabilitation procedures to help formerly psychotic individuals overcome their doubts and anxieties about ability to sustain the demands of a work schedule; the use of sublimative activities to permit proper expression of aggressive drives when pathological defenses are weakened or where an already excessive charge of a drive must be diverted into acceptable outlets; active sports to provide such outlets. Body mechanics and dancing are also of value, as are art activities, painting, ceramics and music. Volunteer social services may provide an outlet for effeminate drives which otherwise would be unacceptable to the individual. Care must be exercised that these recommendations do not create conflict at the same time they seek to ameliorate it. A person with a latent homosexual problem, for example, might not be advised into swimming programs that would expose him to homosexual stimulation in lockerroom circumstances. Bellak and Small also include travel and vacation recommendations as a manipulation that enables the patient to achieve a distance between himself and his conflict; the patient is thus enabled to indulge in a certain amount of pleasurable gratification that he otherwise would not let himself achieve.

Erlich and Phillips (55) used environmental manipulation among other techniques in short-term psychotherapy of aviators with considerable success. Hoch (100) directs attention to the use of various social resources in abbreviating psychotherapy, Koegler (121) finds that environmental manipulation, particularly in the treatment of children where adjustments in living arrangements and living patterns are indicated, may be the therapy of choice. Wayne (236) reports environmental manipulation as contributing to a reduction of duration of in-hospital treatment.

Wolberg (242) notes that most emotional problems involve an environmental condition of stress or deprivation, and that one task in many therapies is to enable the patient to turn away from damaging or depriving forces. Wolberg mentions varied possibilities: recommendation of sports, hobbies, social recreation; financing of medical and dental expenses; referrals to appropriate clinics, and agencies; achievement of better housing; obtaining proper care for a handicapped child; psychological testing for a child failing in school; providing outlets for parents with nothing better to do than to attempt to dominate the patient; child adoption for childless couples who feel bereft; introduction to social facilities.

Coleman (47) comments that practical help in the form of jobs, housing, family counseling, all may be extremely useful in achieving balance in a patient's life to the point where he can cope with psychological factors that before seemed overwhelming.

Environmental interventions and manipulation are advocated by Normand *et al.* (163) as the therapeutic approach of choice in working with persons of lower socio-economic groups. Straker (219) also found that intervention into the environment of the lower-class outpatient facilitated stabilization. Wolk's (248) approach to the use of environmental intervention to increase dependency of economically and culturally deprived patients has already been mentioned in the section on Dependency.

Helgesson, reporting on his work with college students at the Chicago Brief Psychotherapy Council (174), observed that he came to feel that interpretations based on dynamics were not as practically useful as certain environmental shifts which got patients who were striving beyond their social and/or intellectual depth back down to the level where they were able to function without tension. Environmental manipulation is used by Blaine (11) in treating college students, including both changes of school and work with parents. Waltzer *et al.* (231) use manipulation of the environment to improve the patient's feelings of support, particularly when his relationship to his world needs improvement. Fenichel (60) speaks of environmental manipulation as "situational therapy" and indicates that it is most effective where the neurosis has not yet been firmly internalized, as in the case of children. He indicates, for example, that both fear and excitement can be mitigated in children by changes of environment.

The valuable contributions of the social work profession to the techniques of psychotherapy are many; the success of meaningful interventions into a patient's environment is a clear illustration of psychotherapy's indebtedness to social work and its functional partnership with that profession.

Evocation of intense neurotic responses

This technique advocated by Wolpe (249) may be classified as an arousal technique. Repeated unreinforced evocation of neurotic motor responses or emotional habits contributes to their elimination. Wolpe reports on the extinction of various motor habits by the repetition of such behaviors as tics and stammering. He also employs a sub-technique he identifies as "emotional flooding," which seeks to arouse the vividness of the patient's anxiety by the intense presentation of anxiety-arousing stimuli. Wolpe cautions that the technique is unpredictable and that some patients are made worse. The reader will be interested in considering this idea in relation to Ferenczi's technique of increasing emotional tension for the purposes of achieving insight. One should also have in mind the assessment of ego functions advocated as part of the diagnostic appraisal to precede therapy.

Exhortation

This approach reported by Barten (12) may be considered an arousal technique. Vividness and intensity of expression are designed to heighten the experience for the patient.

Exposure, graduated

Stekel (214) recommended that the therapist experiment with reality situations, particularly with the phobic, encouraging the patient to involve himself in a graduated exposure to the dreaded situation —a technique anticipatory of the hierarchies advocated by the behavioral therapist.

Extinction, experimental

This is a behavioral-therapy technique described by Wolpe (249); repeated non-reinforcement is used progressively to weaken a habit.

Family therapy

Wolberg (245) among others is concerned with the problems arising from a patient's interactions with members of his family. Where these interactions are pathological, the patient may be imprisoned, and indeed may be the person in the family who least needs psychological help. Where the difficulty in the patient's life arises from pathological interactions among members of the family, the preferred course of brief intervention may be to bring the family together for a group discussion of insight into and resolution of their joint problems.

Kaffman (112) suggests that family therapy may be a viable technique for extending psychodynamic aid to the large masses of people. Believing that many children and adults with emotional disturbances can be helped satisfactorily without resort to longer-term methods, he describes his work with family therapy in Israel. He finds the technique particularly applicable in the treatment of children, where the child's pathology cannot be separated from the family's. The first interview is a joint family one attended by the child and the parents and other significant members of the family. A long session, perhaps two to three hours, it aims to help everyone, including the child, to obtain a clear view of their most distressing problem. No fixed formula is then established for subsequent interviews; different members of the family may also be seen separately in the course of the same initial interview. Short separate meetings with the child may then take place. In most instances the initial interview process embraces four meetings: (1) the whole family; (2) the child alone; (3) the parents; (4) the entire family again. At the end the therapist summarizes in a concise way to all members of the family whatever has become evident about their problems; he adds specific suggestions and recommendations if they are necessary. Subsequent interviews allowed the same degree of flexibility, meeting with either individual members or the family as a group. The procedure in each interview tends to be similar for all members of the family: (1) redefining of the problems; (2) a summary of what has been established in preceding sessions; (3) analysis of recent events; (4) further scrutiny of factors which may be causing failure in the treatment; (5) a realistic appraisal of the situation; (6) realistic statement of expectations from the treatment; and (7) specific identification of gains and improvement. Kaffman favors a single therapist for all members of the family individually and as a group, believing that this approach is significantly economical in time and effort, that it provides a more cohesive view of the family dynamics, leading, therefore, to a more consistent therapeutic intervention.

Gelb and Ullman, (75) noting that a patient's problems and dysfunction probably occur within a disturbed system of human interaction, recommend bringing the family into the treatment situation.

Variations in approaches to family therapy are numerous and ingenious. They reflect the personalities of the therapists, the situations in which they practice and the age and status of the central client, patient or concern.

In family therapy, notes Paidoussi (165), the therapist's emotional involvement is with a larger number of people. Family therapy thus presents an urgency, a complexity and a challenge requiring a great capacity to detect hierarchies. The family therapist is inundated by the interactions of the family members of different ages and different sexes. Visual cues are significant. The therapist must train his eye to perceive and record non-verbal communications. He is among people whose patterns of relationships have been formed long in the past, who often communicate non-verbally. A crucial ingredient of family therapy is the readiness of the therapist to assume leadership, to involve members of the family in a common theme, to insist that they stay with it in such a way as to develop in each of them a concern and a feeling of responsibility for the whole family. He regards family therapy, in contrast with individual therapy, as demanding from the therapist greater emotional, intellectual and gestural coordination, greater tolerance for confusion, greater adaptability and flexibility.

The techniques of five gifted and experienced family therapists are presented by Haley and Hoffman (94). Virginia Satir offers enough "ego enhancements so that what is ego assaultive can be tolerated." She assumes leadership quite naturally, actively interpreting behavior, and conveys the essential importance of collective responsibility early in the initial session. She elicits a history. Don Jackson does not seek historical data, but acts as a model to show the family how each member can handle the other in regard to inconsistencies in communication. He believes, however, that the adolescent prefers having a private therapist, who does not see the rest of the family; he considers treatment of the adolescent to be addressed largely to that "part of them that is leaving home." Otherwise, the adolescent may see family therapy as continuing their imprisonment of childhood. Jackson attempts to reach the father first, since fathers are the hardest to keep involved, and to have him mediate between mother and child. Jackson says that he uses an autocratic approach, but "in a way that is not objectionable." Whitaker acts as an iconoclast in a dramatic and provocative fashion, deliberately beginning the session by provoking a fight. He seeks to control the course of therapy, but not necessarily the lives of the family members. Usually he introduces a stranger into the family interview, believing that this technique exposes the family to the whole world. A major technique is playfulness, which might be likened to Coleman's banter technique with sadomasochistic features. Pittman, Flomenhaft and DeYoung use family therapy as a brief psychotherapeutic approach to patients in acute psychotic crises. Their effort is to keep the patient out of the hospital; they view hospitalization as regressive and stigmatizing. It isolates the patient as the problem in the family, and contributes to the family's rejection of him; it turns over a family responsibility to the state. In the family session, they focus on the member who seems least willing to acknowledge responsibility and involvement. Fulweiler employs two rooms, one in which the family meets, and one from which he can observe. He moves between the therapy room and the observation room. He believes this facilitates the control of countertransference, since behind the observation screen he does not have to control his responses or avoid taking sides; by leaving the room he also facilitates family responsibility.

Treatment of the family may proceed separately from but parallel to the treatment of the central patient. Levy (134) has developed an interesting variation of the utilization of the family, which is described extensively in Chapter 4 (see p. 62). Concurrent with a patient's first visit to his mental-health clinic at the Maine Medical Center in Portland, the family is interviewed by a social worker, who during the session phones the psychotherapist to relate important family history, personal history or current events. The therapist is then able to utilize them immediately in his session with the patient. Levy believes that many families are themselves disturbed and must be treated simultaneously with the treatment of the patient. His recommendation is a corollary form of treatment rather than a group treatment of the patient and his family simultaneously.

Wayne (236) considers immediate and ongoing involvement in the family an essential component in a shortening of inpatient treatment. The effort is to modify the family structure rather than to modify the patient's adaptation to the stress situation in the family. Family conferences are pursued with the goal of imparting to the entire family insight into the interlocking contributions to a mental illness.

Shall one person treat the entire family? Shall the central patient be seen by one therapist while the rest of the family is seen by another? In the treatment of children, Lester (133) finds separate therapists for child and parent to be fragmenting and a handicap to a brief approach. She urges, therefore, that the same therapist treat both parents and child in separate or in joint interviews. Joint interviews are the treatment of choice where symptoms are obviously reactive to external factors or internal limitations or both. Separate treatment of the child is preferable where neurotic formations are manifest.

Goolishian (81) uses variations of family therapy in the treatment of adolescents. He may see the family as individuals, then in a joint conference or in various combinations of members of the family, depending upon the current dynamics. Overlapping interviews of the family may be scheduled with different therapists, or each member of the family may see a different therapist.

Using co-therapists in family treatment is the pattern discussed by Mitchell (155); she views it as one of the many techniques that have evolved out of practical necessities. Often the difficulties of working with a particular family gave rise to the need to share responsibility, or for a helping colleague to deal with the chaos in a particular family. At other times amorphousness, lack of clear psychosexual differentiation within the family, seemed to call for a therapeutic couple, for both male and female therapists. Co-therapists must be complementary to each other, fitting well together, and respecting each other. Care must be exercised with some families not to raise a threat by the presence of both male and female therapists, particularly in the parent of parallel sex who may fear usurpation of his or her role.

Multiple-impact family therapy is described by Ritchie (186). The clinic team, consisting of psychiatrist, clinical psychologist, psychiatric social worker and a resident clinical psychologist, meets together before the family arrives, reviews information available about the patient and the family. There is usually some preliminary speculation about the dynamics of the family and the origins of the presenting problem; some tentative plans are made for the distribution of responsibility among the team members during the first day. The family then meets with the team for about an hour. Introductions are made, the tape-recording equipment is identified, seating arrangements are suggested and the distance of positions from microphones is established. Chairs are provided so that members of the family will not sit together on a couch. The family is then asked to explain its trouble, to bring the team up-to-date. As one member usually will act as a spokesman, the others are encouraged to participate. Questions and comments are designed to communicate respect for the opinions and feelings of each person in the family. Wherever a theoretical application to the problem of the family is thought to be helpful, it is couched in simple nontechnical language. After about an hour of such exchange, the family members meet with team members in individual sessions. The pairing-off is flexible at this point, but usually the psychiatrist will see the adolescent patient, the social worker the mother, the psychologist the father, while the resident psychologist will see any other family participant. The individual interview gives the adolescent the opportunity to ventilate, to present his case more freely than he could in the presence of his parents. It enhances the psychiatrist's diagnostic impression. The adolescent is told about the psychological test he will take following lunch. At the end of the first morning the family members are advised to share with each other whatever ideas, reactions or insights they obtained during the morning. They are told the team will confer during lunch period for the same purpose. The same recommendation is made at the end of the day. Ritchie notes that some of the most dramatic improvements take place when the family is away from the office. In the afternoon of the first day the adolescent is tested, while each parent is seen by the team member who saw the other parent in the morning. The emphasis is on definition of the role of each member of the family. Parents are encouraged to "rediscover each other." The father's confidence in his ability to function as the head of the family is built up in him and in his wife. The mother's need for feminine satisfactions is presented to both parents. Unconscious exploitation of the child by the parents is delineated. The second day is similar to the first, only more accelerated; it starts with a brief conference of the team and the family, followed by both individual and joint sessions. The adolescent may be present at the final conference, but not necessarily. Specific recommendations are discussed, and insights gained are highlighted in relationship to the "back-home problem."

Focus or focal technique

Concentration upon selected problems or symptoms was advocated by Stekel (214). The idea appears with great frequency in the literature, both among therapists with psychoanalytical orientation and those who practice behavioral therapy. French (4) lucidly defined neurosis as a person's attempt to solve contemporary life problems with efforts that in the past had been ineffective with similar problems. Focus upon the resolution and correction of the here-and-now problems, he held, is "emotional reeducation"—the task of psychotherapy.

Wayne (236) advises that brief therapy focus upon symptoms rather than upon the underlying character disorder, since the latter effort will prolong rather than shorten therapy. His recommendation finds support in the work of Hoch (100), Kaffman (112) who advises focusing upon the problem by definition, review, appraisal and reappraisal, and Wolberg (245). Wolberg urges that brief therapy focus upon symptoms and areas of immediate concern to the patient that are likely to yield the greatest return within the shortest period of time—"target symptoms." The recommendation of focusing upon immediate problems is found also in Bellak and Small (20), Goolishian (81) and his work with adolsecents and their families, Koegler (120) in brief-contact therapy, in Keeler (115) who practiced short-term group therapy with hospitalized psychotic patients focusing upon current problems, Schoenberg and Carr (198) who maintain a focus upon contemporary events, and by Visher (227) who recommends that the focus be on current reality problems. Among others supporting a focused approach are Semrad, Binstock and White (202), and Barten (12). Deutsch (52) is known for his sector-therapy approach, which focuses attention upon symptomatology by encouraging associations in that area through guided interpretations.

Malan (144) provides the most thoroughgoing analysis of focal techniques based upon psychoanalytic theory. He keeps in mind an aim that ideally is formulated as "an essential interpretation on which therapy is to be based." This focus is pursued throughout the therapy; the patient is guided to it by partial interpretation, "selective attention and selective neglect." The implication is that the therapist will direct the patient's attention, and reinforce this direction by responding with either verbal or non-verbal communication when the patient's associations or insights follow a path that is congruent with one predetermined by the therapist; conversely the reinforcing communication will be absent when the patient takes a divergent tack. Malan adds that when the material appears to be overdetermined, the therapist selects the causality that is congruent with his preselected focus. He avoids being diverted by other material, however interesting and tempting it may be.

Focus, centrally, defines the process of concentration, of selection and exclusion, in the effort to conclude a therapy within a short period of time. Secondarily, there is involved the nature of the selection and exclusions. Are they conservatively oriented, treating current reality, superficial symptoms? Or are they, as Malan found practical, relatively radical and directed to conflict resolution and transference interpretation?

The focal technique may mean goal limitation, focusing upon a selected limited goal. Malan advocates this approach as well, as one which helps avoid passivity and perfectionism in the therapist. It counteracts the sense of timelessness, the effects of over-determination and the development of transference neuroses. Treating a case of impotence, Sabin (194) describes how he contracted to meet with the patient five times after their initial session to discuss his question, "Why am I so afraid to be a man?" Sabin maintained focus upon this target by reminding the patient of this agreement when his thoughts turned by free association to his homosexual fantasies.

Present-directiveness is essential, McGuire (145) states: it matches the patient's need for direct answers to practical problems, and serves to delay the development of transference neurosis.

Gillman (76) emphasizes both focus and activity in keeping the considerations on current reality in brief psychotherapy. Behavioral therapists focus upon symptoms as concrete, discrete behavioral variables. Phillips and Wiener (172) advocate a focused technique which they identify as "structured behavior change." They develop a structure for the patient to approach his problem behavior as directly and as efficiently as possible, and they realign the variables as the need develops.

The patient's level of abstraction as a guide to the nature of interventions is suggested by Sullivan *et al.* (222). They suggest that for patients not capable of higher levels of abstraction it may be advisable to concretize therapy from the outset in a structured way, to set specific time limits, and to define problem areas that will be worked on. Periodic summing-up focused on the problem areas can be introduced. The therapist steers the efforts at rehabilitation, making minimal demands on the patient for self-awareness. Instead he would focus on the more concrete alternatives available with the patient's current ability for perception and behavior.

Harris, Kalis and Freeman (96) treat stress situations by focusing upon the conditions which precipitated the stress, with a thorough explanation of the conflict involved in that episode. Their effort is to identify and isolate the factors that precipitated that stress situation and to explore and work through the conflicts involved in the stress.

Miller (152) warns that focusing upon the traumatic episode in the life of an adolescent and the motivations and events which led up to that event may increase anxiety and confusion about identity. It is more effective to show interest in the adolescent which has the effect of diminishing his reaction to the trauma, to explore current life events with which he is able to cope successfully and identify those with which he has problems, to recognize and identify the working-through process that must always follow, and where necessary to explore earlier life events which may be blocking current adaptation.

Courtenay (50) concludes that while there are factors in the patient which are crucial to the success of focal therapy, success in large measure depends also upon the capacity of the therapist to establish a "good doctor-patient relationship early in the treatment," in essence a positive transference relationship.

Achievement and maintenance of focus can be regarded as the single most important technical aspect of brief psychotherapy, also the most demanding of the therapist's powers of concentrated thought. Its importance and difficulty warrant the repetition inherent in bringing together at this point five guidelines for attaining and sustaining focus.

(1) *The "essential" interpretation.* This is Malan's (144) technique, in which the therapist selects an interpretation central to the patient's dynamics, preferably one which demonstrates the pattern of repetition, *i.e.*, the dynamic is visible in a number of aspects of a patient's contemporary life or in a series of situations in his history. The interpretation must be clearly conceived by the therapist and so worded in the therapist's mind as to assure comprehension by the patient, whose capacity for abstraction must be considered.

The therapist may never offer the interpretation as he has conceived it, but will hold it before himself as the goal in an individual's therapy. Employing selective attention and neglect, he responds reinforcingly to remarks by the patient that tend to converge upon his essential interpretation, and does not respond to those remarks that are not so converging.

(2) *The real life goal.* The therapist selects a real life goal that is reasonably realizable (one is tempted to call this the three R goal: real, reasonable, realizable), for example, a job or habitation change, arrangements for child or health care. The goal is explicitly identified for the patient. Diagnostically, the therapist identifies for his own guidance the forces within and outside the patient that block realization of this goal and the interventions for coping with these forces. Interventions emphasize learning techniques focused upon task identification, so that the patient will acquire a technique of problem solution applicable to other situations in his life.

(3) *Participatory planning.* Enlisting the participation of other minds in task identification and/or intervention selection is often an economy. Asked to do so, a patient himself may be able to state precisely what needs to be altered in his life and how the alteration may be realized. Doing so concretizes the problem and its solution for him; mastery is a thrust away and therapy now need only facilitate the thrust.

The participation of a social worker frequently helps a therapist exclude the unrealizable. The social worker may see the patient separately or may be used as a consultant by the therapist who alone sees the patient.

The team evaluation is another application of participatory

planning. Each member of a mental health team sees the patient separately; the team then meets to evolve a focus and to select interventions. While costly of staff time, the benefits of different points of view are obvious. When a patient is not likely to be overwhelmed by numbers, the team may see the patient jointly. The team method is an excellent vehicle for training the therapist in brief approaches.

(4) *The ego function assessment.* This approach is described in the chapter on Diagnosis. The benefits of the ego assessment are at least twofold: (a) focus on the healthy functioning aspects—the intact residue—is assured; (b) the tendency toward oversimplification of the effects of pathology is minimized when one employs an approach based upon the understanding that not everyone suffering a psychosis or neurosis is affected in the same way, and that not every condition is treatable by a single procedure, *e.g.*, not everyone will benefit from uncovering.

(5) *The psychodiagnostic formulation.* Described earlier in Chapter 5 is my use of a set of implied questions the therapist asks himself to order both the diagnostic inquiry and the data it produces. The effect of these unspoken questions is to provide a systematic approach to the understanding and treatment of emotional disorders. The questions focus first upon identification of the complaint, its history and the conditions that evoke it. The origins of the symptoms—manifestations of the complaint—are stated hypothetically in relation to origins in psychodynamic, neurological, physiological, genetic and cultural determinants. The meaning of the symptoms are postulated in both generic and individual terms. The ego system is assessed, the shifts needed to restore homeostasis are identified as are the means (interventions) for doing so, and the order of approach to the therapy is stated in a general way.

Gratification of needs

Meerloo (147) recommends the use of oral gratifications as an adjunct to therapy of traumatic situations to induce a mood of receptivity. His patient may be offered soup, biscuits, cigarettes and sometimes bromides. Alexander (5) suggests that gratifying a patient's dependency needs is a useful procedure during stress situations. Bellak and Small (20) note the oral significance of drugs in producing a placebo effect; this may also be fostered with soft drinks, coffee, weak alcoholic beverages, fruits, cookies, and the like. The approach is useful with deeply depressed patients, who usually respond with a better therapeutic alliance and rapport and the feeling of being in a friendly atmosphere.

Gratification of needs is utilized by Chafetz (37) in the treatment of patients from lower socio-economic groups. The gratification must be within reality limits, but includes such varied items as a place to sleep, dentures, or indeed any reality need that will have to be satisfied before the patient can undertake the psychotherapeutic procedure. The author terms these "constructive utilization of dependency needs." Minimizing reality frustrations is an important corollary, so care is exercised to avoid lengthy waits, fragmented contacts with a number of staff personnel or impersonality in tone.

Group therapy

This technique is used widely alone or in conjunction with individual therapy. Recommendations for its use appear in writings by Bellak and Small (20); Cook (49) for the treatment of hospitalized patients; Crabtree and Graller (51) in a military setting, Goolishian, (81), Kaffman (112), Keeler (115), and Wolf (247) who specifically writes of short-term group therapy. His review of the literature on group therapy, however, makes the process seem rather long term. In a chapter on short-term group psychotherapy he reports experiences extending over a two-year period.

Group psychotherapy, as used by Dr. Pearl Rosenberg, is reported by Klein and Lindemann (118) as a preventive intervention at a predictable point of crisis in the lives of young people, in this case girls who were entering the nursing profession. The recurrent emotional concerns among this group were found to include separation from homes, problems of intimacy with others that stimulated both homo- and heterosexuality, encounters with death, disease and messes, forming of relationships with authority figures, and strong doubts about personal competence in a demanding profession. Ventilation and catharsis were provided, in important ways, sanction to individuality was given just when the young women were having to conform to rigid group norms. Success in diminishing dropouts from nurses training was established by their work.

Fenichel (60) believes that therapists have turned to group psychotherapy in an effort to meet the needs of large numbers of patients needing treatment. He notes that the transference relations become much more complicated in the group. "Object relations of members to each other, such as love, hatred, jealousy, envy, as well as identifications and the influences of 'good' and 'bad' examples, complicate the picture." But despite these he believes that favorable influence is to be derived from a group psychotherapeutic process. He notes that Freud (67) called the hypnotic situation a "group of two," indicating that in a group the interaction between people is similar to that obtaining in a hypnotic relationship. Fenichel states that the patient may identify with the behavior of others and the overcoming of resistances may be fostered. He questions the insight value of the group and is inclined to ascribe to it more of a repressive and inspirational influence than an analytic one.

During the past twenty-five years approaches to group therapy have proliferated; each modification is related to the parent idea but different in its own way: T-groups, sensitivity training, the encounter, the marathon. Self-awareness, awareness of others, awareness of how others are aware of you, relating to others, others relating to you are among the goals cited. Talking, holding hands, touching, pushing, yelling and nudity are among some of the behaviors encouraged in efforts to reach goals. Leaders lead or participate as members of the group. They lead alone or with a co-leader. Where a co-leader, they discuss their cooperation before or away from the group. Permutations of goals and techniques are numerous. (128, 187, 199)

The T-group experience provides the model for the many group approaches. Learning in the T-groups is achieved through "The crucial process of feed-back" (32). The process is facilitated by anxiety about one's limitation in interacting within the new situation (the group) and a permissive, psychologically safe environment or climate.

Rogers (187) in a popular article describes the "intensive group experience" as the "rich, wild, new tapestry," that helps to: (1) combat the alienation and isolation of modern life; (2) achieve psychological fulfillment when material needs have been gratified; (3)

reduce tension in a conflict-laden culture; and (4) achieve the existential goals of living fully in the present.

The marathon encounter, an intensive group experience, perhaps
comes closest in general time concept to identification as a brief
psychotherapy. While goals and techniques are as varied as for any
other of the newer group methods, it is of the encounter that such
"post-mortem" comments are reported as "I got more out of my five-
day work shop at Esalen than I ever got out of my five years of
psychoanalysis." (177)

The therapeutic agent in the marathon encounter appears to be
the effect of concentration in intensifying affect experience that may
lead to insight and improved cognition. Quaytman, a therapist, has
written of his personal journey to Big Sur (177). He reports expanded
awareness and improved ability "to feel, to know, to experience, to
be, to grow." Whatever he did or said seemed "right" for him. He
was, he said, "not ashamed of anything" he felt or did.

Modifying the patient's superego was held by Strachey (218) to
be the effective therapeutic action of psychoanalysis "from which the
other alterations follow in the main automatically." In analysis, the
change is affected by a large number of small steps, the "mutative
interpretations" made by the therapist in his roles as a target of the
patient's id-originating impulses and as the patient's lend-lease superego.

Strachey's view may provide a more fitting theoretical model for
the therapeutic effectiveness of the marathon encounter than the
cognitive impact of intense affect. The time condensation may reduce
the number and increase the size of the steps; the group members,
leaders and co-leaders as object of impulse and as auxiliary superegos
are both more numerous, more varied and more active than the psychoanalyst is in the protracted one-to-one role prescribed by the
psychoanalytic process.

Rapidly available, rapidly escalating affect is dangerously disruptive for some individuals. This effect is observed as a result of fortuitous events both in real life and in therapeutic interventions of all
kinds. Rogers acknowledges the possibility of provoking a psychotic
episode in a group participant. His solution is to provide correction
after the fact rather than prevention before. He advocates follow-up

after the intensive group experience in order to take care of such serious events.

Professional responsibility mandates that the therapist strive to reduce the frequency of fortuitous disruptions by the selective application of interventions derived from a diagnostic assessment. Where admission into marathon encounter groups is possible through procedures as loosely selective as mail applications, the approach cannot be legitimized as a psychotherapy, and one's attitude must remain *caveat emptor*.

The formation of groups of patients in crisis as developed by Martin Strickler and Jean Allgeyer is described by Morley and Brown (158). Since the inception of the crisis group approach in January, 1966, the Venice branch of the Benjamin Rush Center in Los Angeles has seen about 1,300 "consultees" in groups. Each patient is seen in an initial individual session. If the patient is found to be free of serious suicidal and homicidal impulses, without psychosis, and English speaking he is placed in a group for five sessions. In the group he is encouraged to identify his crisis. The group supports, suggests alternative methods of coping and expresses feelings. Suggestions of maladaptive and destructive coping approaches are discouraged, as is discussion of chronic character problems. While the powerful tool of analysis of group process is not available in the crisis group, it offers a number of advantages over the traditional group-therapy approach: (1) many people are able to accept the help with real-life problems provided by the crisis group who would not accept the connotation of being ill that sometimes goes with the traditional group experience; (2) many people become involved for a short-term process who would avoid the longer haul; (3) the universality of the language of crisis cuts across the class barriers that might ordinarily separate the therapist from the blue-collar patient. The authors compare the crisis-group approach with the treatment of individuals in crisis. They find that the advantages for the group include greater support, more effective suggestions of alternate coping behaviors which in turn are more acceptable to the patient when made by a peer than by a therapist, and more successful encouragement of the expression of feelings. To counterbalance these advantages, the group is less effective in maintaining focus upon the crisis, less able to identify the "correct" crisis, and more likely to offer maladaptive coping behaviors,

Guidance and counseling

The Chicago Brief Psychotherapy Council (174) considered guidance a valuable technique in the brief procedure. The encouragement of the patient into new life experiences is useful, but psychoanalytic comprehension of and alertness to emerging dynamics is important in order to protect the patient against untoward effects. Gelb and Ullman (75) find that a well-trained, experienced and perceptive therapist can, on the basis of a brief exploration, guide the patient towards methods of behavior and interaction different from his customary mode, and thus lead him into new forms of experience which will result in a more satisfactory and productive life.

While seemingly related to the techniques of advice-giving and directiveness, counseling and guidance should perhaps be best understood as a process involving problem definition and consideration of alternatives, with the patient making his own decision on the basis of data provided. Thus the therapist's statements are short of being recommendations; they are more often posed as alternatives accompanied by predictions of the consequences involved in each.

Home visits

Friedman *et al.* (69) extend brief psychotherapy to emotionally disturbed people in their homes. No additional nor novel techniques of therapy are practiced. The extension reaches otherwise inaccessible individuals. They report also that the practice is an excellent educational device for the personnel of cooperating social agencies, representatives of whom accompany the therapist on the visit.

In commenting upon the home-treatment services of the Meyer Memorial Hospital in Buffalo, Resnick (182) stresses the need for a network of unusual communication sources (churches, the next-door neighbor) to pick up the "cry for help" that otherwise might go unheeded. Success in such a venture, he believes, will reduce the need for hospitalization and provide more humane care.

Hospitalization, brief

A period of hospitalization of no more than a day in the emergency room of a general hospital was found useful in the evaluation and management of psychiatric patients by Kritzer and Pittman (125). The technique allows for extended evaluation when needed. Acute situations may be resolved quickly, thereby preventing longer hospitalization. Prompt alleviation and management of acute organic conditions and the safety of severely disturbed suicidal patients are obtained.

Fenichel (60) emphasizes that a hospital or sanitarium stay is in itself a doubtful measure as the only curative force. He observes that an environmental change may be useful if accompanied by psychotherapy, provided the shift places the patient in a more favorable and benign environment. Management and interrelationships must be geared to the patient's dynamic needs, such as abreactions, transference or reassurance needs. Hospitalization is clearly indicated for a period of emergency which must be weathered, as in acute depressions. In some situations, gaining time can be most constructive by providing opportunity for the ego to restore its equilibrium.

Suicidal possibilities always raise the question of the advisability of hospitalization. Miller (150) comments on this need among severely depressed patients. Sometimes patients with fixed paranoid delusions who are acutely disturbed or who are overtly assaultive must be hospitalized until there is a mending and improvement of the pathology.

Bellak and Small (20) found situations in the course of emergency treatment of the suicidal and the incipiently psychotic patient where proceeding with out-patient treatment was not safe. They report that a brief period of hospitalization in a general hospital provides protection for the patient with conditions of safety and scrutiny which enable the therapist to make vigorous depth interpretations, thus producing both catharsis and ego-mending as a result. They report that acute delusional states of recent precipitation may be treatable under these circumstances.

Hypnosis

Wolberg (244), long an advocate of the therapeutic use of hypnosis, recommends the technique for brief interventions. He finds that hypnosis improves rapport by creating a positive parent-child atmosphere, that it enhances the suggestibility of the patient by extending the influence of the therapist, that it expedites cathartic experience, that it helps lower blocks to verbalization.

He finds also that hypnosis improves motivation by lowering tension, expands efforts at exploration by reducing anxiety, catalyzes transference phenomena, facilitates working through by helping convert insight into action, and, he believes, more quickly enables termination because it helps transfer responsibility to the patient.

Wolberg advocates a hypnosis technique based on four steps: (1) deep breathing exercises, (2) progressive muscle relaxation, (3) visualization of a relaxed scene, and (4) slow counting to 20.

Bellak and Small (20) report the use of hypnosis to facilitate communication. They caution against using the technique where the patient may be threatened by his passivity and has excessive needs to be passively cared for, or with patients who are likely to progress into disassociated states or paranoia.

Frohman (70) and Haley (93) advocate use of hypnosis to abbreviate the therapy process. Meerloo (147) uses hypnosis as a facilitation of catharsis in crisis and traumatic situations. He also teaches auto-hypnosis for achieving muscle relaxation. Wolpe (249) uses hypnosis in order to induce abreaction.

Extensive experience in the hypnotherapy of frigidity and related sexual problems is reported by Richardson (183, 184). He employs direct hypnotic suggestion for symptom removal; "hypno-analysis and hypno-psychotherapy" are employed when there is evidence or suspicion of an underlying problem. Eye fixation techniques of induction were used in all cases.

Information giving

Miller (151) in treating adolescents recommends the provision of information that encourages the adolescent to take full advantage of normal societal processes (clubs, *e.g.*) in an attempt to relieve the adolescent's inhibition. He finds that the technique requires as much skill as does the making of interpretations.

Insight facilitation

Bellak and Small (20) note that psychotherapy traditionally has sought to ameliorate by conveying insight about the nature and causes of an individual's fears and concerns, his impulses and defenses, his unconscious motivations. The rationale of this approach rests upon its observable effect in producing a dynamic realignment of the personality, resulting in a stronger ego and more effective ego functioning. Strict use of language requires that one consider that insight is a goal, while methods for imparting insight or facilitating its achievement are the technical aspects of the intervention. The direct interpretation as a technique will be considered separately. Here we report on other methods for facilitating the achievement of insight. Bellak and Small stress the importance of timing in gaining acceptance of the insight, timing involving the readiness or set of the patient. Economy in presentation also facilitates the acquisition of insight, so that short, direct statements are more effective than wordier, more literary illusions. They recommend the use of colorful language for its heightening effect, language which may long be remembered by the patient. They advocate the use of stories and jokes and point out that great teachers used parables for good reasons. They encourage active learning by asking the patient to formulate and repeat and integrate propositions with other facets of his situation that are under consideration. They use role playing, asking the patient to switch roles with the therapist. Drugs are also useful in facilitating insight insofar as they decrease anxiety and tension, tighten thought processes and interfere with the push of raw impulse. These authors also use the Thematic Apperception Test to supply repetition as an active learning principle; they may read the patient's TAT stories back to him and ask for his own interpretation.

Intellectualization

Bellak and Small (20) believe that the prestige of psychoanalysis has produced some degree of condescension toward the use of intellectualization as a therapeutic intervention. The emphasis upon the cathartic experience accompanied by affective changes relegated intellectualization to a minor position. They argue, however, that the encouragement of any defense previously used to a small degree by the patient which decreases the use of a more pathological defense is in effect producing a psychotherapeutic change; therefore some intellectualization has a proper place in the armamentarium of the psychotherapist. Knowledge which replaces misinformation, reality which replaces distortion and fantasy, may do much to relieve the anxious patient. Diluting the intensity of a patient's fear that his symptoms or fantasies mean that he is uniquely bizarre, or combatting distortions about masturbation are prime examples of treatment by information. Intellectually delineating the origins of anger and fear often helps the patient resolve a conflict situation in shorter order because he is dealing with the causal affect. Where denial is not too rigid, intellectualization may help cut through and set the stage for a more insightful type of learning. Much apprehension is produced by symptoms before which the patient feels helpless, as if attacked by an unseen antagonist or force. Intellectually delineating the cause of depression, of displacement and somatization in hysteria may impart optimism and increased motivation to cooperate with insight psychotherapy. Intellectualization, in short, becomes a way of giving a patient a new look at his behavior and his symptoms. Treating intellectualization as a defense is suggested by Coleman and Zwerling (45); they found the technique useful with women suffering postpartum obsessional panics that approximate psychoses, by intellectualization of their negative feelings about their babies.

Coleman (47) notes that intellectualization facilitates repression and recommends its use as a maneuver to encourage and support the use of existing defense mechanisms. He believes that only those patients who have used intellectualization before can be encouraged to increase the use of the defense.

Intellectualization may help patients who have suffered illnesses and physical trauma to uncover misconceptions about their illnesses and injuries; the approach improves cognitive understanding of the situation, thus identifying and correcting "cognitive blocks" that otherwise retard emotional restabilization. Stein *et al.* (213) find this a frequent necessity in treating emotional reactions to physical illness. They cite their experience with a man whose emotional recovery from a cardiac arrest was impeded by his misconception of blood circulation: he believed an artery from the heart to the brain originated precisely at the point of his myocardial infarction and that it had been closed by scar tissue. The therapist drew the patient's conception of his heart (a more valid view of the patient's conception might have been assured if he had been willing to draw it himself) and then spent much time in slowly and carefully correcting first his misconception of the circulation to the brain and then his fear that occlusion of this non-existent artery had caused damage to his brain.

Alexander (5) observes that intellectualization is useful as a supportive measure when the ego's impairment is temporary or caused by acute emotional stress.

Nolan Lewis at the Chicago Brief Psychotherapy Council (174) maintained that many methods, including explanation, when used by well-trained people with a knowledge of psychoanalytic theory, are more precise, hence more dynamically effective, than when used without such theoretical basis.

Hoch (100) recommends giving intellectual explanations of dream phenomena in brief psychotherapy in order to avoid lengthening the process. Baker (9) includes intellectual clarification of the patient's problem as the first step in the brief psychotherapeutic process. Semrad, Binstock and White (202) use intellectualization in teaching problem-solving techniques to patients. Tannenbaum (223) in a paper entitled "Three Brief Psychoanalyses" used psychoanalytic theory in an intellectual explanation of masturbatory guilt and misinformation. Terhune (224) reports an intensive six-day course of residential treatment with industrial executives which appears to be largely intellectual in technique, involving lecture discussions and academic approaches to mental-health problems.

The experience of an encounter with a therapist strengthens the synthetic and adaptive functions of the ego, fosters intellectualization in which new rational information can be received and insight into previously unconnected matters can be learned, states Gillman (76).

Sequential perceptual ordering is a technique described by McGuire (145, 146) in which the therapist actively organizes the patient's already-conscious perceptions and emotions. The therapist is very active here, no matter how he conducts later sessions. His activity is designed to get started, to set limits. This is primarily an intellectual procedure and actually seeks to teach the patient a method of insight.

Coddington (39) employs intellectualization in preparing a child for an operation. He discusses the situation with the child in the mother's presence. The child's knowledge and concept of anatomy and physiology of the area involved are explored, and misconceptions readily corrected. Using a surgeon's cap and mask and a small anesthesia mask, some of the more frightening and mysterious elements are explained and the child acquainted with them.

Interpretation

Traditionally, psychotherapy has employed interpretation as a technique for achieving amelioration or cure by conveying insight to the individual concerning the nature and causes of his fears, his impulses, his defenses against them and his motivations that are beyond the level of awareness. Bellak and Small (20) make the point that the rationale for this relatively universal approach is based upon the observable effect of insight in promoting a dynamic realignment of the personality, resulting in a stronger ego, essentially in more effective ego functioning. Traditionally, insight has been reserved for individuals for whom long-term psychotherapy such as psychoanalysis has been considered suitable; other interventions are generally indicated in the treatment of the psychotic, the individual with a character disorder, the person in a crisis situation or the acting-out individual. Nonetheless, they maintain that insight therapy, and therefore the interpretation, is an important technique in brief psychotherapy which must be judiciously used.

They consider the use of interpretation to be among the greatest skills of psychotherapists, and have developed certain cautions for it. Simultaneous change in several personality variables are usually required for success in psychotherapy; the interpretation therefore must not be oversimplified through a singleness of purpose. The therapist needs to ask if a drive should be made ego syntonic in all respects or whether certain restraints need to be built-in simultaneously. In brief psychotherapy particularly, the therapist must attempt to predict the effect of his interpretation and incorporate necessary safeguards. Uncritically encouraging the uncovering and expression of instinctual impulses is misapplication of the interpretation technique. It is important in psychotherapy to strengthen as one uncovers. The often reckless pursuit of affect expression in the patient is based upon a misapplication of the long-established observation that insight accompanied by an affective change is most effective in producing therapeutic changes. These single-purpose strivings, however, lead to the device of confrontation without consideration of its impact upon the patient, the capacity of the ego to tolerate, to incorporate the insight and to apply it in realistic terms. Among the consequences of confrontation may be increased denial and repression and more seriously, panic, deep depression, serious acting out and even suicide. Bellak and Small emphasize the need for estimating the patient's readiness and ability to accept and use insight. Use of an interpretation relative to a drive, for example, must be predicated upon conviction that the patient is ready and able to accept the impulse as an essential part of his personality, is able to experience it, and above all is able to discharge it in a nondestructive manner without experiencing incapacitating anxiety and tension that had formerly been part of its repression. If a patient can do this he achieves a reorganization of the forces in his personality. The reader may wish to consult the section on mediate catharsis in which modifications of interpretations are presented.

A number of writers (6, 76, 202, 227) advance the interpretation as the keystone of brief psychotherapeutic approach, seeking to achieve insight in a general way.

Specific focus on the consequences of the narcissistic injury accompanying severe physical illness and trauma is practiced by Stein et al. (213). These include severe anxiety, rage and hostility. Displacement of the anger to the physician and family is common, and the patient frequently suffers increased anxiety from sensing disruption in these relationships he now needs more than ever. The affect and its displacements are carefully brought to the patient's attention.

In the literature of brief psychotherapy one detects a "school" of active interpretation; such activity in offering interpretations is essentially what many writers mean by the increased activity of the psychotherapist. Saul (195) seeks to communicate through active interpretation a nucleus of insight which enables the patient to continue to expand his awareness and emotional growth with new experiences. Malan (144), an outstanding advocate of the focused technique in brief psychotherapy, recommends the use of interpretation to expose directly the resistance aspects of the transference, dependency, the childhood roots of neurosis and grief over termination. Gould (83) notes that in the treatment of crisis situations, active, forceful, repetitive interpretation of the reality situation facilitates the stabilization of the traumatized patient. Lewin (135) advocates the direct and active interpretation of defenses, finding that work with these is essential to success in brief psychotherapy, as it is in longer-term psychotherapies.

Other workers in the field seek to safeguard the patient in their pursuit of insight by limiting the depth of the interpretation, a technique that may be viewed as different than one which seeks to build in safeguards through providing appropriate social outlets. Bonime (25) used this limitation in treatment of traumatized merchant marine men. Erlich and Phillips (55) restrict the depth of insight to certain forms of recognition, including connection between disassociated feelings and symptoms and a general recognition of emotional problems. Harris, Kalis and Freeman (96) in relieving stress quickly find it is necessary to resolve conflict; consequently interpretation of the conflict is an essential component of their treatment.

Rosenthal (191) does not believe that limiting depth of interpretation is feasible in emergency psychotherapies, maintaining that the traumatized patient must be helped to comprehend the symbolic meaning the situation has for him; repression, she is convinced, must be avoided in such cases. She believes, however, that the patient should be "steered" to an insight. This is similar to the "graduated approach" that Bellak and Small (20) suggest in the form of a focusing technique (as in the use of the microscope) whereby the therapist introduces the general area in which he is going to make his interpretation, then makes a series of partial interpretations that enable many patients to make the final leap themselves. If this does not happen, the patient at least has been prepared, and the therapist has opportunity to evaluate whether anxiety or tension or other pathologicalness of defenses are increasing.

Interpreting "with" or "against" the current is made an important distinction by French (4). Going with the current implies that the content of the interpretation is reassuring rather than disturbing; the therapist indicates that he understands the patient's situation, that he is sympathetic, and finds the patient's reactions reasonable and natural. When the therapist decides to interpret against the current, he has decided that defenses must be undermined to lay bare the conflict, that the patient must be forced to give up partial, ineffective solutions before he has acquired more complete, more effective ones. The therapist must rely heavily upon a positive transference to help the patient endure the predictable anxiety of the interim between ineffective and effective solution. In brief psychotherapy the frequency of contact may be increased at such a point.

The interpretation of distortions of contemporary reality on the basis of earlier experiences is urged by Mintz (154) in the treatment of depression and suicidal individuals.

The interpretation of dreams during brief psychotherapy has concerned a number of workers. Bonime (25) advocates their interpretation but favors limiting the depth. Rado (179) argues that limiting the dream interpretation to a long-term psychotherapy is indefensible. Stone (217) advocates a directive approach in the interpretation of dreams. An inherent principle of most brief psychotherapies appears to be that association to the dream is not encouraged without some control by the psychotherapist, who probably will select aspects of the dream for association or discussion.

Wolberg (245) notes that the use of dreams, like the use of any other personality production, is dependent upon the therapist's comprehension of dynamics as well as his comprehension of technical applications. Bellak and Small (20) predicate the interpretation of dreams upon evaluation of the patient's ego strength whenever there is concern that the drive inherent in a dream should not be fully elucidated. In questionable situations, they may elect to work only with the manifest content, relating it to contemporaneous events, or to deal with the fear of the counterdrive rather than to produce insight into the wish for gratification of the pressuring drive. Wolf (247) finds that in short-term group therapy dreams are an important guide to what is going on in the patient unconsciously, but does not recommend that they be used for depth exploration.

Several workers specifically use the interpretation to connect present with past events. (175, 223)

Working with adolescents, Miller (151) uses interpretations based on psychoanalytic concepts to clarify the patient's actions that produce unsatisfactory relationships.

The interpretation of resistance in brief psychotherapy is advocated by Baker (9), Hoch (100), Wolberg (245), and Malan (144).

Interpretation of the meanings of symptoms is found useful by Saul (195), a technique he couples with direct advice for handling the symptom.

The role of the interpretation as an uncovering technique is central to Alexander's (5) distinction between uncovering therapies and supportive measures. Theoretically the interpretation expands the ego's perceptual capacity, facilitating concomitant expansion of its integrative and executive functions.

The interpretation of transference manifestations is also advocated by a number of workers whose approach is grounded in psychoanalytic theory. Bellak and Small (20) accept the positive transference as a working ally but are alert to early manifestations of negative transference and interpret them quickly, so that they do not become an obstacle to the progress of the therapy. Malan agrees, in that he finds transference interpretations especially necessary where there are negative components. Baker (9) and Stone (217) also note the importance of transference interpretations in brief psychotherapy. (See also *Transference, management of.*)

At the Chicago Brief Psychotherapy Council (174) Gerard observed that the interpretation in brief psychotherapy is made much earlier than it would be in analysis, and more superficially. Also prediction of reaction is built into the interpretation in order to carry the patient between sessions. At the same conference, Grinker and Spiegel cautioned specifically that interpretations be kept superficial, particularly in relationship to severe loss in war neuroses, *e.g.*, where a soldier had lost a buddy. This situation could not be interpreted in a brief period, because handling the unconscious hostility present in any ambivalent relationship takes time.

Coleman and Zwerling (45) found that accurate knowledge of realistic precipitating circumstances enabled interpretations that helped even incoherent and disorganized schizophrenics to restabilize. They give as an example that learning that such a patient's wife was pregnant enabled them to make an interpretation of his regression which enabled him to recover. Coleman (47) reports that in acute depressions of recent origin where the lost object can be identified, interpretation can be effective when aimed to mitigate the effect of a severe superego and to deflect from the ego the aggressive drives and lessen the pressure of oral demands. The therapist may simultaneously employ a transference of omnipotence in order to permit and accept the anger which is disclosed toward the lost object, and the rage which arises when passive oral wishes are frustrated. A note of interest concerning the giving of drugs arises here. Coleman found that the actual relationship with the therapist, or his giving of drugs or advice, may so gratify the oral wishes that pointing them out is not necessary. This finding is a clear example of the way in which a psychoanalytically-based awareness of dynamics may permit moves, seemingly superficial, which nonetheless are effective.

In the same report Coleman categorizes interpretations into three distinct groups:

(1) The exact interpretation—where the timing and the area interpreted are precisely correct and the patient responds quickly;

(2) The correct interpretation—where the interpretation is correct but is not on the level of the present conflict. (Glover (78) has called this the "incomplete interpretation.") An example is a quick interpretation of the present situation in terms of the past, such as in postpartum obsessional states, where interpretation that the hatred of a sibling has been displaced upon the child facilitates recovery. This approach, he notes, supports repression and could be classified as a supporting of a defense.

(3) The inexact interpretation—where the intervention becomes a form of suggestion that Glover says functions as an egosyntonic displacement system. This is too unpredictable to be used deliberately, and can only be identified accurately in retrospect. It operates to support repression and thus the defense.

Stein (213) relies heavily upon the interpretation in helping patients with emotional reactions to physical illness to work through denial, and on to a direct discussion of the causal relationship between their emotional symptoms and the narcissistic injury resulting from the physical illness.

In a related fashion, Gelb and Ullman (75) recommend that the therapist bring to conscious awareness modes of thinking and behavior clearly destructive to the patient's well-being, that are the cause of his difficult real-life situation.

Exploration of the dynamics of a panic following calming through sedation and reassurance is advised by Stern (215). He recommends the same approach in treating acute hysterical episodes.

In addition to the patient's seeming capacity for insight, his education, capacity for abstraction, vocabulary and socio-economic background influence the form and timing of interpretations. Wolk (248)

in working with economically deprived patients observes that interpretations must be geared to leave such a patient at the end of each
session with a minimal amount of anxiety; they must also complete
the problem or topic which has been under discussion. Within this
context, when interpretations are used, they are kept short. They
are made specific and do not touch too many topics or areas at one
time. The interpretation is used frequently in what Wolk calls a
"Kernel Interview," but never used obliquely. He believes that the
interpretation must be "additive," that it must move from a preceding
interpretation on to a somewhat higher level of understanding, but
always within the comprehension of the patient. Other workers view
this as a focusing or graduated approach that prepares the patient to
accept an insight that might otherwise mobilize anxiety by preceding
the full development of the insight with statements of lesser emotional content.

The interpretation is seen in a special way by McGuire (145). It
is not used essentially to uncover, but more often to consolidate what
has already been perceptually ordered and discussed in the therapy.
This might be called a partial, or consolidating interpretation. Content, construction and timing are important components of the interpretation, since it is often desirable to avoid, dissect out or hold back
problems which the therapist wishes to exclude. Partial interpretations
may be given to clarify understanding, because the perceptual ordering of the therapist may be incomplete. He may not understand the
patient fully; the patient's defenses may stress one aspect of a conflict
not amenable to treatment so that the interpretation would not further therapy; or a factor of "experience bias" in the patient may be
interfering with both perceptual ordering and acceptance of the
interpretations. McGuire defines "experience bias" as the repetitious
way in which the patient orders his life experiences. He may see himself as subjected, which would lead to introjection, or as subjector
which would lead to projection. McGuire observes that these are not
clinical equivalents of psychoanalytic concepts.

The optimal time for interventions is determined by McGuire
via a "phase model." The variables of his model are:

Positive transference. The patient unrealistically loves the therapist and "follows" the therapist; a decrease is seen when such following
falls off.

The transference neurosis. This is indicated by an expansion of associations to "infantile oedipal references," sudden blocking, or associating the therapist's sex with that of the opposite parent.

The experience bias. This is part of the patient's character and is present throughout therapy as in all stress situations.

The symptoms. An increase suggests unrecognized feeling toward the therapist and that the previously encapsulated conflict is becoming more diffuse.

The phases in the model are: perceptual ordering in which the therapist sets goals, notes the experience bias, dissects out the problems, and during which positive transference begins; perceptual re-ordering, where there is an attempt to introduce new perceptual relationships, the re-ordering of conscious material, clarification and some confrontation. New or unfettered thoughts and emotions are interwoven. Termination is seen when the patient fails to expand the material, rejects suggestions openly, or when his associations suggest intense, unverbalized anger.

Burdon (29) judges an insight successful if it leads to a real and new action, such as making a decision, facing a situation, taking a move in one direction or another in what before was an impasse.

Multiple therapists

An intensification of the therapeutic process is obtained by Goolishian (81) in the treatment of disturbed adolescents by using psychiatrist, psychologist and social workers as multiple therapists for the same patient. The patient may see the different therapists consecutively, alone or with members of his family, or simultaneously; he may see one therapist while members of the family see another.

A "network" of therapists is deployed by Rabkin* in family therapy. A team of therapists works with the family. Therapists and family members both freely move from observation behind a one-way screen to participation with the group. The flexibility facilitates disclosure of pathological modes of communication. In an accepting fashion, the therapists candidly express their observations. Therapists may disagree before the patients.

Gelb and Ullman (75) initially place the inexperienced therapist

---

* Personal Communication from Marcia Pollack.

as an observer with a more experienced one, providing opportunities for supervision and participation in therapy in a manner not usually accomplished through indirect reports. However, they give no indication of benefits for the patient from this procedure. Such a procedure might be expected to give some people more of an "institutional transference" and to tend to dilute dependency somewhat. Co-therapists are advocated by Normand *et al.* (163) to prevent a stereotyped approach to individuals. When one of the co-therapists is a social worker, the environmental and social forces get full weight.

Behavioral therapists have been successful in efforts to enroll the parents of a child as therapists in operant conditioning procedures. Wagner (228) reports his reinforcement of parents' efforts at reinforcement of independent behavior in an 11-year-old girl with severe school and home problems. His decision to adopt this approach was predicated upon the motivation of the parents to cooperate, the fact that the problems appeared more related to interaction precipitated when the girl became ill and less to maladjustment of the parents, and that the older siblings appeared well adjusted.

A cooperative father was the co-therapist of Holland (101) in eliminating fire-setting by a seven-year-old boy. As desirable changes in the boy's behavior appeared, the mother, initially resistant, began to cooperate with the program.

Natural grouping

This ingenious approach developed in a hospital setting by Crabtree and Graller (51) combines group therapy and multiple therapists with autonomy for both patients and therapists. Four to seven patients and staff members select each other for participation in group therapy. Everyone participating is conceived of as a therapist; suicidal patients may be coupled with fellow patients who have a capacity for caring about other people, a schizoid patient may be seen along with the only other person he has been willing to talk to at the hospital, and a paranoid patient may be seen in groups of people who have had some sort of status importance on the ward. The first session is addressed to ward problems or to some personal crisis that a patient may be experiencing. Subsequent sessions are addressed to therapy that is unrelated to either crisis or to a conflict. The group is guided by these rules:

(1) Respect for ability to help each other is paramount.
(2) The therapist is available to the group only as a group, not to any individuals.
(3) Group members work together on problems outside of the therapy hour.
(4) If a member of the group is too upset to leave the hospital, the group assumes responsibility for him.
(5) New members who may be either patients or staff are selected by the group as a whole.

Non-verbal communication

Meta-communication, described by Dreiblatt and Weatherly (53), can be viewed as one form of non-verbal communication, in the sense that more is communicated in a conversation than its manifest verbal content. Koegler (120) observes that brief-contact therapy communicates at a non-verbal level and is particularly useful for people who tend to be limited in their verbal communication ability. Visher (227) follows the practice of not arranging a regular schedule; instead he makes appointments at the end of each session, on the basis that this indicates non-verbally that the therapist sees the treatment as limited in duration.

Placebo

The placebo effect is advocated by Patterson (168) as a powerful therapeutic technique. Factors such as attention, interest, concern, trust, belief, faith and expectation are recognized as placebo effects in the treatment of physical disorders. Psychotherapy, while not excluding these effects, generally considers them to be insufficient, holding that a technique must produce effects which exceed those obtained by placebo in order to be judged effectively useful. Patterson argues that the extraneous nature of the placebo effect in the treatment of a physical disorder is not applicable to psychotherapy. The disorder here is psychological; therefore, it is logical that the specific treatment for a psychological condition should itself be psychological. He suggests that the placebo effect be harnessed and maximized in psychotherapy. Some interesting aspects of the placebo effect are reported by Frank (65). These are discussed in the section on Expectation Theory in Chapter 3.

Philosophy of life, development of

Wolberg (245) considers life philosophy to be an essential component of brief psychotherapy, especially for its successful termination within a reasonable period of time. He includes in a proper philosophy of life: ability to separate present from past; an attitude of tolerance for some tension, anxiety, hostility, frustration and deprivation; the attitude that the person will undertake to correct what is correctable and adjust to the unalterable; to stop self-destructive activities by will power; to curb unreasonable demands upon the self; to challenge one's own devalued self image; to seek to obtain the utmost pleasure possible from life; to develop an attitude of acceptance of one's social role. One may argue that this teaches value systems, and that another therapist might offer quite a different content for a life philosophy. I know, for example, of one therapist who contends that a patient is not cured until he has become a revolutionary.

Prediction

This method uses the patient's past performances to predict what the future may bring if the past continues to be relived. Sifneos (207) suggests its use in anxiety-suppressive therapy. Bellak and Small (20) use it when necessary to alienate the patient rapidly from undesirable, self-destructive forms of behavior; they paint the outcome in unattractive terms to induce the patient to make an effort to avoid what would otherwise be a predictable consequence.

Prodding

Garner (74) uses this as part of an active approach to encouraging patients to undertake problem solving efforts. (See also *Exhortation.*)

Promptness of intervention

The title for this aspect of technique is an attempt at a name for a basic principle in emergency psychotherapy: the patient should be seen as soon as possible after a traumatic event. Harris, Kalis and Freeman (96) advocate that every effort be made to see the patient within a maximum of 24 hours following a traumatic episode. Rosenthal (191) who has worked with those who have experienced bombing or accidents advocates seeing the patient as soon as possible following a trauma even if the patient should still be in shock. Meerloo (147) believes that the initial interview with traumatized patients should be as long as necessary, up to three and four hours even, in order to utilize the heightened tension of the situation and to assure that efforts are made to prevent the damming up of affect. Quick availability of a therapist enables immediate and active confrontation with impaired functioning, state Gelb and Ullman (75); if the help is empathic and accurate it will be more effective than passive working through.

Bellak and Small (20) advocate reaching out to the victims of traumatic events (fires or explosions, for example) to provide quick emergency help to the victims, an intervention that would have preventive ramifications. With this same aim, the Beekman Downtown Hospital in New York City now has a mobile psychotherapeutic out-reach unit.

Reality testing

Bellak and Small (20) note the importance of memory and learning in the development of reality testing and adopt these techniques in treating impairments in this area. They advise the technique of recollecting former, more appropriate responses and contrasting them with the present maladaptive distortion. Or they make predictions of outcomes of behavior accompanied by suggestions of alternative approaches or interpretations, or give an indication that a person described by the patient may have motivations other than those the patients ascribes to him. They comment that among young people particularly, awareness of role position or status may not be adequately developed, and pressures may arise from misinterpretation of one's role. Correction of the distortion tends to modify maladaptive behavior. They advise the therapist to be aware that even neurotic patients may present distortion or denial of perception of both external reality and internal striving, and that a mild paranoid reaction may be found among people who are not psychotic but are using the dynamic in the service of masochism.

The gradual reworking with a patient of the events and their

significance of an acute physical illness is employed by Stein *et al.*
(213) to combat the pessimism that frequently floods a person when
his denial mechanisms are weakened or break down. They liken the
therapist in this process to the "protecting parent" who makes a harsh
and ominous reality more tolerable for the child, enabling the child
to confront and cope with the unpleasant world. Stein and his colleagues persist in a carefully measured, "graduated" approach over a
period of time—they "titrate" denial with reality.

Green and Rothenberg (84) advocate the use of reality structuring in treating children. Waltzer *et al.* (235) note its importance
when the patient's relationship to reality must be improved. Coleman
and Zwerling (45) report that reality testing helps overcome obsessional thoughts in postpartum disturbances about the condition of
the child that has recently been born, *e.g.*, the fear of mental retardation in the child may be combated by such an intervention.

Reassurance

Reassurance may be viewed as an oral offering, in the sense that
the patient incorporates the benignity of the therapist and his succor-
ing proffer. Green and Rothenberg (84) advocate its use liberally
where a child has either witnessed an accident or been slightly injured
in one; active reassurance as to the outcome and the limits of injury
to himself are important here. Mintz (154) reassures the depressive
or suicidal patient as to the lmitations of the current crisis, so that
the patient will not feel he is caught up in an interminable process
of pain and deprivation. Bos (26) suggests that the careful taking of
a history is reassuring to the patient, conveying the feeling that he
is in the hands of a competent and responsible individual. Tannenbaum (233) advocates reassuring patients about specific guilt reactions
based on misinformation, as in masturbation for example. Bellak and
Small (20) report this procedure also. One often encounters a patient
who fears he may be crazy or homosexual, and they may be proffered
direct reassurance that he is neither of these. Universalizing the fear
is also reassuring, helping the patient see that he is not unique and
bizarre.

Bellak and Small further note that reassurance and support may
be either implicit or explicit. The statement of the therapist's availability at any time day or night to the panicky or suicidal patient

is a good example of implicit support, the offer communicating to the patient that he is not alone and that the therapist is available as a source of help. In their experience, most individuals use the proffer judiciously; some need to be reassured several times that the proffer is sincerely meant. Where the proffer of availability is exploited, the situation is ameliorated by interpreting the patient's testing of the therapist or his excessive passive needs. They note also that the therapist may explicitly reassure by expressions of approval or of identification with the patient's feelings, statements or overt behavior. They identify "vestibule anxiety," experienced on the threshold of a new situation. In these circumstances the patient may be reassured that his anxiety on approaching a new situation will be of limited duration.

Awareness of the need of the physically ill person for reassurance that a troubling phenomenon may be functional rather than organically caused is stressed by Stein *et al.* (213). This approach was part of their treatment method with a post-myocardial-infarction patient who feared that his memory difficulties were the result of brain damage arising from an occluded "fantasy" artery. Psychological test findings were used to demonstrate to him that his faulty memory was caused by intense anxiety instead.

Reassurance and emotional support are found useful with aged persons between the ages 80 and 90 by Goldfarb and Turner (79). They report that the approach appears to combat the tendency toward increasing helplessness in the elderly, a self-perpetuating evil, since increased helplessness contributes to a loss of self-esteem which in turn generates more feelings of helplessness, and so on.

Reassurance is considered critical in the acute phase of panic states along with sedation, before there is an exploration of dynamics, according to Stern (215).

Reconditioning, positive

This is one of the basic procedures of behavioral therapy. Wolpe (249) notes that new behaviors may be needed in a situation or context that do not invoke anxiety; he cites Skinner's conditioning techniques for the removal and replacement of undesirable habits. In this approach, new desired behaviors are rewarded, while the undesired behavior is either consistently not rewarded or punished.

Relaxation, physical

The encouragement and teaching of physical relaxation is an inherent part of the behavioral therapist's armamentarium (249). Ferenczi (62) early advised the use of physical relaxation techniques to overcome inhibitions and resistances to associations; Freud's early ventures with putting his hand on a patient's brow to calm him were of the same order. Wolberg (245) more specifically teaches patients progressive muscle relaxation to facilitate the induction of hypnotic states.

Self-esteem reconstruction

A frequent concomitant of depression, lowered self-esteem has been noted in many individuals seeking psychotherapy. Mintz (154) advocates that special attention be paid to the reconstruction of self-esteem in depressive and suicidal patients. Bellak and Small (20) view the necessity to increase self-esteem as an almost universal requirement in brief psychotherapy. The very necessity to ask for help for an emotional and mental problem is found to be traumatic to many individuals, a blow to their self-esteem. The feeling that one is inadequate to deal with one's own problems is often concomitant with decision to ask for help. Others see the necessity for seeking psychotherapy as opening them to rejection and to a sense of failure. Bellak and Small advocate that the positive features in his life should be pointed out to such an individual, with recognition that he has accomplished something, that he has been able to endure difficulty and that he has done something especially reasonable in seeking help for his problem. They suggest that the therapist reveal himself to the patient as being a human with frailties and difficulties similar if not identical with those the patient is encountering. They caution, however, that the approach can be neither insincere nor overdone.

In group therapy, Wolf (247) holds sessions in which the members of the group point out each other's positive qualities in an effort to build up each others' self-esteem.

Coleman and Zwerling (45) carefully observe and report to the patient the strengths in his life history, to bolster the self-esteem of the depressed; at the same time they evoke affective expression.

The effect of helplessness in damaging self-esteem is reported by

Goldfarb and Turner (79); Nelken (Gwartney *et al.* (92)) eloquently describes how an acute emotional condition isolates an individual from contact and relationship, increases hopelessness and misunderstanding and turns to self-abhorrence.

Socarides (211) emphasizes that self-esteem is increased through insight and provides motivation of sufficient impetus to carry the patient toward the beginning solutions of neurotic conflicts.

Increased self-esteem is found by Sifneos (208) in the majority of cases who improve with anxiety-provoking therapy. He believes that this results from the learning of new and better coping and problem-solving behavior

Semantics, general

Frohman (70) used the systems and approaches of general semantics in helping individuals comprehend the symbolic meaning of many situations and life experiences.

Sensitization to signals

This technique described by Bellak and Small (20) consists of training patients to recognize and perceive both internal and external signals. The process may well fall under the rubric of reality testing, but merits special attention as a therapeutic intervention. Careful and detailed review of a situation will often enable the therapist to point out to the patient that advance notice of an impending emotional response was either detectable in themselves or in the other person, and had the patient been alert to the signal, the painful situation could have been averted or modified.

Social milieu, use of

The use of the social milieu is especially important in the treatment of identity crises in the adolescent, writes Miller (152). The therapist must attempt to aid the adolescent to take full advantage of the normal societal processes available to him, usually relationships with peers and discussions with them of mutual problems.

Aid from the environment will be needed if hostility is the most marked feature of a grief response (Lindemann, 137). A member of the family, a minister, social worker or physician may be useful in urging the patient to continue seeing the therapist in order to work through the hostility.

Bellak and Small (20) and Mintz (154) urge the advisability of involving other members of the family in a suicidal crisis, to chaperon the patient, to prevent acting on impulse, and to provide companionship for combating the sense of isolation.

Structuring

Taking over and organizing the patient's life is seen by some therapists as a means of permitting for a time a dependency upon the therapist that enables repair of traumatic damage. Mintz (154) does not hesitate to permit depressed and suicidal patients to lean upon him by organizing a detailed daily schedule which he then admonishes them to follow strictly. The effect is to keep them occupied, to interfere with obsessional dwelling upon their unhappy condition and to facilitate the discharge of aggression. Wolberg (245) also employs the technique of structuring plans of action for the patient as preliminary to his developing his own strategy for an activity program. (See also *Activity of Therapist* for an elaboration of some aspects of structuring.)

Suggestion

Haley (93) pursues a very active course in brief psychotherapy, seeking to establish control by the therapist over resistance and the symptoms themselves. He employs suggestion techniques, reinforced by hypnosis where he considers it necessary. Semrad, Binstock and White (202) also employ suggestion. Wolberg (245) notes that the use of hypnosis tends to extend the influence of suggestion in the psychotherapeutic process, an influence which he believes operates in all therapy.

Support

This technique is reported with great frequency in the literature on brief psychotherapy. Alexander (5) notes that brief psychotherapy essentially is of two types: supportive and uncovering. Supportive measures are specifically called for in situations where the impairment is temporary and caused by an acute stress. Bellak and Small (20) classify supportive techniques along with reassurance methods, described in an earlier section of this chapter. Baker (9) considers supportive measures one of six essential techniques in brief psychotherapy. Bonime (25) lists support as a crucial technique for traumatic war neurosis. Dreiblatt and Weatherly (53) report the effectiveness of supportive brief contacts in reducing hospital stays.

Miller (151) has found it useful to support adolescents in making their own decisions, so long as these decisions do not involve actions which would seriously hinder the achievement of an identity solution, such as passive submission to authority, leaving school, committing a crime, withdrawing from interpersonal contact and other behavior extremes. Support of constructive decisions has helped adolescents establish a sense of values.

Green and Rothenberg (84) consider supportive techniques important in emergency treatment of children, especially where there has been a death of a close relative or friend. In such cases the child needs to know that the therapist or some other figure can be relied upon as an adult who will be available to the child.

Mintz (154) advocates encouraging the support of suicidal patients upon the therapist to the point of actual dependence.

Rabkin* has developed supportive measures for aiding patients who find themselves unable to deal with some aspect of society's bureaucracy (Welfare, Medicaid). Sometimes the therapist must leave his office to accompany the patient and engage the bureaucratic process for him to show that it can be mastered. The patient observes and learns by modelling himself after the therapist. The learning is reinforced by a discussion of the proceedings after the fact. Rabkin calls this the Advocate Approach.

"A dynamically-oriented supportive psychotherapy" is described by Coleman and Zwerling (45), one that employs a variety of therapeutic interventions in order to assist a patient to reestablish defensive structures that were effective for him prior to a crisis or breakdown. Coleman (47) has developed this technique even further, particularly as the support pertains to the strengthening of defense mechanisms. It is important never to attack an important defense of

---

* Personal Communication from Marcia Pollack.

the patient in a brief psychotherapeutic intervention, but preferable to praise and give narcissistic support to those defenses that combine with adaptive gratifications, and to discourage without attack those that appear to be maladaptive. The solution can be delicate, since the conflict area may be close to the surface and may need interpretation. If symptoms are intensified by interpretation, the wise therapist will re-evaluate his approach to the therapy of the individual, obviously moving to defensive support rather than to interpretation thrust. Coleman also comments on the total support provided by a hospital setting, if the hospital is one respected by the patient; the availability of help through the 24-hour period of the day and night is of itself a critical supportive element.

Supportive measures were found useful to Levy (134) in preventing hospitalization among newly disturbed individuals. Waltzer *et al.* (235) advised the extensive use of supportive rather than expressive techniques when the patient's relationship to reality must be improved.

Tactics

Tactics in a non-military sense is the term suggested by Regan (181) for his approach in the brief psychotherapy of depression. He defines tactics as "methods of procedure, especially adroit devices for accomplishing an end." In practice those described are relatively straightforward operational procedures, methods which have been proved through experience and careful testing. Often simple, lacking the "grandeur" of theoretical formulations, they include protection of the patient, the need for preparatory exploration, the interruption of the ruminative cycle, the use of physical therapy, the initiation of attitudinal change, and effective collaboration with other resources.

Time limits, definition of

This technique is one of the distinguishing features of brief psychotherapy; the establishment of time limitations at the very beginning of psychotherapy creates the expectancy within both the therapist and the patient which exercises an influence on the outcome. Kaffman (112) makes this point most succinctly.

Some patients, often those coming from lower socio-economic groups, cannot comprehend a fact recognized by more sophisticated individuals: that unlike physical ailments, emotional disturbances may require prolonged and intensive treatment. Thus less sophisticated individuals tend to become uncooperative at the prospect of long-term psychotherapy, while in sharp contrast the sophisticated patient may be disappointed and even skeptical if short term psychotherapy is offered instead of intensive treatment.

Bellak and Small (20) report on the use of time-limitation technique with more than 1,400 patients seen in the walk-in emergency clinic of a large public hospital. Seitz (201) set time limits at the beginning of treatment in working with psychosomatic skin ailments.

Malan (144) working with a "focal" therapeutic aim used time-limitation techniques but in a less structured way. His patients are told at the beginning that the therapist plans to go ahead with treatment for a few months to see what happens; the patient is told that the situation will be reviewed at the end of that time and if he needs more treatment he will be transferred to a longer form of treatment. In a reported few cases, however, Malan did set an exact time limit in advance and reports that the limit did not make the work impossible; rather, in accordance with Phillips and Johnston (171), it seemed to give a definite structure of "a beginning, a middle and an end" to the treament. Malan also believes that setting an exact time limit facilitates the task of dealing with patients' feelings about termination.

Stekel (214) was among the early activists in psychotherapy and advocated time definition in order to facilitate the progress of therapy. Straker (219) indicates that early setting of time limits counteracts the lengthening factor of termination resistance.

Levy (134) is also among those advocating this technique. His clinic employs the technique to prevent hospitalization in acute situations; at the first interview the therapist states concretely that the purpose of the therapy is to help the individual avoid hospitalization and that this goal is to be accomplished in a maximum of six sessions.

Transference, management of

This technique is inherent in brief psychotherapy when practiced by psychoanalytically-oriented therapists.

Malan (144) has extensively studied the literature of brief psychotherapy and that of transference particularly. He calls attention to a conservative view voiced in the extreme by Rogerians that brief therapy is only possible if the therapy is without the transference relationship—hence non-directive therapy. Pumpian-Mindlin, also a conservative on this point although a psychoanalyst, cited the tendency in brief therapy to avoid an "intense transference" and to diminish it when it appeared, by less frequent sessions and by concentrating only upon the presenting problem. Malan's studies identified also a radical view, exemplified by Alexander and French (4), in which transference interpretation may play any part; it may be used or not; in some cases transference phenomena may be handled by acceptance, in others by interpretation, or by a "corrective emotional experience" in the patient's relationship with the therapist.

In his study of 21 cases, Malan quickly found it impossible to avoid the development of intense and powerful transference feelings; accordingly, an initial fear of making a transference interpretation was soon overcome and ignored. He and his colleague soon learned also that transference interpretation did no harm, that fears of disturbing the patient were groundless, if partial interpretations prepare patient and therapist to advance together to the ultimate interpretation. His conclusion was that transference interpretation of both positive and negative features was necessary to success in brief therapy.

Bellak and Small (20) begin a chapter on basic procedures with a discussion of transference. They urge the necessity to distinguish general transference phenomena from the sharply defined psychoanalytic concept of a transference neurosis, "a brief recapitulation of earlier phases of conflict and development with sentiments projected on to the analyst which once were held to other figures, especially the parent." In brief psychotherapy they advocate that the therapist direct his attention to transference phenomena, defined as the "non-rational sentiments of the patients toward his therapist, including hopes, fears, likes, and dislikes." They add that the therapist must understand that negative sentiments toward the therapist need not be unreasonable ones. They consider a positive transference as essential to brief psychotherapy, one whereby the therapist is viewed as likeable, reliable, understanding and accepting, and which leads the patient to expect that the therapist will be able to help him. The emphasis is to establish and maintain in the patient a view of the therapist as benign, interested and helpful. Care therefore must be exercised that the clinging, overly-dependent patient is assisted to counteract this effect. The therapist may do this by lengthening the intervals between sessions, and upon termination by arranging for a prearranged telephone contact to avoid feelings of rejection. To maintain positive transference, negative features must be dealt with when they arise; in fact they should be dealt with promptly, effectively and with good grace. In addition to the dependent clinging personality, Bellak and Small note other patients requiring management of the positive transference. With adolescents, spatial proximity and physical contact may be considered unwise; with a flirtatious young woman, a male therapist may need to become somewhat more formal, more polite; an obsessively isolating person who is reserved and inhibited may benefit from a more direct, salty approach.

The "therapeutic alliance" is the keystone of the carefully measured attack upon denial practiced by Stein et al. (213) for patients suffering emotional reactions to severe physical illnesses. Without this alliance, their implied conclusion is that the fantasies attendant to illness cannot be brought into congruence with reality.

The development and maintenance of positive transference are advocated also by Baker (9) and Visher (227). Rosenbaum (188) believes that the mechanism of early relief is quick identification with the therapist, permitting a transference cure based upon object substitution. Sifneos (207) finds that the development of a positive transference is necessary in his anxiety-provoking techniques in order to encourage the patient to undertake problem solving. Wolberg (245) seeks to develop a working relationship as rapidly as possible. He finds that this process is facilitated by "an unqualified acceptance of the patient" and the ability of the therapist to communicate to the patient a confidence in his methods and the belief that he can help.

Sifneos (207) notes the necessity of preventing the formation of a transference neurosis. Stone (217) refers to developing a "limited" transference and interpreting it only when necessary; his emphasis is on demonstrable reality, not on fantasy. Gillman (76) recommends that the therapist's attitude be one of "attentive neutrality" in order to avoid encouraging dependency and ambivalent transference features.

Howard (102), whose paper is titled "Of Gimmicks and Gadgets in Brief Psychotherapy," adopts what might be called a "forced" transference in which the patient is not permitted to develop his own view of his problems, but is urged to adopt the one presented to him by the therapist. The patient must write and sign a statement of his reaction to the therapy which Howard believes shows the patient's acceptance of the view of the problem advocated by the therapist.

Lewin (135) actually seeks to arouse negative transference at the very first session by direct interpretation of defenses. This he finds arouses masochistic defenses and fears of expressing anger; when these are elicited quickly and interpreted, movement takes place.

Fenichel (60) cautions against the use of positive transference to induce improved behavior on the basis that it may be equated by the patient with "good behavior," earning him love, protection and participation with the God-like doctor. Coleman (47) also notes that many dramatic changes are presumed to relate to a positive transference, but warns that these are not predictable and the benefits are fortuitous, hence not under control. Nonetheless, he comments that the manipulation of the positive transference often makes it possible to effect changes in the patient's life; this is especially clear in the use of drugs where the prescription by an "omnipotent" psychotherapist may produce what he probably considers to be placebo effects on top of whatever direct physiological benefit is obtained.

At the Chicago Brief Psychotherapy Council (174) Levine discussed certain aspects of transference behavior as difficult to label. These involve what might be considered a "one-two" manuever, in which on the one hand the therapist refused to respond to the patient's pathological defenses or efforts to intimidate, possess or engulf him. He also refused to be omnipotent, to be preferential, to feel rejected or to reject. Instead he counterposed this with expressions of warm responses to the patient's fundamental decency, showing liking and respect for the patient. Where there was a strong positive transference, Levine believed the therapist could successfully employ guidance techniques, if needed.

Grinker, at the same conference, stressed that identification with the therapist is not just a step toward viewing the world as hospitable, but more importantly is dynamically an aid in reducing the hostility of the superego and in keeping the person from hating himself, as a failure and coward. This was particularly true among those in combat.

McGuire (145, 146) reports Sifneos' speculation that there is an optimal time for achieving aims in brief psychotherapy. It is that period when a positive transference exists but before a transference neurosis develops; it is a limited interval of time.

Transference interpretation at the initial interview is advocated by Socarides (211); he stresses the importance of appraising such manifestations rapidly. If accurately and forcefully interpreted, they can "fascinate" the patient by their exactness, and motivate him toward more insightful work. The patient comes to regard the therapist not only as completely understanding him but also as his agent in his struggle for freedom from frightening neurotic processes.

Consideration is given to the discouragement of regressive dependency or ambivalent transference (Gillman, 76). The power of transference to achieve symptomatic improvement may be due to the transference either to a good parent with dependable protection and love, or to a threatening parent, which would motivate an increase in repression. The improvement obtained from this approach, Gillman notes, remains only so long as the image of the therapist is retained undisturbed by the patient.

Burdon (29) uses transference feelings as they arise, relating them to reality events in order to prevent their becoming unwieldly in the course of treatment.

Interpretation of transference and defenses is important in the treatment of children, according to Lester (133), and replaces the earlier emphasis on symbolic interpretation.

The importance of working with transference distortions in lower-class patients is stressed by Jacobson (105). Such distortions tend to vary inversely with the availability of reality testing. The more unfamiliar a situation is, the more readily is it colored by unconscious fantasies. A tendency for the lower-class patient to see the therapist as a parent, because the therapist is "above him" in the social ladder, is reported. This in turn may reinforce the patient's tendency to see himself as bad, as well as frightened. All of this may lead to the fear of rejection, and would interfere with the effectiveness of brief therapy. Jacobson observes that crisis therapy minimizes cultural differences that lead to negative transference manifestations, because crises evoke universally shared childhood experiences, which both the therapist and the patient have experienced and which both understand no matter what the social stratum.

Ventilation

This is a metaphor describing the act of freely expressing one's emotions, feelings and thoughts, particularly about a problem. It is similar to the cathartic experience but has less structured anticipation that incidents of the past will be relived and the tension attendant to them discharged.

Erlich and Phillips (55) report on the use of ventilation as one of five essential techniques in working with grounded aviators. Keeler (115) describes the ventilation of feelings about current problems as an essential group-therapy technique with hospitalized non-psychotic patients. Lewin (135) seeks particularly the ventilation of anger in his techniques employing the arousal of negative transference. Schoenberg and Carr (198) focus on the expression of hostility in the brief treatment of neurodermatitis. Seitz (201) describing treatment with psychosomatic skin disorders reports on the ventilation of rage, guilt and inferiority feelings. Cook (49) uses ventilation techniques with hospitalized patients in both individual and group therapy. Green and Rothenberg (84) advocate the use of ventilation in first-aid psychotherapy with children. Hansen (95) has found ventilation of anxiety, sorrow and other affects crucial in treating a variety of medical emergencies where the patient's feelings about the illness or the procedure undergone or imminent is essential to stabilization and adjustment.

Levine at the Chicago Brief Psychotherapy Council (174) recommended the use of confession and ventilation short of true catharsis in the brief psychotherapy encounter. Grinker at the same conference reported on the well-established use of narcosynthesis in stimulating ventilation and bringing about the release of unconscious tensions. Greenblatt *et al.* (86) are among those recommending the technique as a widely useful one in community mental-health services.

Lindemann's (137) study of the symptomatology and management of acute grief indicates that ventilation will enable the patient to accept the pain of bereavement, require that he review his relationships with the deceased and become acquainted with the alterations and his own modes of emotional reaction. Fear of insanity, of accepting the startling changes in his feelings, especially the overflow of hostility, have to be worked through. The patient must express his sorrow and sense of loss, and he will have to develop an acceptable formulation of his future mental and emotional relationship to the deceased person. Feelings of guilt will have to be verbalized. The technique is essentially ventilation, with some insight.

Ventilation is employed by Coddington (39) as a technique with the mothers of children in brief psychotherapy in a pediatric practice. He reports that ventilation allays the anxiety of parents of a sick child, and is useful in both home calls and office practice. Parents develop self assurance in their ability to cope with a mildly ill child.

Writing therapy

This technique, developed and described by Phillips and Wiener (172), arose from theoretical considerations that sought to minimize interpersonal effects in psychotherapy, and also to reduce the pressure of waiting lists for the services of a university psychological clinic. The technique requires that the patient be reasonably articulate, is able to write with some clarity, and, of course, is willing to accept writing as the therapeutic intervention. The patient is given specific guiding instructions which include scheduling a given hour when he is to write his statements as if he were having an appointment for a personal interview. He is told to write out his ideas, to define his problems as clearly as he can, and to think of ways in which he has tried to cope with these problems. The therapist responds to the patient's statements. He may request more discussion, make a suggestion or provide information. The authors believe that the technique is focal, that it tends to reduce to a minimum the nonessential in the therapeutic transaction.

CHAPTER 7

Termination

In brief psychotherapy the patient's wish to end treatment is seldom questioned as a "flight into health." No confusion is possible if patient and therapist enter into a compact specifying termination at the very moment treatment is begun.

Bellak and Small (20) rely on a carefully cultivated positive transference for smooth transition in ending brief psychotherapy. They advise that the patient be made to understand that he is welcome to return. The positive transference minimizes the sense of rejection, and permits the therapist to be retained by the patient as a benign, introjected figure, thus motivating the patient to continue to do well for the sake of the therapist. The availability of the therapist is stressed, while at the same time the patient is urged to apply for himself the lessons he has learned. He is assured that he has become better because he has learned to understand some of his problems; he is advised to get in touch with the therapist before any future situation becomes unmanageable. Helping the patient anticipate future problems that may arise as a consequence of patterns of behavior he has recognized in himself tends to reinforce the learning accomplished. A request for periodic follow-up reports by letter or telephone helps maintain the positive transference and reassures the patient of the therapist's availability.

Malan (144), tracing the historical development of psychoanalysis, relates how recognition grew that the early relief of symptoms occurred primarily because of transference cures and gratification of the patient's need for love, that relapses often occurred at termination and could be reversed only when the negative transference, the anger at being abandoned, was interpreted. He notes that while termination and follow up are not very much discussed in psychoanalytic literature, Stekel discussed the emergence of resentment at termination. In Malan's approach, the transference and its infantile roots are frequently explored. Following a study of especially difficult cases, he and his colleagues decided that the negative transference had to become an essential part of almost every therapy, particularly the anger which develops at termination or in relationship to the loss of the therapist for any other reason. They found that negative transference over termination was a major issue in six of the 21 cases studied. Such anger is considered by Malan to be one of the primary lengthening factors in psychotherapy, so that comprehension of it and it satisfactory interpretation are essential to conclusion.

Aldrich (2) recommends erring on the side of premature termination, rather than unwarranted continuation of treatment: "Early termination of psychotherapy perhaps should be perceived as calculated risk, to be undertaken when the potential benefits outweigh the potential liabilities. . . ." Treatment may be resumed following termination without much damage to the patient's self esteem, provided termination is managed properly. He concludes "I would rather have a few patients return following premature termination than have many others continue in treatment past the time when they are able to carry on without outside assistance."

Socarides (211) observes that brief psychotherapy leaves the patient with a conviction that he has an omnipotent agent in his therapist, ready to help him with future conflicts, in sharp contrast to the psychoanalytic goal of achieving freedom from all authority figures.

The tapering termination, a course he recommends with the "average neurotic patient," is preferred by Hoch (100), a view which will not find great support among psychotherapists experienced with brief work.

Termination when the patient expresses satisfaction or when he hints that he wants to continue treatment is advised by Sifneos. (207)

Alexander (5) believes that "transference cures" may be long lasting even after very brief psychotherapeutic contact; he likens termination to the vacations in longer-term therapies and comments favorably upon the benefits resulting from these.

Wolberg (245) also emphasizes the ongoing application by the patient of the lessons he has learned during psychotherapy. He suggests that the therapist and the patient have different viewpoints in considering readiness for termination. The therapist's view will depend upon whether his objectives have been achieved. From the patient's point of view, termination is in order when he has achieved the following: (1) decrease or resolution of anxiety; (2) amelioration of other disturbing symptoms; (3) a degree of insight into the sources of his difficulty including conflicts, personality patterns of a troublesome nature and inadequate coping mechanisms; (4) comprehension of what is needed for him to make a better adjustment and a willingness to make the effort in that direction; (5) a greater tolerance for frustration and deprivation; (6) increased mastery of troublesome aspects of his environment and a willingness to accept essential demands made upon him; (7) a change in outlook on life; (8) any ability at self observation and self-relaxation; and (9) ability to terminate the treatment. Above all, Wolberg appears to emphasize the need for self observation and for the active challenging for one's own neurotic patterns. He also prepares the patient for the eventuality of a setback and arms the patient with a follow-up responsibility for reporting at a stated interval.

Miller (152) is succinct: terminate when satisfactory adjustment to the present has been achieved; let the future take care of itself.

CHAPTER 8

Studies of the Process of Brief Psychotherapy

Little material is available that analyzes process in brief psychotherapy; there is much theory but little research. Two investigations —Malan's published in 1963 (144) and Bellak's in 1965 (20)—are magnificent exceptions.

Malan explored and developed "the focal technique," the pursuit of a formulated objective. More significantly, he has shattered the shibboleth of the sanctity of the transference interpretation as the exclusive territory of longer-term, more intensive therapies. He demonstrates what many other therapists have stated—transference manifestations of all kinds must be dealt with quickly and effectively if brief therapy is to succeed within its time definitions.

He carefully investigated the rather widespread "conservative" position that transference interpretations would produce troubling consequences in brief psychotherapy and hence would be dangerous. He analyzed the therapies of 19 patients according to their "transference orientation," using a four-point scale to compare the "importance" of the transference work with non-transference work. The importance of any kind of interpretation was judged to be high when: (1) many such interpretations were made and a clear response came eventually, or, (2) the patient was manifestly working with an interpertation step by step, or, (3) more qualitatively when a marked response apeared to either one or to a few isolated interpretations. On the basis of these evaluations, he found that a high degree of transference orientation is "a necessary condition to success" in brief psychotherapy. All cases were rated on a four-point scale for the degree of resolution of their main problem. Scores 3, 2, and 1 indicated varying degrees of favorable resolution. A score of 0 indicated no change, or all other changes which could have been negative. All cases that received an outcome score higher than zero were found to contain some successful work on negative transference. Six of ten cases that received a 0 score showed either no response to interpretations of negative transference, or no evidence that negative transference work had been done. Additional research indicated that transference work was not only associated with favorable outcomes but also did not intensify dependence of the patient, since only one of the seven cases in which transference played the most important role failed to terminate.

Thereafter, Malan undertook a form of content analysis of the written case records in an effort to meet the criticism that the preceding transference hypotheses were produced by a single observer studying his own clinical judgments. He attempted to quantify measures of transference interpretations, using as a method the "ratio of the number of transference interpretations to the total number of interpretations recorded." The study explored the proposition that the "higher the proportion of a given interpretation in the case record, the more does the case record tend to be that of a successful therapy." Malan cogently and forthrightly reviews the objections to an *ex post facto* study, but insists that in the face of these his approach had one advantage: since the content analysis was conceived long after the therapies had been completed, the therapists at the time of recording could not have been guided by the research intent. He acknowledges the common error that an observed relationship may be offered as proof of a hypothesis, then argues in reply that evidence from *post facto* reasoning can be quite strong, if enough coincidence can be found in it.

He concentrated upon the content of the interventions, that is, on interpretations. He defines an intervention as a passage in the record, however long, however many different elements were contained in it, in which what the therapist says is located between two passages in which the patient is reported as saying something. Since the therapeutic technique employed was almost entirely interpretive, the interventions were divided into only two groups: interpretations and non-interpretations (exploratory questions, reality testing, advice and reassurance). He identified four categories of persons toward whom an interpretation can be directed: the parent, the therapist, the non-parent and a linked category in which the parent and the therapist were combined. Malan himself rated all of the cases. (Subsequently five cases were rated by another judge.) Differences never exceeded 6 percent between the two judges on any proportion of patient-directed or therapist-directed interpretation. The relationship between the total number of interpretations recorded and outcome produced a zero correlation. When the three unsuccessful therapies were removed, a positive correlation was obtained at a 5 percent level of significance. The relationship between the average number of interpretations as reported for each session and the outcome was slightly negative. This particular evidence of intensity of communication, or of the therapist's interest, was in itself not correlated with successful outcome. The essential conclusion is that in the therapies studied, the necessary conditions for success were interpretation of the link between transference of feelings and its relationship to one or both parents of the patient and whether or not this link became a major issue in the therapy.

Bellak (20) and colleagues report an intensive evaluation of short-term, psychoanalytic psychotherapy in which repeated judgments on a complex series of increasingly detailed variables were studied in one case. In a second case, repeated judgments were made on the same variables and upon specifically designed *ad hoc* questions plus a number of short-range predictions on other variables. Among the six raters were four psychoanalysts, graduates of the New York Psychoanalytic Institute, a training candidate at the Psychoanalytic Institute of New York Downstate Medical Center, and a psychologist trained at the William Alanson White Institute. The two therapists were well trained and experienced, one a psychiatrist, the other a psychologist.

Both sought to conceptualize their treatment approach along the following model: (1) obtain a general understanding of the patient, his complaints and his present life situation; (2) select and define the problem areas to be worked with; (3) formulate a dynamic appraisal of the problem into a description of reality, dynamic and genetic factors and how they converged to produce the presenting problem; (4) devise a treatment plan intended to alter the balance of these forces so as to eliminate the symptom or reduce its severity. This plan in itself would then constitute a prediction. Variables were defined to obtain quantification of these procedures and modified throughout preliminary try-outs in which the treatment of patients was not part of the experiments. The raters were trained. The two patients were selected by the research staff for their apparent suitability for dynamic psychotherapy and for the likelihood that they would remain for the course of five sessions of treatment. The patients gave permission to have their interviews taped. The tapes were transcribed and each interview was presented to the judges. When a judge had rated one interview, the next was presented to him.

Two methods of analysis were employed, the first utilized a set of rating scales, the items of which were based upon a psychoanalytic model of personality. Three areas were established for study: (1) Dynamic Appraisal of the patient's illness; (2) the Treatment Plan; (3) the Patient's Status in each session.

In the Dynamic Appraisal area subscales were devised to record notations of: (a) a precipitating event; (b) impulse arousal; (c) modifications of impulse, ego, and superego in response to the preceding events. The following elements were rated by the scales: primary impulses, drives as defenses, affects and feelings, ego defenses, superego reactions, impairment of ego functions. Each of the scales consisted of a number of relevant items.

The sub-scales in the Treatment Plan area were similar to the dynamic appraisal scales and included the following: drives, affects and feelings, ego defenses, superego reactions, strength of ego functions. These scales were designed to obtain an objective description of those aspects of personality functioning which required alteration in order to help the patient achieve a more comfortable way of living. Explicit statements were made concerning the problems selected for therapeutic attention, and those to be ignored or avoided, and the reasons for either of the decisions. Methods of intervention were made explicit, as were areas of intervention.

In the third area, Session Observation, a scale was adopted for recording session-to-session changes which was identical to the one used for the Treatment Plan, with additional items describing the patient's behavior in the interview.

Patient A, a housewife, complained of depression and suicidal fears; patient B, an unmarried graduate student, complained of anxiety and indecision in social relationships. The ratings of patient A were used in training the raters and in exploring and resolving difficulties. All judges met together when the sessions of patient A had been rated, and then embarked upon independent ratings of the sessions with patient B. The six raters here were divided into three judges and three predictors. Both judges and predictors rated the patient on Dynamic Appraisal and Treatment Plan for interviews one and two. The Session Observation scale was used by the judges for all five sessions. The predictors predicted the status of the patient at the succeeding session; having listened to the recordings and read the transcript for the first interview, the predictor used ratings to anticipate the status of the patient in the second interview.

A mean reliability co-efficient of .80 was obtained for the combined ratings of Dynamic Appraisal for all raters. The reliability co-efficient for the judges was .81, for predictors .78. The findings indicate that therapists can arrive at a highly reliable estimate of the psychodynamics of the patient within one or two interviews, an essential requirement for an effective brief psychotherapy. For Treatment Plan ratings, the mean reliability co-efficient was .77, and for Session Observation ratings it was .78. The relative reliability of the judges ranged from .80 to .94 and was greater and more cohesive than the reliability of the predictors, which ranged from .63 to .84, indicating that prediction is less reliable than judgment.

The second method was an effort to assess the ability of trained clinicians to predict the effects of a specific psychotherapeutic intervention upon a patient's functioning. The interventions of the therapist of patient B were extracted from the transcripts of all five interviews and were broadly classified as interpretations, suggestions, advice, etc.

The therapist recorded his intentions in making each intervention, trying to state the effect he expected each to have on the patient. Of a rather large total, 19 interventions were finally selected. The effects anticipated by the therapist were identified in 43 categories which were recast as dimensions of behavior and then combined into a questionnaire that covered three major categories: (1) Insight Variables; (2) Problem Areas, and (3) Therapy Behavior. The judges rated the patient's responses as Insight Variables, Problem Areas and Therapy Behavior for each session. The predictors had a much more complex task. Given the 19 interventions and the 43 effects provided by the therapist, they were asked to predict the effects of each intervention. These were identified as Specific Predictions. Beyond this they were required to predict the effects of the session as a whole, arriving at General Predictions. Both judges and predictors achieved satisfactory levels of agreement among themselves, with mean reliability co-efficients ranging from .75 to .76. No significant differences were obtained between predictors and judges or between Specific and General Predictions. The reliability of both judgments and predictions of Insight Variables was found to be less than those for Problem Areas and Therapy Behavior.

Each of the 43 content variables had its mean numerical rating computed at each interview, so that each variable could be described as increasing, decreasing or unchanged. A similar procedure was followed with the predictions. The percentage of correct predictions was derived for each of the five General Predictions and the 19 Specific Predictions, by comparing the mean predicted directional change with the actual mean change. Fifty-one percent of the General Predictions and 46 percent of the Specific Predictions agreed with the actual direction of change as rated by the judges. Pure chance would have expected 33 percent agreement; the differences are significant at the 5 percent level of confidence. In general, accuracy of prediction was not found to be significantly related to the position of the interview in the series of five. Therapy Behavior was not predicted as accurately as were the other variables. Ability to predict direction of change was lower than the ability to agree on the presence or absence of a variable. The authors conclude that the data indicate that prediction of direction of change in response to psychotherapy is possible in a statistically significant way.

The import of these two rather complicated studies is that independent well-trained clinicians are able, to a highly significant degree, to agree on the formulations of psychodynamics, a concise treatment plan and upon the actual process of psychotherapy. Further, they show that brief, well-conceptualized, psychoanalytically oriented therapy has both a demonstrable rationale and a success, and therefore merits a place in comprehensive mental-health programs.

In comparing the effects of length of psychotherapy in two groups of patients, one seen six to ten times and the other more than 21 times, Errera and colleagues (56) shed some light upon the question of whether short-term therapy is essentially supportive while longer-term is exploratory. Thirty patients in each category were studied. A six-point rating scale derived from Knight's discussion of supportive and exploratory psychotherapy was devised. It contained clinical appraisal of the patient, items relating to supportive therapy, items relating to exploratory therapy, overall evaluation of the therapeutic technique, and a "resonance" scale reflecting therapist and patient interaction. Three independent raters were employed. The median test applied to the data indicated that the two groups were not dissimilar. All P values were less than .005 with the exceptions of intelligence, the patient's comprehension and use of the therapist's attempts to clarify and interpret material, and the patient's indication that he felt he was understood. Patients in longer-term therapy were more likely to comprehend and utilize the therapist's attempts to clarify and interpret the material. There were no significant differences in improvement rates, either as recorded by the therapist, or as evaluated by the rater. Examination of the five cases which received the highest global ratings for exploratory treatment indicated that the therapist here was considered more interpretive, and the patients were considered better able to examine their thoughts and feelings and to have generally greater assets of intelligence, control and work performance.

Similar examination of the cases rated highest for supportive therapy suggested that the therapists here were found to be more reassuring, to give more advice, and to be more manipulative; the patients appeared to be more desirous of these therapist activities. Essentially, however, results of the groups are the same and could not be differentiated into a short-term supportive therapy group and a long-term insight oriented therapy group. Patient qualities such as intact ego controls, self-awareness and ability to reflect on experience and the tendency to connect present with past experiences—generally considered prerequisites for exploratory therapy—were similar in the two.

The study of comparative effects of client-centered and structured therapy by Batrawi (15) is suggestive of the variety of interactions in different kinds of treatment process. During a school term, 26 high school students received client-centered or "unstructured" therapy, while 26 others were given "structured" therapy in which they had problems defined and acted upon and outcomes were evaluated. Pre- and post-therapy tests were administered. The groups were similar in educational development, mean intelligence, and dispersion of intelligence. Excerpts of the treatment were judged in each case for their adherence to the stated types of procedure, that is, for their validity. In the post-therapy results, the structured-therapy patients showed a higher educational development on Edwards Personal Preference Schedule. They showed greater development of orderly and achievement oriented behavior. The client-centered group changed more toward introspection and affiliation. Batrawi suggests that the client-centered therapy manipulated the patient's verbal behavior through the therapist's "unconditional positive regard and acceptance." Perhaps this could better be characterized as learning through identification.

III

POPULATION CHARACTERISTICS, DIAGNOSIS AND PROGNOSIS

The reports surveyed in this book provide an overview of the demonstrated ultility of the briefer psychotherapies.

What are the characteristics of the people who have been treated? Are the briefer techniques addressed to a particular educational, cultural or socio-economic group? What are the sizes of the populations reported?

What conditions have been treated? In what numbers? Has the therapist practicing brief psychotherapy tended to limit his efforts to particular kinds of disturbances?

What kinds of conditions respond best to brief therapeutic interventions? What is the prognosis for a specific condition? Can a prognosis be established for a specific intervention?

CHAPTER 9

Population Characteristics

A review of the available epidemiological characteristics of the populations described in published reports, while actuarially weak, gives a reasonable view of the variety of persons to whom brief psychotherapy has been made available. A true statistical analysis defies the best of intentions: age and socio-economic status, for example, are noted too erratically to permit it.

POPULATION SIZES

The sizes of populations vary from single-case reports to 3,128 (75). As might be expected, the smaller populations tend to be reported by individuals practicing privately, the larger ones from clinics and other public facilities. Significantly, the larger populations are reported in the more recent papers, the smaller ones, for the most part, in papers dating back several decades. This trend reflects the response of mental-health professions to public need and demand.

Populations can be roughly and somewhat inconsistently grouped as follows:

Population sizes and bibliographical references:

single case reports (25, 195, 211, 227)
2 to 10 cases (76, 93, 96, 102, 104, 120, 121, 140, 191, 217, 223)
11 to 30 cases (4, 144, 188, 198, 201)
50 to 100 cases (12, 39, 183, 202, 212, 232)
101 to 200 cases (79, 153, 174, 184, 204)
201 to 300 cases (174)
301 to 400 cases (226, 235)
401 to 500 cases (134)
601 to 700 cases (162)
701 to 800 cases (171)
1001 to 2000 cases (8, 20, 37, 45)
3001 plus (75)

AGES OF PATIENTS SERVED

The bulk of the studies report services to adults between 20 and 59 years of age. Specialized services have reported on children (8, 37, 39, 76, 86, 112, 121, 191, 204) and adolescents (8, 81, 86, 93, 112, 121, 144, 151, 191, 193, 198, 201, 204, 217, 226). Services to older individuals are also reported. The numbers of patients at the upper end of the age range are fewer, but the reports show that they can be served effectively by brief psychotherapy. The following upper age brackets are reported: 60 to 69 years (93, 120, 193, 198, 201, 226), 70 to 79 years (37), and 80 to 89 years (37, 79, 226).

SOCIO-ECONOMIC STATUS

Very few studies report patients from the topmost economic brackets. A few came from the upper-middle class and a large number from the middle class. These groups are reported largely from private practice or from a special hospital situation. Most brief psychotherapy offered to members of the lower class and lower-middle class groups is through clinics and other public facilities. Group Health Insurance study (8) reports that 67 percent of their population earned between $4,000 and $8,000 a year, while 13 per cent earned less than $4,000.

Bellak and Small (20) observed that 50 percent of their population had no earned income and lived on pensions, unemployment insurance or welfare, while 38 percent earned between $3,000 and $6,000 a year. Authors describing private-practice experience almost always are reporting patients of the middle and upper-middle class. Hollingshead's classifications are often used. The following groupings (with associated bibliographical references) roughly correspond with those classifications: lower socio-economic status (8, 20, 37, 105, 106, 162, 188, 201, 219, 235, 248); lower-middle class (8, 20, 37, 102, 223); middle-class (8, 20, 93, 96, 121, 151, 188, 191, 195, 201, 223, 227); upper-middle class (204, 224).

NON-WHITE PATIENTS

Bellak and Small (20) note that the Trouble Shooting Clinic of the City Hospital at Elmhurst, Queens, New York, served a larger proportion of non-whites than the proportion residing in the community, suggesting that the facilities were perceived favorably by non-whites. Four other studies report serving non-white populations. (106, 162, 201, 226)

COLLEGE STUDENTS

The university appears to be one major center for the development of brief psychotherapeutic procedures to meet the emergent needs of relatively large and cohesive populations. (89, 104, 153, 174, 212, 239)

REPORTS FROM OTHER COUNTRIES

Brief psychotherapy is reported with patients in England (50, 144, 191), Scotland (116), Israel (112) and Holland (132).

SETTINGS IN WHICH BRIEF THERAPY HAS BEEN OFFERED

The situation in which the service is provided tells something about the populations to whom brief therapy has been directed. Freud provided the most unusual locales for practicing the brief procedures: on a mountain during a vacation (27) and on the streets of Vienna while strolling with Gustav Mahler (110). More conventional settings are listed here with associated bibliographical references:

Hospital out-patient clinics (6, 16, 20, 37, 38, 56, 105, 106, 123, 144, 153, 158, 162, 163, 205, 206, 208, 235, 241)
Social service agencies (12, 152, 166, 180, 186, 204)
Mental-hygiene clinics (101, 107, 120, 122, 156, 194, 221, 222)
College services (24, 57, 89, 142, 212, 239)
Day-care program (125)
Military installations (12, 51, 55, 174, 175)
Private practice (17, 39, 70, 76, 143, 183, 184, 204, 211, 249)
In-hospital (1, 12, 30, 49, 53, 153, 232, 237)

CHAPTER 10
Diagnosis

Scanning the literature for diagnostic categories of patients treated by brief psychotherapy presents some difficulty. Authors often fail to differentiate between complaint, symptom and diagnosis, and at times will report either one of these or any combination of them. Thus, "confusion" may be a complaint or symptom; it is not a diagnosis. "Depression" may be a complaint, but not a diagnosis until one has qualified it with terms such as "reactive," "neurotic," "psychotic," "acute," "suicidal," "moderate," etc. Sullivan *et al.* (222) decided not to present diagnostic data at all, concluding that diagnoses were "too unreliable and too contaminated with legalistic procedures . . ."

Coleman and Errera (44) believe that no diagnostic problem exists in emergency psychotherapy other than the necessity to decide whether or not to refer the patient for mental hospitalization. They are perhaps uniquely sanguine. Can the efficacy of brief psychotherapy be determined without being scrutinized in relation to specific types of disturbances? Is it universally applicable except for people who appear to need hospitalization? Should it be used in the hospital? Or is it best restricted to certain conditions? The following sections will present the evidence as clearly as the literature permits.

LISTING OF DIAGNOSES, SYMPTOMS AND COMPLAINTS TREATED

This section first lists the complaints, symptoms and diagnoses reported, adhering nearly as possible to the several authors' usages. I have taken very few liberties in modifying words and titles to arrive at categories; consequently a term listed separately is often very similar to others, and may appear not to merit separate status. Many authors report brief psychotherapy conducted with one or a small number of cases, or do not cite population size at all. Yet population size is an important datum in judging the usefulness of brief psychotherapy in certain diagnostic categories. Therefore, following this listing, a number of studies are presented that report frequencies of complaints, symptoms and/or diagnoses among the population served. The intent of this section is to survey the bulk of problems to which psychotherapists have addressed themselves.

Abortion attempt, reaction to (226)
Acting out (20, 120)
Addiction (31)
Agitation, acute (116, 120, 226)
Air sickness (55)
Alcoholism (8, 37, 226)
Amnesia (31)
Anti-social behavior (188)
Anxiety (8, 20, 211, 226)
Anxiety in adolescence (151)
Anxiety, free floating (55)
Anxiety hysteria (144)
Anxiety neurosis (144)
Anxiety reaction (134, 202, 219)
Anxiety, situational (145)
Anxiety states (194, 227, 231)
Anxiety states, reactive (47)
Autistic disorders (55)

Manic Depression (86, 162, 174)
Marital adjustment (8)
Marital problems (20, 86, 144, 226)
Masturbation, public (229)
Medical diagnosis (226)
Melancholia (76)
Mental strain (8)
Middle-age problems (8)
Mourning (76)
Nervousness (8)
Neurodermatitis (198, 201)
Neurosis (8, 12, 20, 22, 53, 71, 79, 174, 176, 188, 212, 224, 226, 249)
Neurosis, chronic (75)
Neurosis, conversion reaction (212)
Neurosis, depressive reaction (212)
Neurosis, obsessive-compulsive (212)
Neurotic anxiety states (96)
Neurotic crisis (96)
Neurotic homosexual panic (96)
Neurotic reaction (162)
Nightmares (211)
No assignable cause (86)
Obesity, gross (23)
Obsessive-compulsive symptoms (115)
Panic, endogenous and exogenous (20)
Panic state (76, 215, 231)
Paranoid problems (116, 224)
Paranoid delusions (76)
Paranoid involutional state (195)
Pathological personality (150)
Pathological stealing (144)
Peeping Tom (31)
Personality disorders (12, 79, 86, 162, 212)
Personality disorders, transient situational (20)
Phobias (8, 131, 249)
Phobia, school (86)
Phobic symptoms (76, 226)
Phobic anxiety (144)

Stress reactions, acute (116)
Suicide attempts (20, 31, 174, 226)
Traumatic neurosis (114, 147)
Traumatic neurosis of war (25, 114, 147, 172)
Traumatic reactions (191)
Tuberculosis, traumatic reactions to (20)
Unreality feelings (226)
Voyeurism (103)
Work problems (20)

REPORTS OF FREQUENCIES OF DIAGNOSIS

Therapists and clinic directors embarking upon brief-psychotherapy programs may be interested in the percentage of complaints, symptoms or diagnoses to expect in any given population. A number of studies recording such data are presented here. However, the reader will not find everything he might like to know, since reporting varies in both precision and fullness.

An investigation of the applicability of brief psychotherapy in neurodermatitis (198) judged initially that 13 of 26 patients were susceptible to psychotic decompensation; two patients were diagnosed as overtly psychotic.

Grotjahn (174) reports that of 129 patients treated by brief psychotherapy according to psychoanalytic principles at the Institute for Psychoanalysis in Chicago, 34 persons were diagnosed as psychoneurotic with symptom formation, six as homosexual, 55 as character disturbances, nine as having psychosomatic problems and 25 as psychotics.

Among 92 patients described by Semrad et al. (202), diagnostic frequencies were: 45 neurotic depressions; nine involutional depressions; one psychosis; 14 schizophrenics; six situational reactions; four anxiety reactions; 13 other types of behavior.

Malan (144) reports extensively on a population of 21 individuals who received a total of 29 diagnoses: six phobic anxiety, five depressive reactions, four character disorders, two anxiety hysteria, two homosexuality. Each of the following occurred once: anxiety neurosis, borderline paranoid psychosis, compulsion neurosis, frigidity, hysterical personality, marital problem, pathological stealing and post-traumatic syndrome.

In a study of brief psychotherapy in a private pediatric practice, Coddington (39) found psychoneurotic traits in 34 cases in his population of 86, personality disturbance in 19, while in 18 instances the pathology rested primarily in the parents; the remainder included psychophysiologic disturbances, developmental variations and behavior problems secondary to congenital handicaps.

Frequency of diagnostic categories among college women students treated with brief psychotherapy is reported by Speers (212): psychosis, two; psychoneurosis, personality trait disturbance, 31; acute situational adjustment reactions, 23.

Avnet (8), describing 1,115 patients seen in brief psychotherapy under a group-health insurance plan in New York, relates that all types of problems and symptoms were presented. Most frequent were depression, anxiety, muscular strain, nervousness, phobias, marital adjustment, family conflicts, single-status problems, blighted romances, postpartum problems, middle age and retirement adjustment problems. Somatic complaints were not as frequent; relatively infrequent were complaints about alcoholism, drug addiction and homosexuality. Twenty percent were diagnosed as psychotics.

Sullivan et al. (222), while withholding diagnostic data for 286 VA hospital patients because the data were confusing and contaminated, observe nonetheless that their population consisted largely of neurotic and psychomatic cases, and that only about 25 percent were schizophrenic.

A Denver VA hospital study of brief psychotherapy is reported by Dreiblatt and Weatherly (53). Of 44 patients who had had no previous hospitalization, 22 were diagnosed as psychotic, 10 as neurotic, and 12 with character disorders; of patients who had had some previous mental hospitalization 35 were diagnosed as psychotic, 21 as neurotic, and 18 as character disorders.

Erlich and Phillips (55) treated 42 Navy aviators who had been temporarily grounded and referred for brief psychotherapy. Of these, 24 were diagnosed as having psychophysiological symptoms, six suffered from air sickness, three from depression, four from poor performance, three from autistic disorders, one from free-floating anxiety, and one from altered consciousness under G-stress.

Straker (219) reporting on brief psychotherapy for general hospital out-patients in lower socio-economic groups in 1963 recorded 33 percent depressive reactions, 19 percent anxiety reactions and 11 percent schizophrenic reactions.

Ungerleider (226) attempts to differentiate the presenting problem from diagnosis in reporting six months' experience at a hospital consultation service. In 378 cases the presenting problems were: psychotic break with suicidal attempts or thoughts 20 percent; depressive symptoms 18 percent; anxiety symptoms 7 percent; somatic symptoms 7 percent; disorientation or confusion 6 percent; disturbance of consciousness 4 percent; others, including homocidal thoughts, hyperactivity, alcoholism, etc., 19 percent. These figures do not add up to 100 percent; frequently more than one diagnostic category or presenting problem is recorded for a single patient. The 378 individuals seen received a total of 530 diagnoses: 40 percent neurosis; 20 percent psychosis; 17 percent character disorders; 10 percent acute brain syndromes; 3 percent situational reactions; 3 percent medical diagnosis. In the neurotic group the order of decreasing frequency was depressions, anxiety, disassociative reactions, conversion reactions, phobic reactions. Comparable order in the psychotic group was: schizophrenia, paranoia, acute and undifferentiated psychosis, chronic psychosis, simple psychosis, schizoaffective psychosis, catatonic, hebephrenia, psychotic depressions, manic-depressives, manic reactions, paranoid psychosis, paranoid states, involutional psychosis, and postpartum psychosis.

A study of 1,414 patients is described by Bellak and Small (20) from the walk-in clinic of a city hospital. The frequency of complaints was the following (many individuals presented several different complaints): anxiety 53.5 percent, depression 50.4 percent, marital problems 29.7 percent, somatic problems 26.4 percent, miscellaneous family problems 25.2 percent and work problems 21.4 percent. Actual diagnoses were: psychoneurotic disorders 45.5 percent, character disorders 28.5 percent, psychotic disorders 21.1 percent, transient situational personality disorders 11.6 percent.

Greenblatt et al., (86) describing the application of brief psychotherapy to prevent hospitalization at the Boston Mental Health Center, report the following percentages of presenting problems among 400 patients: marital 20 percent, child-parent 10 percent, physical fitness 10 percent, job problems 10 percent, sex trauma 5 percent, responses to death 5 percent, boy-girl stress 8 percent, legal problems

3 percent, difficulty with or loss of therapists 5 percent, postpartum problems 2 percent, no immediate cause assignable 20 percent. Diagnostic frequencies for this same population are: schizophrenia 20 percent, manic depressive psychosis 5 percent, other depressions 30 percent, personality disorder 35 percent, others including character disorders and borderline states 10 percent.

A six-months study of 183 emergency patients (153) observed 42 percent to be "dangerous" emergencies and concludes that "emergency patients often had poor emotional and impulse controls."

Persons availing themselves of an emergency service at the Massachusetts General Hospital totaled 1,271 for the first quarter of 1964. Psychiatric problems were presented by 56.9 percent, alcoholic problems by 36.7 percent, medical problems by 4.6 percent, while the essential problem was unknown in 1.8 percent.

Approximately 60 percent of 392 patients seen in the emergency service of Kings County Psychiatric Hospital during a six-month period were psychotic (235). Anxiety states and depressions were the most frequent syndromes.

The walk-in clinic at Metropolitan Hospital in New York City saw 682 patients during its first six-months of operation in a "highly deprived community" (162). No diagnosis was made for 85 patients; mixed diagnoses were made for 29. The frequency of diagnostic categories among the rest were: schizophrenic reaction 40.5 percent, psychoneurotic reaction 22.4 percent, personality disorder 15.5 percent, chronic brain syndrome 4.6 percent, depressive involutional state 4.1 percent, psychotic depression 2.8 percent, psychophysiological reaction 2.3 percent, transient situational disorder 1.9 percent, acute brain syndrome 1.9 percent, psychotic reaction 1.7 percent, manic-depressive psychosis, depressed, 0.9 percent, paranoid involutional state 0.7 percent, mental retardation 0.7 percent.

Use of brief psychotherapy, it becomes clear, has not been confined to simple or easy problems. The variety of human difficulties reported here is extensive; many are complex and serious. How well have they been served? How effective are the brief therapies? The next chapter explores prognosis.

CHAPTER 11

Prognosis

What outcomes can be expected from the application of the brief psychotherapies? Are certain types of individuals more responsive than others to brief psychotherapy? Are there some situations in which a brief psychotherapeutic effort should not even be attempted? Prognosis, like diagnosis, has always been a vague area. This chapter attempts to establish a few guidelines from available experience.

Some writers state that diagnosis is of little value for predicting outcome. Fuerst (174) is pessimistic about the ability of conventional psychiatric diagnosis to help in the prediction of success. Nosological systems are presently unable to tell us how the patient will respond to treatment, contends Wolberg (245), ". . . few diagnostic yardsticks can be set up to prognosticate results"—while every patient may be helped in some measure. He observes a relationship between diagnosis and prognosis when "reconstructive change" (seldom an objective in brief therapy) is the goal.

Avnet (8) reporting on the outcome of brief psychotherapy with more than a thousand patients concludes that diagnosis is hardly a clue to prognosis. She relates some impression that psychophysiological problems are harder to reach, but such problems accounted for only 2 percent of the reported population of 1,115 patients. Three classifications—psychoses, neuroses and personality disorders—account for 86 percent of the diagnoses and each were found to have the same rate of improvement or non-improvement; four out of five benefited from the brief psychotherapy.

Such findings are not congruent with other points of view. Grotjahn (174), for example, reflects the view that brief psychotherapy is applicable to those who either are too sick or too well for psychoanalysis. He also states that brief psychotherapy offers more in the treatment of psychoses than does psychoanalysis.

Other workers are not at all sanguine about the effectiveness of brief psychotherapy, and regard it as an approach that is simply better than nothing. Rado (179) writes, "In general, nothing responds better to short-term therapy than to longer treatment, but brief therapy may be available in cases where long-term therapy is not. The most important criterion is emergency, where an important but temporary change is needed.

Stein *et al.* (213) would probably contest Rado's views. They state that brief therapy is the treatment of choice in "many instances." In their experience a major such instance is that group of individuals who suffer emotional reactions to "physical illness, trauma, or surgery," when these reactions are acute, relatively severe and of recent onset, and when treatment goals are limited to restoration to a former psychological and social level of adaptation and to the relief of symptoms.

Gelb and Ullman (75) reflect on their experience with brief psychotherapy for a clinic population: "Our experience has been that we can help these 'sicker' patients" (*i.e.*, those with severe chronic neuroses or schizophrenic reactions) "if we focus on maintaining them in the community." Barten (12) reports that the results with the brief psychotherapy seem as good as long-term therapy for symptom improvement, but not for achieving self understanding. Other therapists believe that brief psychotherapy should be offered to all patients applying at a psychiatric clinic (96), the concept being presumably that the brief procedure serve as a sieve, so that those who do not respond to the brief method may be offered other or more extended treatments.

Malan (144) in reviewing the literature on prognosis identified *radical* and *conservative* points of view. The radical view holds that "good results can often be achieved in severe, longstanding illnesses. Brief methods have their own positive indication and may in certain cases be more suitable than long-term methods." The conservative view postulates that, "Only acute illnesses in basically well-adjusted personalities are suitable. Brief methods should be used only when long-term methods are not available for practical purposes."

Consensus is not apparent. Some claim that only the very sick should be treated by brief psychotherapy, others that only the very well integrated are suitable candidates for a brief intervention, still others aver that the extremes of the continuum of adjustment provide the most suitable candidates. Reports are difficult to judge because the rigor of the research which has gone into the studies varies markedly, population sizes are spread over uncompressible range: one study offering a prognostication may be based on two subjects, another on more than one thousand cases. There is no manifest agreement as to the variables to be considered in assessing prognosis.

Harris and Christiansen (97) comment on the looseness of criteria used for prediction in current psychotherapeutic thinking. They find that prognosis is sometimes related to diagnosis, in statements like, "psychoses are less promising than neuroses" or "within the neuroses, the transference neuroses seem more promising than do narcissistic ones"; and "hysterias are more favorable than obsessive compulsives," or "some character disorders are thought not to respond well." They find that some non-nosological features are used in prediction: the amount of anxiety, the adequacy of characteristic defenses, the presence of ego strength, the acuteness of onset, the age of the patient, the patient's intelligence and characteristics of his situation. They reasonably observe that prognosis must be based on a complicated set of judgments, that response to therapy is a function of many variables in at least three major categories: (1) patient variables; (2) situational variables; and (3) treatment and therapist variables. Probably no study of prognosis has attempted to incorporate all three approaches. Harris and Christiansen address their own study to the patient variables.

The contradicting results of research of outcome in psychotherapy are attributed by Sullivan *et al.* (222) to the large variety of factors that may affect outcome. These they classify into three groups similar to those above: (1) patient characteristics; (2) therapist characteristics; (3) situational variables (*e.g.*, length of treatment, clinic policies, forces in patient's life).

PROGNOSIS, THERAPEUTIC ORIENTATION AND THEORY

This section reviews reports by advocates of types of brief psychotherapy who are proponents of a variety of theoretical positions.

Behavioral Therapy

Wolpe and Lazarus (249) state boldly ". . . behavior therapy is effective in all neuroses . . ." Morton (159), also a behavior therapist, finds a good prognosis for the seriously maladjusted when the treatment is brief psychotherapy conducted in a ". . . rational manner, following systematic theoretic orientation and utilizing vehicles appropriate to theory . . ."

Anxiety Management Therapy

Sifneos (207) has delineated two kinds of brief psychotherapy centered around the management of anxiety. Anxiety-provoking therapy, an uncovering approach, he declares is best applied to individuals of above average I.Q., with at least one meaningful relationship with another person during their lifetime, who are flexible and able to interact during the interview, who have a chief complaint, are motivated to work and have realistic expectations.

The counterpart is anxiety-suppressive therapy, which is supportive; it uses medication and poses the therapist as a helping person. For Sifneos it is the treatment of choice for individuals who have severely disturbed character defects with a history of rapid, recent decompensation from a previously precarious balance, who while complaining of lifelong difficulties are nonetheless able to maintain a job, who make a strong appeal for help, who recognize the psychological origins of their symptoms, and who are cooperative with the treatment.

Psychoanalytically-Oriented Therapies

Fenichel (60) believes that "acute difficulties of life present the first and foremost field of indication for brief psychotherapy . . ." Next in order of suitability are neuroses in a childish, immature person, where the repressing forces are represented by anxiety about external danger and are not yet internalized. Summing up his prognostic opinions, Fenichel offers conditions with decreasing probability of success: the traumatic neuroses and acute conflicts; immature personalities who need reeducation; hysterical types who are ready for a dramatic transference and easily accept "magical influences."

Kardiner (114) has found that no judgment of prognosis in a traumatic situation is possible without a trial at therapy. Even epileptiform conditions respond well if there has been no injury to the brain and treatment is begun immediately.

Burdon (29) is convinced that almost all patients can benefit from brief psychotherapy. Some will need no further treatment, others will move into more intensive psychotherapy or require various medical or physical treatments. He urges a therapeutic trial at brief psychotherapy with almost all patients and observes that prognosis has to do with ego functions, not with diagnostic categories.

Gillman (76) advances two criteria for the selection of suitable patients: (1) the patient sees his former functioning as adequate; (2) the therapist believes regression should not be promoted.

Bellak and Small (20) considered three classes of variables in arriving at prognosis for brief psychotherapy in a study of 1,414 patients: (1) patient demography, (2) symptomatology and clinical status, (3) treatment factors. They found that the "individual" with the most favorable prognosis for psychoanalytically-oriented brief psychotherapy of no more than six sessions would be female, unmarried, 18 to 30 years of age, in a higher occupational level, with a problem in the work area, with a diagnosis of neurosis, who receives psychotropic drugs along with psychotherapy, whose troubles are characterized by relative lack of chronicity and who uses more of the sessions offered.

Wolberg (245) relates prognosis to the goals of both the therapist and the patient; these are based upon the therapist's evaluation of the patient's presenting problem and his general personality organization with its strengths and weaknesses. The goals which offer the most favorable prognosis for brief psychotherapy are those: (1) where a rapid restructuring of homeostasis is sought in an acute neurotic disturbance; (2) where it is desired to stabilize the person with a chronic personality disorder who has suffered an acute upset; (3) where reconstruction is needed in a person who is unsuited for or unable to avail himself of long-term psychotherapy. By contrast Wolberg identifies conditions suitable for long-term psychotherapy, hence negatively prognostic for brief psychotherapy: (1) extensive personality reconstruction is needed; (2) dependency is so great that prolonged support will be required; (3) the person exhibits persistent and uncontrollable acting-out tendencies; (4) the person is subject to constant uncontrollable anxiety.

Malan (144) identifies a number of favorable prognostic signs in both the therapist and the patient, and relatively independent of diagnosis: (1) the material is understandable; (2) a therapeutic plan can be formulated; (3) the patient shows evidence of ability to work with interpretation; (4) there are signs of a developing transference although it is neither too dependent or too demanding; (5) motivation starts high and shows a rapid increase, (6) the therapist has high enthusiasm; (7) transference emerges early and becomes an important feature of treatment; (8) termination is accompanied by grief and anger (presumably a *post facto* recognition). Malan sees the prognosis best when both patient and therapist are willing to become deeply involved and are able to bear the ensuing tension of the therapeutic encounter.

Straker (219) also emphasizes the importance in prognosis of the "interested, active" therapist; this is the therapist, Straker reports, who enjoys the lowest drop-out rate and the highest rate of improvements.

Courtenay (50) following Malan's lead in brief psychotherapy in his own work with married couples specifies "static" and "dynamic" indices of prognosis. His list of "static" indices incorporates: (1) a mild and limited pathology—the individual with a three-person oedipal problem rather than one with a two-person oral problem or one with severely depressive difficulties; (2) ego strength evidenced in ability to cope with reality and tolerance for frustration and conflict; (3) evidence of satisfactory personal relations in the past; (4) a problem of recent onset or a "propitious moment" in a relatively chronic illness. The "dynamic" indices à la Malan include: (1) understandable material; (2) motivation starting high and/or accelerating early; (3) evidence of positive transference neither too dependent nor too demanding; (4) evidence of capacity to work with interpretation. Courtenay comments that ". . . sharpness of the focus, the degree of motivation, and the capacity for insight" are "patient" factors, while an important "therapist" factor is "skill in establishing a good patient-doctor relationship early in treatment."

Courtenay also derives lists of favorable and unfavorable prognostic indices. The favorable ones are: (1) reasonable ego strength; (2) reasonable relationships; (3) recent exacerbation; (4) readily identifiable narcissism; (5) no previous breakdown; (6) good motivation; (7) disturbance at the genital level; (8) motivated to come for treatment; (9) responds to interpretation; (10) asks for help. The unfavorable indices are: (1) narcissism evidenced in a disturbance at the pregenital level; (2) disturbance life-long; (3) demand for help on his own terms; (4) strong resistance to interpretation and lack of cooperation; (5) evidence of poor relationships; (6) antagonism demonstrated in interview; (7) rigid character structure; (8) severe and generalized pathology; (9) reflection of a passive mood of referral; (10) passive agreement with interpretations; (11) exhibitionistic manner of communicating.

Johnson (174) reporting to the Chicago Institute Council offered the following criteria for identifying patients most suitable for brief psychoanalytic therapy: (1) a wish for help is essential but is no guarantee of success; (2) a strong ego helps but is also not essential; (3) little secondary gain is a good sign—a high degree is unfavorable; (4) little ambivalence is demonstrated—more ambivalence will lengthen required therapeutic time; (5) the problem is recent and acute, but a long-standing underlying neuroses is not to be overlooked simply because the problem seems to have appeared recently; (6) the therapist's aims and attitudes are optimistic but not too highly hopeful.

Dunbar (174) reported the following criteria for good response of somatic problems to brief psychoanalytic psychotherapy: (1) no recognizable neurosis prior to the appearance of somatic symptoms (the more crystallized the problem, the more time is required for treatment); (2) good prior adjustment; (3) strong ego; (4) early acceptance of an emotional basis to the somatic problem; (5) quick acceptance of the therapist.

Supportive Psychotherapy

Visher (227) reporting on his experience in a mental-hygiene clinic identifies these criteria for the selection of suitable candidates for brief psychotherapy: (1) readiness for change, in that the patient should be at a crucial point where the life situation has changed drastically, so that he needs and hence may be amenable to a new orientation; (2) acuteness of the presenting problems; (3) evidences of environmental stability and adequate previous adjustments; (4) a positive reaction to the initial interview. Visher's indications of a poor prognosis are : (1) marked familial or marital difficulties; (2) characterological problems; (3) poor rapport.

Directive Therapy

Brief psychotherapy with 26 neurodermatitis patients by Schoenberg and Carr (198) resulted in this statement of prognosis. For a directive therapy with a contemporary focus, and major emphasis on encouragement and reinforcement of the expression of hostility toward the figure who is the current source of the patient's trouble, successful treatment is related to: (1) the availability of aggressive ideation observable in the initial interview and on the Rorschach content; (2) the patient's ability to follow the therapist's advice to express the hostility in a focused manner toward the central figure in the current conflict.

Group Therapy

Experience with hospitalized non-psychotic patients has led Keeler (115) to establish criteria for prognosis in short-term group therapy. The prognosis is best, he reports, when at least half of the patients in the group are between the ages of 20 and 40, they are all members of one sex or sex distribution is even, and they present a combination of diagnostic types. The prognosis is poor with an entire group made up of obsessive compulsives, or a mixture of obsessive-compulsive and hysterical patients.

Hope and Expectation Theory

Frank (65) reports placebo (68) studies indicating that anxiety and depression states are most responsive to the patient's expectations that therapy will help him. He cites other studies (238) indicating that attitudes of the therapist influence the patient's improvement, particularly with schizophrenics, where the following attributes in the therapist appear to be important: empathy, flexibility and self-assurance, combining into a capacity to help the patient overcome his essential distrust and thereby stimulate his hopes and expectations for finding help.

Prognostically, Frank concludes that the weight of evidence is that the elevation of the patient's hope and of corresponding therapeutic effectiveness is not determined solely by the patient's characteristics or the therapist's, but rather by the interaction between "certain permanent or transient properties of the patient, the therapist and possible other aspects of the therapeutic situation." Without precisely saying so, Frank seems to indicate that psychotherapy is applicable to the individual who expects and hopes that the process will benefit him. For the hopeless individual Frank sees the major therapeutic interventions deriving from the biochemical and neurophysiological effects of the drugs and electroconvulsive therapy.

Time-Fantasy Theory

The fantasies of time in relationship to an individual's life have intrigued McGuire (146). These are easily found with careful listening; they are repetitious ideas, similar to compulsions, which people "use as a focal point to order and explain their experiences." They exist before the person becomes a patient in psychotherapy, but they influence the patient's comprehension of and response to "briefness" when it is a short-term therapy that is offered to him. Categories of "time-life" fantasies identified by McGuire are said to influence response to brief therapy, as follows:

> *"Return of the past" fantasy*—Patients with this fantasy are pessimistic; they expect that painful experiences of the past will return in the immediate future. Informed of the brevity of therapy, they become more pessimistic than before.

"Expected moment of realization" fantasy. These patients tend to be falsely optimistic, believing that the immediate future will bring their longed-for happiness. Because much time and energy must go into reality testing, they are difficult to treat successfully with the briefer psychotherapies.

"The present is alone" fantasy. For these persons the present is a petrified state, unconnected with either past or future, the one recalled as painful, the other anticipated as such. McGuire finds them the least responsive to therapy, since neither past nor future exerts motivating influence; the present is their chief concern, yet lacks significance for them.

"The present is the door to the future" fantasy. In this fantasy both immediate and distant future are significantly tied up with the present. Hence, commitments have great consequences, an emphasis that must be diluted somewhat in the therapy. These patients usually are initially enthusiastic about brief therapy, and later somewhat uncertain about its worth.

"The present is the inevitable result of the past" fantasy. Easily humiliated, these patients tend to feel rejected and disparaged by the offer of brief therapy. Life to them is a continuation of past pain and suffering.

PROGNOSIS IN BRIEF PSYCHOTHERAPY OF CHILDREN

Lester (133) lists these states as having a favorable prognosis: (1) acute phobias; (2) regressive states of short duration; (3) inhibition of instinctual or ego functions (manifested in eating, sleeping and play); (4) neurotic acting out; (5) phase-adequate exaggerated binding of anxiety and guilt. Examples of the last are: reaction formation against masturbation during the latency period; denial and magic play warding-off of separation anxiety in the preschool child; aggressive acting out in an early latency boy; bossiness and over-industriousness in an early latency girl. Unfavorable states according to Lester are: (1) characterological disorders; (2) developmental retardation; (3) complex neurotic structure (a common example she reports is the child whose early maternal object was shifting and unstable and who shows therefore a defective ego and syntonic patterns of abnormal behavior); (4) multiple phobias. Lester succinctly sums up the indicators for a favorable prognosis: (1) the ability of the child to move forward through successive developmental stages without serious fixations or regressions; (2) the flexibility of the family; its capacity for change and accommodation to the changing, developing child.

FACTORS INDICATING A FAVORABLE PROGNOSIS

Here are listed, along with bibliographical references, factors reported as prognostic of a favorable outcome. They are in four groups: diagnostic indices, patient characteristics, therapist characteristics, and situational factors (those relative to the setting).

Diagnostic Indices

This section presents the nosological groupings that have been reported as successfully treatable with brief psychotherapies. Symptoms and complaints sometimes confused with diagnostic categories (*e.g.*, aggression, homosexuality) are placed in the following section, *Patient Characteristics.*

Neuroses (8, 20, 249)
   anxiety reaction, acute (29, 71, 174)
   conflicts, acute (29, 60, 76, 91)
   depression state, acute (71)
   depressive reactions (212)
   conversion symptoms (174)
   hysterical types (60)
   neurotic disturbances (245)
   neurotic reaction to environment (100)
   neurotic symptoms of recent origin (104)
   organ neuroses (22)
   panic states (215)
   phobia, school (231)
Immature Personalities (60)
Personality Disorders (8)
Psychoses (8, 174)
Schizophrenia (with preceding well-organized obsessional structure) (29)
Psychosomatic Disorders (174)

Situational adjustment reactions, acute (29, 76, 212)
Traumatic Neurosis (60, 114)

Patient Characteristics

Age: 18-30 years (20, 145)
Ambivalence, slight (174)
Chronicity, lack of (20)
Conflict, libidinal rather than aggressive (145)
Conflict, tolerance for (50)
Confidence in the therapist (29, 211)
Coping ability (50, 176)
Ego strength (3, 5, 29, 50, 97, 174)
Employed (35)
    job satisfaction (185)
Expects a change in his own personality (29, 168)
Fear, lack of (11)
Female (20)
Former functioning seen as adequate (76)
Frigidity (174, 183, 184)
Frustration tolerance (50, 176)
History of adequate prior adjustment (50, 227)
Homosexuality, guilt abnormality (174)
Homosexual panic (100)
Hopes for improvement (168)
Impotence (22)
Insight, capacity for (50, 144, 148, 211)
Integrative capacity to focus on current problems (76)
Masochistic symptoms, moderate (22)
MMPI scores, lower (222)
Motivation—for change; starts high; increases rapidly; wishes help
    (50, 144, 145, 174, 227)
Narcissism, little (174)
Object relations—reasonable; satisfactory (35, 50, 176, 185, 189)
Occupational level, higher than the lowest (20)
Oedipal problems (50)
Onset, recent (50, 91, 174, 185)
Pathology, limited (50)
Pathology, mild (50)

Reality contact, good (11)
Reaction, acute (5, 47, 60, 100, 144, 174, 227)
Secondary gains, limited (174)
Self-esteem (11)
Sexual adjustment, good (189)
Situational aspects of problems are visible (35, 145, 174)
Socially functional in accustomed role (35)
Stability of pre-morbid personality (76)
Stability-modifiability factor in personality (97)
"Time-life" fantasies, optimistic (146)
Transference, capacity for (50, 114, 144)
Unmarried (20)
Work problems (20)

Therapist Characteristics

Ability to make interpretations vivid (211)
Ability to understand the patient's conflicts quickly (50, 135, 144, 188,
    211
Active (16, 219)
Empathy (65)
Enthusiastic (144, 219)
Flexibility (65)
Focal sharpness, skill in developing (50, 144)
Interest in the total human being (29)
Self-assurance (65)
Skill in developing good patient-doctor relationships (50)
Willingness to accept early termination (188)

Situational Factors

Adequate number of clinic staff (174)
Drugs and psychotherapy offered (20)
Environmental stability (167)

FACTORS INDICATING AN UNFAVORABLE PROGNOSIS

Diagnostic Indices

Adjustment problems of adolescence, severe (152)
Agitated depression (139)

Pregenital disturbance (50)
Secondary gains, considerable (100, 119, 174)
Sexual aberrations, marked and extended (100)
  sadomasochistic (100)
Stammering, as result of trauma (114)
Super-ego, rigid (174)
Symptoms masked (211)
"Time-life" fantasies, pessimistic (188)
Transference capacity, poor (227)

Therapist Characteristics

Enthusiasm waning (144)
Fear he cannot do enough (188)
Fear he will reject patient (188)

CHAPTER 12

Studies of Outcome

Studies of outcome serve to give substance to the speculations about prognosis, when brief psychotherapies are attempted in a variety of situations and with different populations.

PSYCHOANALYTICALLY-ORIENTED THERAPIES

Because of the affiliations of their authors, the first three studies reported have an essentially psychoanalytic flavor. To say this, however, is not to state that they are evaluations of "brief psychoanalysis." Also, the studies are separated by more than two decades, Grotjahn reporting to the Chicago Psychotherapy Council in the early 1940's, Malan and Courtenay publishing in the 1960's.

At the Chicago Brief Psychotherapy Council, Grotjahn (174) reported the outcome for more than 100 patients who had been treated with courses of "brief" psychotherapy (which in a few cases ranged up to 200 hours). Thirty-two percent were rated as greatly improved;

44 percent as benefited. Of 34 patients with psychoneurotic symptoms, 20 (60 percent) were benefited or greatly improved; four of six (66 percent) patients with homosexual problems were so classified; 33 of 55 (60 percent) with character disturbances were rated in these categories; of nine patients with psychosomatic problems, seven (78 percent) and of 25 patients diagnosed as psychotic, 13 (52 percent) were judged benefited or greatly improved.

A four-point scale was used by Malan (144) to evaluate outcomes in 21 patients treated by brief psychotherapy in England. His work produced strong evidence against the conservative view that the results of brief psychotherapy are only temporary. Studied continuously in a follow-up of three to five years, the outcomes in individual patients tended also to dispute another conservative view that the results of brief psychotherapy are only palliative and consist merely in symptom improvement. Malan found changes in longstanding neurotic behavioral patterns of exactly the kind which more intensive and longer psychotherapies strive to achieve. Favorable changes were observed in a variety of pathological conditions, confirming the "radical" view that good results are obtainable in a wide spectrum of cases other than those with mild pathology and symptoms of relatively recent origin. The study concludes that these results can be obtained in from 10 to 40 sessions.

Courtenay (50) adopted eight criteria from Malan's static and dynamic hypotheses concerning suitability for brief psychotherapy (see page 193). Courtenay rated the eight factors for each of 27 cases treated by brief psychotherapy in his study on sexual discord in marriage. In his 3-point scale, +1 is favorable and —1 is unfavorable, and 0 represented "the nullpoint, where the factors balance." The highest score possible was +8, the lowest score —8. A —1 and a +1 cancelled each other out, a 0 score had no effect on either +1 or —1. Of eight patients whose total was on the plus side, one was found to have an uncertain outcome and two were considered to be failures. Conversely, of nine patients whose total was on the negative side, the outcome of one was judged to be uncertain and there were no successes in this group. Courtenay interprets his results to support the value of a clear focus in establishing a positive prognosis. He notes that of 13 cases which had a positive prognosis (total score on the plus side), only three had a diffuse focus; of nine cases showing a negative prognosis only three were judged to have a clear focus. When all eight criteria are taken into account, the higher the score in Courtenay's method, the more likely a successful focal therapy. He notes that if clear focus is employed as the sole criteria of prognosis, success was obtained in 61 percent of the 13 cases for which a favorable prognosis was established.

ANXIETY-MANAGEMENT THERAPIES

The need for suiting therapeutic approach to the patient, the kind of person he is and the kind of problems he has, is the theme of the study of Sifneos (207) of the effects of anxiety-provoking and anxiety-suppressive brief psychotherapies. Anxiety-provoking therapy was indicated for patients who had realistic expectations, were motivated to work, had a recognizable chief complaint, seemed flexible, were able to interact with the interviewer, had at least one meaningful relationship with another person during their lifetime, and were of above average intelligence. Anxiety-suppressive therapy was indicated for persons with severe character defects, with a history of recent and rapid decompensation from a former precarious level of functioning, who complained of lifelong difficulties, but who also showed a strong appeal for help, had ability to hold a job, were willing to cooperate with the treatment and recognized that their symptoms were psychological in origin. Generally, the patients receiving the anxiety-provoking therapy were seen for two months to a year at weekly sessions of 45 minutes; where the anxiety-provoking technique was used in crisis intervention, the patients were seen for periods up to two months. The same time factors operated in the provision of anxiety-suppressive therapy, except that the patients might be seen as much as three times a week in sessions running from several minutes to 45 minutes.

Follow-up was not systematic, being based entirely on the reports of patients. Those who had received anxiety-provoking therapy tended to report moderate symptomatic relief with new adaptive patterns and more realistic expectations. Patients who were seen in crisis usually had overcome the crisis and had achieved a new level of integration. The patients who had received anxiety-suppressive therapy were not followed up as extensively as the others. They appeared to have experienced marked symptom relief, and had learned to avoid anxiety-provoking situations. No dynamic changes were observed; they tended to view the clinic rather than the therapist as the supportive agent, an interesting case of transference to an institution rather than a person.

Behavioral therapy is evaluated in outcome studies of phobias, sexual problems and "maladjustment." One study compares behavioral therapy with a variety of analytic treatments; the latter fare badly.

The outcome of systematic desensitization treatment with 39 patients is reported by Wolpe (249). The records of these patients were extracted from the therapist's files in random fashion by a visitor to his office. A rating scale was applied. The rater is not identified, and there is no indication that reliabilities were checked. Treatment was judged to be effective in 35 of the patients. Among the 39 patients, a total of 68 phobias was identified. The mean number of sessions required for the treatment of each phobia was slightly more than 11. Forty-five phobias were judged to have been overcome, 17 markedly improved, a total of 91 percent improved or better. Six phobias, 9 percent, were judged to be unimproved. Wolpe reports another study in which sexual inadequacy (impotence or premature ejaculation) was treated by "manipulating sexual situations so that sexual responses were as far as possible kept dominant over anxiety." Thirty-one cases are reported, 21, or 67.7 percent are judged to have reached entirely satisfactory performance sexually, and 6, 19.4 percent, were able to function in a manner acceptable to their partners. The number of sessions is not given, but the mean time to achieve the result was 11.5 weeks.

Lang *et al.* (129) measured the effectiveness of therapy in desensitization of students with severe phobic reactions to harmless snakes. The results were compared with two control groups: one received no treatment, the other was exposed to "pseudo therapy," defined as relaxation training followed by focused interviews on living problems. The authors observe that the experimental group improved "very much more than either of the control groups." Judgments were made by a snake avoidance test and patient's self-rating of his fear reaction to snakes.

Lazarus (131) compares the outcome of a systematic desensitization group therapy with that of a "conventional dynamic group" in treating phobias. Matched pairs of patients were randomly placed in the two groups. At the end of 21 sessions, 72 percent of the patients placed in the desensitization groups had recovered, while only 12 percent in the dynamic groups were judged as recovered.

Comparison of desensitization therapy with two other methods is reported by Paul (169), whose subjects were members of a public-speaking class, all of whom had severe fears of public speaking. He hired the services of five psychotherapists, experienced in various affiliations ranging from Freud to Sullivan. Nine cases were assigned to each therapist. Each therapist was required to use three different methods, each method with three subjects. The methods were: (1) the therapist's usual type of insight therapy; (2) an "attention-placebo" therapy which utilized suggestion and support; (3) systematic desensitization in which the therapist was trained beforehand. Each patient was seen for five treatment sessions. Paul reports that 86 percent of the patients treated by desensitization were rated as much improved and 14 percent improved. This contrasts with the insight group of whom 20 percent were rated as much improved and 27 percent improved. In the attention-placebo group, 47 percent were rated improved and none very much improved.

An experiment with brief psychotherapy based upon Rotter's social learning theory is described by Morton (159). Forty subjects judged to be socially and personally impaired by personality maladjustment were treated by vocational counselors. The author reports that 97 percent of his experimental group and 47 percent of the controls improved; he concludes with an extremely high degree of confidence that "brief psychotherapy conducted in a rational manner, following systematic theoretical orientation and utilizing vehicles appropriate to the theory, will result in striking and lasting changes of adjustment in subjects who were seriously maladjusted."

Smoking behavior has received the attention of a number of behavioral therapists. Results of reciprocal reinforcement of graduated reduction of smoking is reported by Nehemkis and Lichtenstein (161). Eight married couples were trained in the procedure on a day-to-day and week-to-week basis. All couples were seen by the same therapist at five-weekly sessions, each lasting about one-half hour. Smoking rates at the end of treatment and at the one-month and six-month follow-up were significantly lower. There was little increase in the first month after the end of treatment, but between that time and the six-month follow-up the smoking rate had increased markedly. No control group was used.

Lichtenstein and Keutzer (136) are not sanguine about the ability of existing behavior-change techniques to decrease smoking rates after a study of 31 non-treated control patients compared with 123 treated patients who had been divided into five treatment groups. They conclude, "Either new methods must be developed or appropriate modifications of traditional ones must be made to meet the unique requirements of smoking behavior."

A GENERAL STUDY

The following is a good example of a general study of outcome with patients bearing a variety of diagnostic labels. Semrad *et al.* (202) report the outcome of brief psychotherapy with 92 patients; 45 suffered neurotic depressions, nine were diagnosed as involutional, one as psychotic, 14 as schizophrenic, six suffered situational reactions, four anxiety reactions, and 13 received a variety of other diagnostic classifications. Length of treatment is not given. The technique is described as problem solving, neither coercive nor permissive. The patient is helped to define his problem; suggestion, abreaction, manipulation, clarification and interpretation are provided. At termination, 35 were judged successful; 23 completed treatment but were referred for continued care; two were terminated and suffered recurrences. Nine were judged unsuccessful and required hospitalization; 11 were judged as unsuccessful but given no further care. Three were judged as unsuccessful and were given further care. Eight discontinued therapy before termination.

THERAPY IN A MILITARY SETTING

In a military setting brief psychotherapy of a variety of complaints among Navy aviators, contrasting a number of methods, was examined by Erlich and Phillips (55). Temporarily grounded and referred for psychotherapy, 24 suffered psychophysiological disorders—such as headache and nausea, six air sickness, three depression, four poor performance, three autistic disorders, one free floating anxiety, and one altered consciousness under increased G-stress. Thirty patients received one to four sessions only, six were seen for more than six months. A follow-up questionnaire concerning their flight status and emotional status was sent to all; half replied, and service records were also used to determine status. The time after treatment is not stated. Thirty-four of the patients were flying; their flight status was used as the criteria of success, and the authors conclude better than 70 percent success. They also studied success in relationship to the techniques employed: of 28 patients treated with insight therapy 25, approximately 86 percent, were considered successful; of six treated with support therapy, three, or 50 percent, were judged successful; of three treated by environmental manipulation all are reportedly successful; one treated solely by hospitalization is considered a failure; three of four treated by ventilation, 75 percent, are considered successful. The high success is attributed to the high motivation of the aviator group resulting from immediate reality threats of economic and status loss.

BRIEF PSYCHOTHERAPY UNDER PRE-PAID HEALTH INSURANCE

The high cost of psychotherapy has been a frequent argument against inclusion of psychotherapy in prepaid insurance plans, or for an increase of their premium payments. Brief psychotherapy appears, in the next study, to be a reasonable counter-argument.

Avnet (8) reports on the short-term psychiatric program of the Group Health Insurance; patients treated in this program were followed up two and a half years afterwards by a questionnaire which was compared with one completed by the treating psychiatrist; 801 recordable questionnaires were received from the group of 1,115 patients. Only 18 respondents failed to record an appraisal of their current mental-health status. Psychiatrist's ratings on the patient's response to treatment was available for 740 of the respondents. The great majority of both psychiatrists and patients recorded ratings in the *recovery* or *improved columns*. Of the 783 respondents, 81 percent saw at least some improvement. The psychiatrists placed 76 percent of their ratings in these latter columns. Of the patients 19 percent reported that they felt the *same, worse* or were *uncertain* of their condition. Of the psychiatrists' ratings 24 percent fell in the *unimproved* or *uncertain* categories. The areas of greatest disagreement involved patients self-rated as *unimproved* by the psychiatrist, 70 percent of the patients rated themselves as *recovered* or *improved*. Of the patients who had rated themselves as *worse* at follow-up, two-thirds had been rated by the psychiatrists as either *recovered* or *improved*. But the important feature is that their analysis produced no factor or common denominator which would have predicted failure in the face of the four-to-one chances in favor of improvement. This was their ultimate result; one in five felt unchanged, uncertain or in some cases worse. Diagnosis was not a clue. The 20 percent of the population who had been diagnosed as psychotic were not the people who preponderantly reported themselves unimproved. Each of the major diagnostic categories—psychoses, neuroses and personality disorders—showed exactly 20 percent in the unimproved and uncertain rating categories.

PREVENTING HOSPITALIZATION

Reduction in the need for hospitalization is one of the widely recognized achievements of brief psychotherapy. Cost savings are significant—in dollars, and in the predictable damages to individuals, families and communities.

Carse (34) reports that outpatient brief psychotherapy helped reduce hospital admissions by 40 percent.

Greenblatt *et al.* (86) report on the effectiveness of emergency psychotherapy in preventing hospitalization among 400 patients seen in a community extension service of the Massachusetts Mental Health Center in Boston. Most of these were very ill; 50 percent asked for hospitalization but only 30 percent proved to need it.

Six months of experience in a hospital consultation service for psychiatric emergencies is reported by Ungerleider (226); 350 patients were seen in 378 separate emergency situations. Of these, only 7 percent were considered to have a presenting problem of longer than one-year duration; 36 percent presented problems that had developed the same day that the consultation took place. Hospitalization was recommended for 52 percent of the patients but effected for only 43 percent. Of those who were given definite appointments for outpatient psychotherapy, 73 percent returned for these appointments.

A feature story in the *Wall Street Journal* by Pinkerton (173) reports Dr. Werner Mendel, director of services for adult patients at the Los Angeles County Hospital, as stating that whereas the hospital ten years ago admitted 95 percent of the patients it saw, it was admitting only 35 percent of the 1,600 patients it now sees each month. Dr. Mendel attributes the decrease to the provision of crisis-intervention services.

Lemkau and Crocetti (132) describe the Amsterdam municipal psychiatric service which provides emergency service to calls from police, physicians, friends and family 24 hours a day. Seventy percent of the patients seen under these circumstances do not require hospitalization; the service produces a significant decline in the necessity for hospitalization. Also reported is a significant decline in calls for service, despite an increase in population. In 1964 the service had 1,419 calls, in 1956 only 411. All the psychiatrists involved in the service observed a decline in psychotic violence. The authors ask themselves whether this significant decline reflects the accessibility of help or other factors; they do not draw any conclusions.

A rigorously organized six-session, crisis-oriented approach is reported by Levy (134) from Portland, Maine. The service, offered to a severely disturbed patient population, required that few people be hospitalized; only seven of 500 patients treated during the first 14 months of the service required commitment.

"Instant psychotherapy" and its effectiveness are described by Gelb and Ullman (75) at the Maimonides Medical Center in Brooklyn, New York. They measured improvement in terms of the patient's ability or willingness to function "within various identified changeable or unchangeable limitations," and concluded that more than 60 percent of 3,128 patients seen during 1965 had improved or had completed necessary treatment within five visits.

CRISIS AND EMERGENCY SERVICES

General outpatient crisis or emergency service is a pressing need in our country, one that is finding some response as public-health concerns press hard against manpower limitations. Bellak and Small (20) report a study of outcome at the trouble-shooting clinic of the City Hospital at Elmhurst, Queens, New York, during a 12-month period. A sample of 472 patients was followed up by both interview and rating scales to evaluate the success of the therapeutic intervention. A symptom checklist was used in patient characterization, to assign an appropriate therapeutic regimen, and as an independent method for evaluating outcome. Of the 1,414 patients seen, approximately 70 percent received brief psychotherapy, 8.8 percent required hospitalization, 23.6 percent did not return, by their own choice. Of the nearly 1,000 patients who received brief psychotherapy, 45 percent were considered not in need of any further treatment, 35 percent were referred for further treatment, 13.6 percent were maintained on medication and 7.6 percent were referred for other types of environmental aid; 8.1 pecent refused further treatment. The symptom checklist enabled the patient to evaluate his relative comfort in 16 subscale categories: somatic problems, anxiety, depression, hostility and aggression, dependency, obsessive-compulsive problems, psychosis, sexual problems, homosexual problems, marital problems, family conflicts, work problems, travel phobia, alcohol problems, drug problems, other problems. The list was administered to the patient on three occasions: (1) immediately before seeing the therapist for the first time; (2) immediately after the final interview; and (3) six months after completion of treatment. Rather elaborate procedures obtained a response from 55.6 percent of the 491 patients who were followed. For this group, the mean score of the symptom checklist at its first administration was 164, at the second administration 143. The difference between these two mean scores was significant at the .001 level. Six months later, at the third administration, the mean score remained 143. The authors conclude "These findings indicate a significant lessening of patient discomfort in response to brief psychotherapy, and that the improvement was maintained for at least six months."

A six-month study of 183 "emergency patients" is reported by Miller (153). Most of these were young single women who were students or unemployed. Forty-two percent were considered to be dangerous emergencies. Slightly more than one-third went back to their own doctors; one-sixth completed treatment with the emergency personnel, making "impressive gains"; and one-fourth went on to outpatient treatment. Approximately one-sixth were found to be so disturbed or so unsupported by their economic and social group that they required hospitalization. Two-thirds of the patients seen in an early-access brief-treatment psychiatric center were reported improved by Jacobson et al. (106) at the Benjamin Rush Center. There were no exclusions of "bad risks."

Of 392 patients seen in a six months period in the Emergency Service at Kings County Psychiatric Hospital, New York, Waltzer et al. (235) report that 38 percent improved; 19 percent were unchanged; 13 percent were hospitalized; and 30 percent were not heard from after the first interview. Approximately 60 percent of those seen were psychotic, the most frequent syndromes being anxiety or panic states and depression. The authors observe that evaluation of treatment results in an emergency clinic is difficult. Two months or less is a very short interval for judging the status of a severely disturbed person. How long a follow-up, they ask, is needed to determine number of instances and rates of subsequent decompensation?

A successful effort to counteract poor prognosis with lower-class patients is described by Baum and Felzer (16). They cite 47 percent dropout prior to the sixth session at Phipps Psychiatric Clinic, 57 percent after the first interview at the University of Maryland Psychiatric Institute and an average of 60 percent during the first five interviews in a national study of 499 clinics. They employed an active approach in the first interview centered around expectations, and drop-outs were down to 35 percent. This was extended to include a "pre-selection process" in which the applicant first saw a social worker who sifted out chronic alcoholics, court referrals, and floaters. Dropouts were further reduced to 23 percent.

The outcome of brief emergency therapy of patients with acute and severe symptoms was evaluated by Gottschalk et al. (82) in a pilot study with 20 patients and a replication study with 33 subjects. Patients were seen for a maximum of six sessions of 25-50 minutes duration. Therapy focused upon the resolution of crises; use of psychotropic drugs was minimized. Several measures were developed for evaluating outcome: (1) The Psychiatric Morbidity Scale measured severity of disability as revealed in a standardized interview; (2) The Therapist Attitude Inventory enabled therapists to rate their attitudes to each patient; (3) Verbal Behavior Scales measured "anxiety, hostility, social alienation-personal disorganization, and interest in human relations" from a content analysis of five minutes of a patient's verbalization; Social Class Ratings were derived from the Hollingshead-Redlich scale.

A high percentage of patients were recorded as symptomatically and "functionally" improved. The therapist's attitude (like or dislike) toward the patient bore no relationship to "degree of improvement." Patients from lower social classes showed more improvement than those from upper class groups.

These factors in patients were associated with favorable outcome: (1) facility and interest in interpersonal relationships; (2) intact thought processes; (3) unalienated; (4) acute distress; (5) lower socio-economic background.

The efficacy of outpatient family-crisis therapy with families of schizophrenic and non-schizophrenic patients is reported by Langsley et al. (130). The study, conducted at the University of Colorado, encompassed one group of 50 families each with a schizophrenic member, and a second group of families each with a non-schizophrenic but "psychiatric" family member. In each group, half the patients were treated by outpatient family-crisis therapy and half by hospitalization of the family member who was psychiatrically ill. After six-months follow-up, the mean number of crises in each group was lower than before treatment. The authors report that the change was more dramatic for the schizophrenic patients treated by crisis therapy than it was for the schizophrenic patients treated with hospitalization. For the non-schizophrenic groups the amount of change was approximately the same in both outpatient and hospital treatment cases. The most apparent difference between the two groups reported is in their respective ability in the management of crises in the family: The non-schizophrenics better manage crisis after treatment than they had before; the schizophrenic patients were less changed in this respect and more often needed an outside source of help in managing the critical event. This was especially true if the patient had been hospitalized before. The authors attribute the difference to the observable phenomenon of withdrawal among schizophrenics, a process which does not lend itself to the successful mastery of crises, so that ordinary stresses are less likely to be resolved within the family. The non-schizophrenic patients do not withdraw from the new action and cooperation needed within the family to resolve the crisis, and so these families are better able to interact in the resolution of their problems.

CRISIS GROUP SERVICE

The group treatment of individuals in crisis has been developed by Strickler and Allgeyer and the outcome of a pilot study evaluated (221). The study was made over a six-months period at the Benjamin Rush Center in Los Angeles. Admission to the group paralleled practices in an adult walk-in clinic. Exclusions were made only when the applicant was under-age, in treatment elsewhere, seriously suicidal or homicidal, or seriously unable to communicate either because of pathology or language limitations. Pathology itself was not an excluding factor since the treatment was oriented towards problem-solving rather than pathology. Thirty patients were served during the six-months pilot period. Group size varied from four to eight individuals. The authors evaluated outcome on three levels: (1) minimum improvement—return to pre-crisis level of functioning; (2) moderate improvement—on return to pre-crisis level of functioning, the patient develops an adaptive means of coping with the emotional hazard; (3) maximum improvement—the patient demonstrates cognitive comprehension of the coping means he used in the past, why these were not effective with the recent hazard, and why his new means are more effective in handling this and similar threats likely to arise in the future. Twenty-five of the thirty patients in the pilot study were judged to have demonstrated one of the three levels of improvement. Two-thirds of these were judged to have shown maximum improvement, and one-sixth each moderate and minimum improvement.

REDUCING HOSPITAL STAY

Does brief therapy result in shorter hospital stays? One study says yes; another says no.

Short-term psychotherapy with hospitalized schizophrenic patients in a VA hospital is reported by Walker and Kelley (232). An experimental group of 44 received psychotherapy; 38 served as controls. Different levels of intensity were employed: sixteen 45-minute interviews once weekly, sixteen 30-minute interviews once weekly, or eight

45-minute interviews once weekly or sixteen 15-minute interviews once a week. Follow up was conducted 90 days after treatment by a social worker. No technique of therapy is specified. Treatment was conducted both individually and in groups. Criteria of improvement were work behavior rated by the staff, discharge from the hospital and symptom improvement evaluated from an interview with the patient and a checklist. No difference in improvement between the psychotherapy group and the controls is reported, except that significantly more controls were discharged within six months of admission (the authors believe more was expected of the treatment patients). No difference of significance were found that bore upon the length of treatment and its relationship to symptom amelioration or length of hospitalization.

Wayne (236) from his experience as medical director of a small private psychiatric hospital observes that over a twenty-year period, short-term psychotherapy has resulted in a reduction in hospital stay; approximately 25 percent of patients now leave after ten days and 60 percent are discharged within 30 days. The approach used is flexible, patient-centered, individually tailored psychotherapy which is essentially "eclectic," relying upon all adjunctive measures available.

STUDIES OF TIME MANIPULATION

Efforts have been made to study the effects of time: how much can brief therapy be abbreviated? With what effects?

Brief Contact Therapies

An evaluation of brief-contact therapy with hospitalized psychiatric patients was undertaken by Dreiblatt and Weatherly (53). Their population consisted of all male patients, approximately 38 to 40 years of age, on the admission ward. One group of 44 had had no previous hospitalization; the second group of 74 patients previously had been hospitalized. Of the patients without previous hospitalization, 22 were psychotic, 10 neurotic and 12 character disorders. These were divided into matched groups which received three five- to ten-minute contacts a week for two weeks, or six such contacts a week for two weeks. The group that had had prior hospitalization consisted of 35 psychotics, 21 neurotics and 12 character disorders; they all received six contacts a week for two weeks. The total length of hospitalization of both control and experimental groups was compared. There was no follow-up after discharge. The technique was non-directive and supportive counselling for the patients without previous hospitalization. The second group with prior hospitalization consisted of four sub-groups: (1) task-centered contact, in which the patient was asked to give opinions, (2) brief non-directive contact which was non-symptom oriented, (3) a brief directed contact which was symptom oriented, and (4) a control group. Patients in both experimental situations were given pre- and post-treatment measures of anxiety, self-esteem and self-concept. The brief contacts were informal, chatty, unscheduled and cheerful, and begun within two days of admission to the hospital. The groups which received brief contacts spent significantly less time in the hospital. In the first experiment, with patients who had no prior hospitalization, the groups which received six contacts a week showed significantly greater decrease in anxiety and an increase in self-esteem; the groups which received three contacts a week showed significant increases in self-esteem, but no decrease in anxiety. In the second experiment with patients who had had prior hospitalization, there were no differences between the group receiving task-centered contacts and the control group in anxiety decrease, in increased self-esteem and self-concept, and in shorter length of hospitalization. The symptom-oriented contact group showed no more change than did the control group. The non-symptom-oriented contact group showed an insignificant decrease over the control group in the number of symptoms reported. The authors conclude that because no therapeutic intent was communicated, there was no placebo effect, and certainly there was no catharsis or insight. They believe that the brief contact conveys an ego-enhancing message to the patient that he is accepted as a person.

The effectiveness of brief-contact therapy combined with drug prescription is described by Koegler (120, 123). The double-blind study of 299 outpatients at the University of California's Los Angeles Neuropsychological Institute offered either 15-minute brief-contact sessions and one of three drugs or a placebo, or a regular 50-minute weekly therapy session. The duration of the treatment is not specified. No differences were found between the group which received weekly 50-minute sessions and the groups which received placebo or drugs and brief contact. All five groups showed improvement when compared to the waiting-list group of patients with similar characteristics. Neither the specific drugs employed nor the length of the interview appear to be crucial. A two-year post-treatment follow-up showed continued improvement in all groups, especially in the waiting-list group which was now no different from the other five groups. There was a trend, however, for the regular 50-minute therapy group to be the most improved. The authors conclude that the waiting-list improvement shows that regular-length therapy and brief-contact therapy merely accelerate a recovery process that would occur without intervention.

Comparative Time Studies

Phillips and Johnston (171) compared longer-term psychoanalytic psychotherapy with shorter-term psychotherapy in which the time limits were set in advance. They report that the shorter-term group produced fewer dropouts and the patients expressed greater satisfaction in the outcome.

A comparison of brief and long-term therapy is reported by Shlien *et al.* (203) in a rather questionable study of the effects of time limitations. Brief therapy is limited to twenty sessions; the longer-term to 37 sessions. Two types of therapy were employed, client-centered and Adlerian. The effects on the two time groups were comparable, indicating that the results enjoyed by the long-term group were achieved in a shorter period of time.

Errera *et al.* (56) compared the effects of six to ten sessions of therapy with that of 21 sessions among patients seen at the psychiatric outpatient clinic of the Yale New Haven Medical Center, a community facility. The clinic sees approximately 800 patients a year. Thirty patients in each group were selected at random.

Independent raters yielded scores with a high degree of agreement. The Chi-Square test showed no significant differences between the groups for age, sex, marital status, religion, race, social class, number of previous admissions or intake diagnosis. Ratings of improvement for the two groups were essentially the same; there was no correlation between length of treatment and improvement, and the authors conclude that reports of a trend toward diminishing returns beyond the twentieth hour of therapy is not supported by their findings.

HYPNOTHERAPY IN THE TREATMENT OF FRIGIDITY

Extensive experience in the treatment of frigidity and related problems by hypnotherapy is reported by Richardson (183, 184). In 1964 he reports 24 percent climaxes in relation to coital experiences in a group of 76 untreated women. Following hypnotherapy the rate increased to 84 percent. Treatment sessions ranged from one to eight, with the average 1.53. Only four persons failed to benefit; the other 72 were "dramatically improved." Follow-up indicated that a post-treatment decrease in percentage of orgasm occurred in only two patients. Subsequently, in 1968, he reports comparable success with 94 of 114 patients. Richardson attributed these excellent results to the motivation of married women suffering a sexual problem and to the absence of any "tempting counter-suggestion" as is present in the treatment of obesity and smoking.

TREATMENT OF SKIN DISORDERS

The ability of brief psychotherapy to affect improvement in skin disorders is the subject of several studies. Seitz (201) studied psychocutaneous excoriation syndromes and their response to brief psychotherapy. His subjects were 12 male and 13 female patients, with a mean age of 45, and range in age from 13 to 67. The population included whites and blacks, Protestants, Jews, Quakers and Catholics. Thirteen were lower class, 12 middle class in socio-economic status. The patient received 12 sessions, at weekly intervals, of very directive psychotherapy oriented toward: (1) the verbal expression of repressed rage generated by the current interpersonal conflict, accompanied by a dilution of associated guilt; (2) verbal expression of inferiority feelings with dilution of associated shame; (3) symptomatic cure of the syndrome. The follow-up was conducted three months, six months and a year after termination. Twelve patients discontinued therapy when the important contemporary conflict had been identified; this generally occurred after the sixth interview. Thirteen patients completed the treatment; of these, 12 showed improvement beginning with a sustained expression of rage appearing about the eighth interview; one patient was judged unimproved after 12 sessions even though the expression of rage had taken place. The patients who completed the treatment showed a higher motivation for therapy, less possibility of psychogenic disorders in the family, and less extensive lesions. As had been predicted, the skin lesions became worse during the third to eighth interviews. Sustained awareness of anger required several expressions of the rage. Fourteen patients experienced explosive rage reactions accompanied by hysterical laughter or weeping. One patient required hospitalization for his skin ailments during the psychotherapy. Three of the 12 patients who improved exhibited marked acting out of hostility. Minor acting out was observed in the other nine. In the follow-up a cure was maintained at the three-month interval. Conceptualization of the treatment was seen as somewhat glib, with masochistic mechanisms again evident. At the six-months follow-up, six of seven had maintained their improved status; details of therapy were recalled. At the year follow-up, four of five contacted had maintained improvement; one had suffered a relapse. Memory of the treatment was considered to be intellectual in nature. Seitz found little evidence that the brief psychotherapy had provided an emotionally corrective experience with permanent effect.

Criteria for the brief psychotherapy of patients suffering neurodermatitis were investigated by Schoenberg and Carr (198) with ten male and 16 female private and clinic patients, with neurodermatitis of two-year duration, varying in degree from slight to severe. Overt psychosis was diagnosed in two, and thirteen were judged as likely to experience psychotic decompensation. Each patient was seen for twelve sessions. The treatment was directive with a contemporary focus; the major emphasis was placed on encouragement and reinforcement of expressions of hostility toward the figure in the patient's life who was the current source of conflict. The follow-up was rather haphazard; while pre-planned, it was not completed. Episodic contact was made with about 45 percent of the patients over a three-year period; findings indicated that the remissions obtained had persisted. They conclude that 16 of the 26 improved, of these 11 markedly, five moderately. Ten patients showed slight improvement or none, or were worse. A significant positive relationship was found between success in psychotherapy and the degree of overt hostility available to the patient. Self-reported psychopathology was significantly greater on the MMPI in the unimproved group. Unrelated to outcome were the following variables: presence of contemporary conflict, likelihood of psychotic decompensation, motivation, verbal resources, likelihood of dangerous acting out.

TREATING THE POST-MYOCARDIAL PATIENT

Brief group psychotherapy with coronary patients (post-myocardial infarction) is reported from a seven-year neurocardiology research project at the University of Oklahoma Medical Center by Adsett and Bruhn (1). Patients were evaluated clinically by a physician at about six to eight week intervals. At each visit they were given several physiological tests—blood pressure, pulse rate, serum cholesterol and serum uric acid. Sub-scales of the Minnesota Multiphasic Personality Inventory measuring anxiety and depression were administered. Test data were compared with those obtained from controls, post-myocardial infarction patients who did not receive group psychotherapy and those patients who refused the group psychotherapy. There were no significant differences in age, education or I.Q. among the three groups. The controls showed higher scores on the hypomania scale of the MMPI than did members of the psychotherapy group. Persons refusing group psychotherapy showed higher scores on the MMPI scales of psychopathy, paranoia and hypomania. No differences in blood pressure, pulse, anxiety or depression were observed between the experimental and control groups during the six-month period in which therapy was administered or the six-months follow-up period. The therapy group, however, did show a significantly higher serum cholesterol both during and after therapy. They also showed higher serum uric acid levels after therapy than did the controls. The researchers find the increase in serum cholesterol and serum uric acid inexplicable. During some group therapy sessions patients were connected to electrocardiogram equipment, and no significant changes in EEG's were recorded during these sessions. None of the patients experienced any distress other than anxiety symptoms such as mild restlessness, sweating and palpitations. The investigators now believe that myocardial patients are able to engage in group psychotherapy without precipitating serious heart consequences. This finding is meaningful, since cardiac patients often tyrannize family life because relatives are afraid cardiac crisis will be precipitated if they oppose the patient or express their feelings to him. Adsett and Bruhn conclude that families should be helped to deal more realistically with a member who suffers a heart attack: "They must learn to respond to the patient on the basis of reality factors rather than be controlled by a fear that the patient will drop dead if they stir him emotionally or encourage him to lead an active life."

CASE STUDIES

Reports of outcome with very small populations—one to three patients—are the following. A very brief psychotherapy with a single case is reported by Saul (195). Ridden with hypochondriacal fears, the patient, a 30-year-old single, middle-class American woman, was seen in two interviews three weeks apart. Saul employed active interpretation and support. She was provided with a nucleus of insight which would permit her to expand her awareness and to grow emotionally with new experiences; the dynamic function of the symptom was interpreted, and suggestions made about how to handle it. Follow-up a year later indicated that she had been helped appreciably. Outcome in two patients treated by brief psychotherapy is reported by Haley (93): a 17-year-old male complained of enuresis; a 65-year-old male complained of insomnia. They were treated with very active directive approach using suggestion techniques and hypnosis. A year later both reported sustained improvement. A single case study is reported by Visher (227). The patient, a 32-year-old female, white, middle-class American, was seen for nine sessions for an anxiety state. Treatment involved supportive focus on current reality problems, interpretations, and advice; non-verbal communication was used to express expectation of a limited treatment duration. Several years later, the patient was reported doing well.

Changes in distress level and styles of adaptation in response to brief psychotherapy were assessed by Jacobs *et al.* (104). Patients rated their own manifest distress preceding each session; the therapist evaluated the level of distress following each weekly session, and transcripts of the recorded sessions were subsequently evaluated by three independent judges for the weekly status of patient's ego strength and degree of incapacitation. Three cases were reported. Patient A, a 20-year-old female college student with a history of psychosomatic disorders, came for treatment of a depression. Seen for a six-month period of 24 sessions, she experienced improvements in her life reflected in decreased self-ratings of distress during the second half of her treatment, a finding paralleled by therapist ratings. Judges' ratings indicated significant improvement in the second half of the treatment. Patient B, a 21-year-old male college student, complained of intense anxiety and difficulty relating to people. He too was treated for six months for a total of 24 sessions. He was referred for psychoanalysis at the end of this treatment but was rejected as unsuitable. He undertook another form of long-term therapy. Neither the patient, the therapist, nor the three judges perceived significant changes in distress level during the treatment course. Patient C, a 20-year-old female college student, complained of self-consciousness and feelings of inadequacy. She was seen 16 times during the six-month period. She made rather dubious improvement and terminated because she felt more sure of herself. Her self-evaluation showed significant improvement, but neither the therapist nor the judges rated significant improvements in distress level, although there was a trend in that direction. The second phase of the study concerned characterological manifestations or modes of adaptation. The authors categorize various reported styles of adaptation, which they call ego strength, into five dimensions, reflecting the individual's ability to: (1) deal with his own impulse; (2) relate to others; (3) function independently; (4) handle feelings and frustrations; and (5) feel adequate as to his own worth, these corresponding with impulse control, interpersonal relations, autonomy, frustration tolerance, and self esteem. A 19-point rating scale was applied by the three judges to the transcripts of the therapy sessions in a weekly evaluation of ego strength. Patient A initially was found to be impetuous, to avoid contact with others, passive and independent, easily shaken, and self-devaluating. Significant improvement was observed in autonomy, frustration tolerance, and self-esteem, but she failed to show appreciable change in ability to control impulses or in interpersonal relationships. From the ratings, Patient B was described as ruminating, obsessive and ritualistic, avoiding close contact with others, passive and unassertive, relatively easily overcome by feelings of frustration and seeing himself as less worthy and effective than was warranted. Only interpersonal relationships were found to have improved significantly for this patient. Deviation scores for the other four factors tended to decrease but not significantly. Patient C appeared from the ratings to be spontaneous and relatively impetuous, capable of forming many social contacts, passive, submissive, and childish, easily shaken by feelings and setbacks, requiring much praise and reinforcement to bolster her self-esteem. Only autonomy appeared to increase significantly. Borderline improvement was noticed in self esteem, the other three areas were unchanged.

An unusual outcome study by Lord (140) employed "before" and "after" Rorschach protocols for two subjects who received psychotherapy for six months. The author concludes "both subjects, a year after the initial contact, displayed observable behavioral changes in the direction of more adequate personal and social adjustment, the criterion of successful psychotherapy." Both patients had manifested problems of such severity as to interfere with both interpersonal and vocational adjustments. The male subject had consistently experienced complete speech blocking since childhood. A year after treat-- ment he was talking regularly before groups; when experiencing some anxiety occasionally he was unable to speak fluently, but for six months had experienced no complete blocking of speech. The second subject, a girl, had complained of loneliness and job instability. She was embarrassed and guilty in the company of females, and when with men suffered severe anxiety; sexual content predominated in her thoughts. A year later she had been elected to officership of a woman's club, and reported that she had a number of female friends of reasonable closeness; she was contemplating marriage as well. Lord concludes that: (1) the basic personality configurations remained recognizably constant despite the successful brief psychotherapy; (2) measurable personality changes do occur; (3) these include more adequate inner balance between intellectual and emotional personality factors, and the emergency of thinking processes that are "in line with community thought."

TREATMENT OF CHILDREN

Children, their parents and their families are the focus of the next group of studies of outcome. Augenbraun et al. (6) noted a decrease in anxiety in parents of children in brief psychotherapy. They report in some cases that the child's symptoms disappeared and were undetectable a year later.

Treatment of children by a university clinic was studied by Maher and Katkovsy (142) with a questionnaire sent to the parent of both treated and untreated groups of children. Treatment was three or fewer one-hour sessions of semi-directive interviews with the parents by a faculty supervisor with diagnostic procedures for the child done by a graduate student; recommendations were then mailed to the parents. Neither group improved in reading, arithmetic, lying behavior or in school discipline. The treated group, however, was reported to have improved in terms of eating pattern, nervous habits, fighting with other children and destructive behavior. Both groups improved in relationship to poor appetite, toilet behavior and sensitivity of feelings.

A follow-up study, one to two-and-a-half years later, of the effectiveness of brief psychotherapy with children having reading problems coupled with schizophrenic manifestations, delinquent behavior and learning problems is reported by Koegler (121). All patients were doing well. Koegler states that an early diagnosis is essential for proper progress of therapy, noting that one schizophrenic patient had symbiotic manifestations which were important to understand. He recommends clearing up learning problems with children before tackling the family problems, since the learning problems may be the causal factor.

Waldfogel and Gardner (231) report successful treatment of school phobia in 14 of 16 cases. But, they add, a favorable prognosis is fostered by, perhaps even dependent upon, early treatment; they observe a striking relationship between remission of the acute symptoms and promptness of treatment.

In a pediatric practice Coddington (39) reports that he found that two-thirds of the cases referred to him for psychotherapy and the *great majority* of the problems he identified in his own practice could be satisfactorily treated on a symptomatic level by a "very brief, direct type of psychotherapy."

A study of brief family treatment at children's clinics in Israel is reported by Kaffman (121). Of 29 families in the study, "remarkable improvement" was obtained in 75 percent. The index was the disappearance of the central symptoms and the problems that led to referral. Kaffman concludes that suitable cases include all forms of child psychopathology up to the age of 16, provided that the emotional conflict has not been totally internalized and that the child has enough ego strength and anxiety to feel motivated to establish a meaningful relationship with the therapist.

IV

SOME ADDITIONAL MATTERS

CHAPTER 13

Hazards in Brief Psychotherapy

Are there any dangers for patient or psychotherapist in the brief psychotherapeutic procedure? A few authors have considered this aspect of the effort; they tend to concur that such dangers are limited, and that the trained therapist is able to deal with them adequately.

The strenuous pace required of the therapist who practices brief psychotherapy can make the process a stultifying and constricted experience for him, according to Barten (12). Barten also fears that the process when it does not solve anything for the patient can simply give him a taste of a relationship that may foster dependency and leave him hanging in midair.

French (174) sees a tendency to be overly eager for therapeutic results, leading to hasty, possibly erroneous moves by the therapist. But he believes the therapist can learn to restrain the urge to be of immediate help until the patient's problem is understood.

The pitfalls in brief psychotherapy are viewed as quite apparent by Coleman (47): (1) a tendency toward wild formulations without clinical substantiation; (2) disregard for the patient's reality; and (3) the tendency for the therapist to perceive and interpret material that is inappropriate and may be harmful. Coleman is optimistic that these pitfalls can be avoided by a rational approach.

Responding to a related concern, Bellak and Small (20) stress the importance of a full history, emphasizing details that contribute to understanding the patient and his problem. The value of the history is to foster comprehension and to provide clinical substantiation for intervention. Specifically, they see in the case of interpretations a danger of oversimplification in the desire to produce quick clinical results. They observe that the interpretation to be effective must often produce more than one kind of change, and must then be geared to seemingly disparate aspects of the personality dynamics. For example, an interpretation may have both to uncover a drive and produce ego alienation from it at the same time. They see a danger of failure to protect the ego while uncovering is going on, and warn that simple direct uncovering is mere confrontation, something to be avoided in brief psychotherapy.

Gelb and Ullman (75) note the danger of overlooking somatic symptoms in the pressing urge to produce psychological changes. In their clinic they feel they guard against this possibility through the availability of psychiatrists to the non-psychiatric staff who do brief psychotherapy. A more effective way would be adequate training in the recognition of major evidences of somatic problems, including neurological ones, a skill there is reason to believe is not too abundant among psychotherapists of either medical or other backgrounds.

Malan (144) cautions that the short time interval and hence the relatively limited exposure of patient to therapist does not preclude the possibility of a rapidly and early developing transference of powerful intensity, and that to avoid this development may be impossible. He urges, therefore, that the therapist be prepared to make transference interpretations. Bellak and Small (20) also identify this danger and also advise that transference interpretations are essential. They warn particularly that negative transference elements should be early recognized and interpreted quickly.

Discussing the relationship of psychoanalysis to psychotherapy in 1969, Wallerstein (233) cites the comments of Eleanor Steele at a little publicized conference in 1952. Faithfulness to psychoanalytic goals may frustrate the analyst who attempts more limited goals and prevent the operation of necessary flexibility. This frustration coupled with the time pressure of psychotherapy makes the analyst more likely to overlook essential events and more likely to act out in the countertransference. Less intensive therapy, she noted, requires both depth of analytic understanding and its ready availability for emergencies. Judgments must be made more quickly, more intuitively than is usual in a formal analysis.

The review of these relatively few comments on dangers in brief psychotherapy would indicate that the potential hazard lies more with the therapist than with the patient. Essentially, the risk for the patient appears to be the development of an intense transference that cannot be resolved in the brief time allowed. The therapist is seen as subject to an oppressive pace, the danger of not comprehending the patient within the short time allowed, and therefore making erroneous interventions, the hazard of overlooking symptoms of a somatic nature in a drive to achieve psychological change, and in acting out in the counter transference.

The best prevention rests in the quality of the training the therapist brings to the brief psychotherapeutic effort, and the opportunity for supervision and consultation available to him in the pattern of his professional practice.

CHAPTER 14
Training for Brief Psychotherapy

Coleman (46) comments on the unpopularity of brief psychotherapy with residents whose orientation toward the psychoanalytic
model heightens their concern about supporting defenses, aiding repression and engaging in social manipulation. They appear to be especially frightened of and antagonistic to the manipulation of the
transference, considering the approach both unworthy and unscientific.
Coleman believes that these objections can be overcome with special
analytic supervision, that experience and analytic training are essential for competence in brief psychotherapy and especially for engaging
the problems of intensity and compression. The therapist must be
able to respond with zest and aggressiveness to the challenge of the
compression; he suggests that the reason so few psychoanalytically-
oriented residents fail to respond in this way "may possibly be found
in the personality types of those who choose psychotherapy as a
career."

Gelb and Ullman (75) and Goolishian (81) employ co-therapy both as a treatment technique and as a device for the training of psychotherapists. They match an experienced psychotherapist with an inexperienced one, who initially acts as an observer. The junior psychotherapist learns through observation and discussion with the more experienced therapist, and after several meetings with the patient the junior therapist may continue the treatment, freeing the senior therapist for "initial encounters with other patients." They find the technique provides excellent opportunity for active supervision through participation and a type of relationship rarely provided by the secondhand reporting that is the method of most supervisor-trainee relationships.

Wolberg (245) delineates the essential formal requirements of a good practitioner of brief psychotherapy as including extensive training, flexibility in personality, and flexibility in approach. Extensive training assures skill in arriving quickly at a diagnosis, in comprehending the basic dynamics, and familiarity with a wide array of techniques. Wolberg does not state that formal psychoanalytic training is essential; he believes this depends upon whatever individual problems the therapist has and brings to the work. Since experience is the essential ingredient in training, the therapist benefits from an exposure to the widest possible variety of problems and patients. Personal flexibility enables the quick establishment of a working relationship; the therapist must be able through his manner to communicate a sense of confidence and make the patient feel stabilized and understood. His flexibility must extend to a sensitivity to the emergence of transference neurosis and an ability to handle it quickly. Flexibility of approach provides freedom to resort to any intervention in the wide armamentarium available. This requires appreciation of the functions, the limitations and values of the various techniques, as well as experience in using them.

Sometimes the special nature of a limited service that a brief-psychotherapy clinic offers suggests a focus to the training beyond whatever preparation may be required for a psychotherapist in general. Courtenay (50) acknowledges his indebtedness to Michael Balint for applying psychoanalytic concepts to feasible short-term approaches. He relates Balint's belief that the general practitioner if treated psychotherapeutically might gain insight into his own personality which would enable him to deal with his patients on a more appropriate level. Thus in Courtenay's clinic where brief therapy was applied to problems of sexual discord in marriage, the workers participated in a seminar which integrated the classical gynecological examination (the anatomical structure of the female genitalia, physiological and pathological functioning) with a psychological study of the emotions and fantasies which women center upon their genitals.

The potentialities for training in psychotherapy provided by a brief procedure are discussed by Bellak and Small (20). They comment that the very length of psychoanalysis and other intensive psychotherapies limits training methods, since to record the full processes photographically and aurally is not feasible. Nor can the student spend years behind a one-way screen observing a skilled therapist. They believe that learning based upon direct observation of a teacher and supervision based upon direct observation of the student would improve the quality of training. Brief psychotherapy makes practical such observation of the student therapist, instead of having him make reports after the fact to his supervisor—reports that suffer from attenuation through time lapse, repression and ego involvement. These authors also reflect that with brief psychotherapy the young therapist has more, and more varied, clinical experiences.

These same authors, describing their recommended requirements for the practice of brief psychotherapy, state without equivocation that "a successful personal analysis and supervised clinical experience are the keystones of therapeutic skill." In addition to, not in place of, these, certain elements of intellectual as well as emotional equipment are important. The therapist must be well trained in psychodynamic theory; training should include a wide range of clinical exposure, and the development of diagnostic skill. The therapist should know learning theory, not to the extent required by an experimental psychologist, but he should be able to incorporate applicable aspects of learning theory in his approach to behavioral problems. Because of the stress placed upon the use of adjunctive interventions, the psychotherapist must be equipped with a thorough knowledge of an array of these measures and have them available. He must be capable of rapid logical thinking, using both inductive and deductive reasoning. Flexibility of approach is basic—he must be able to shift approach and response to the uniqueness of each individual. When only a single approach is utilized, the probabilities for success of the method are diminished; hence the therapist must be able to apply flexibility in the choice and application of intervention as well as in his approach to the patient who sometimes may require kindness, at other times relative sternness. They also call attention to the creative ability of the therapist to experience "regression in the service of the ego," noting that the logic which is "based upon the knowledge of psychodynamics involves an order of causality not available to the ordinary mode of thinking." The therapist must be able to recognize the primary processes which may be operative in his patient's thought patterns. He must be able to identify and comprehend instinctual drives, and the response of drives to various stimuli in a manner which is not generally recognized or acceptable in polite society. This capacity implies by definition "a controlled regression;" such ability facilitates the diagnostic process.

Despite the brevity of the time span in brief psychotherapy, patience and willingness to listen are important, as they are in all psychotherapy, but must not be oversimplified. Ventilation is therapeutic, for example, but it must be used as a matter of choice rather than as the universal approach to all patients. The therapist must have courage to employ the brief process, to assume responsibility for the welfare of another, for his comprehension of the dynamics of his patient, and in the selection of his intervention. He must also have the freedom given by courage to depart from classical models of psychotherapy. Bellak and Small conclude, ". . . there is probably not a person nor a situation that cannot be helped to some extent with the problems that burden them, provided knowledge, ingenuity and willingness exist."

Bibliography

1. *Adsett, C. A.* and *Bruhn, J. G.:* Short-term group psychotherapy for post-myocardial infarction patients and their wives. Canadian Med. Assoc. J. 99, Sept. 28, 1968.
2. *Aldrich, C. K.:* Brief psychotherapy: a reappraisal of some theoretical assumptions. Amer. J. Psychiat. 125:5, 585-592, 1968.
3. *Alexander, F.:* Indications for psychoanalytic therapy. Bull. N. Y. Acad. Med. 20: 319, 1944.
4. *Alexander, F.,* and *French, T. M.:* Psychoanalytic Therapy. New York: Ronald Press, 1946.
5. *Alexander, F.:* Principles and techniques of briefer psychotherapeutic procedures. Proc. Assoc. for Res. Nerv. & Ment. Dis. 31: 16, 1951.
6. *Augenbraun, B., Reid, H.,* and *Friedman, D. B.:* Brief intervention as a preventive force in disorders of early childhood. Am. J. Orthopsychiat. 37: 697, 1967.
7. *Avnet, H. H.:* Short-term treatment under auspices of a medical insurance plan. Amer. J. Psychiat. 122: 2, 1965.
8. *Avnet, H. H.:* How effective is short-term therapy. *In* Wolberg, L. R., (Ed.): Short-Term Psychotherapy, New York: Grune & Stratton, 1965.

9. *Baker, E.:* Brief psychotherapy. J. Med. Soc., N. J., 44: 260-261, 1947.
10. *Barron, F.:* Some test correlates of response to psychotherapy. J. Cons. Psychol. 17: 235, 1953.
11. *Barron, F.:* An ego-strength scale which predicts response to psychotherapy. J. Cons. Psychol. 17: 327, 1953.
12. *Barten, H. H.:* The 15-minute hour: brief therapy in a military setting. Amer. J. Psychiat. 122: 565, 1965.
13. *Barten, H. H.:* The coming of age of the brief psychotherapies. *In* Bellak, L., and Barten, H. H. (Eds.): Progress in Community Mental Health, New York; Grune & Stratton, 1969.
14. *Bartholomew, A. A.,* and *Kelley, M. F.:* The personal emergency advisory service. Mental Hygiene. 46: 382, July, 1962.
15. *Batrawi, S. A.:* The Differential Effects of Two Therapeutic Techniques on Selected Aspects of Client Behavior. Unpublished Doctoral Thesis. George Washington University, 1964.
16. *Baum, O. E.,* and *Felzer, S. B.:* Activity in initial interviews with lower-class patients. Arch. Gen. Psychiat. 10: 345-353, 1964.
17. *Bellak, L.:* The emergency psychotherapy of depression. *In* Bychowski, G. and Despert, J. L. (Eds.): Specialized Techniques in Psychotherapy. New York; Basic Books, 1952.
18. *Bellak, L.:* The schizophrenic syndrome. *In* Bellak, L. (Ed.): Schizophrenia: A Review of the Syndrome. New York: Logos Press, 1958.
19. *Bellak, L.:* A general hospital as a focus of community psychiatry. A trouble shooting clinic combines important functions as part of hospital's service. JAMA. 174: 2214-2217, December 1960.
20. *Bellak, L.,* and *Small, L.:* Emergency Psychotherapy and Brief Psychotherapy. New York: Grune and Stratton, 1965.
21. *Bellak, L.:* The role and nature of emergency psychotherapy. Amer. J. Public Health. 58: 2, 1968.
22. *Berliner, B.:* Short psychoanalytic psychotherapy: its possibilities and its limitations. Bull. Menninger Clinic. 5: 204, 1941.
23. *Bernard, J. L.:* Rapid treatment of gross obesity by operant techniques. Psychol. Reports. 23, 1968.
24. *Blaine, G. B.:* Short-term psychotherapy with college students. New Eng. J. Med. 256: 208-210, 1957.
25. *Bonime, W.:* Some principles of brief psychotherapy. Psychiat. Quart. 27: 1-18, 1953.
26. *Bos, C.:* Short-term psychotherapy. Canad. Psychiat. Assoc. J., 4: 162-165, July, 1959.
27. *Breuer, J.,* and *Freud, S.:* Studies on Hysteria. New York: Basic Books, Inc., 1957 (Published in German, 1895)

28. *Brodsky, C. M., Fischer, A.,* and *Wilson, G. C.:* Analysis of a treatment-decision system. Dis. Ner. Syst. 30, Jan. 1969.
29. *Burdon, A. P.:* Principles of brief psychotherapy. J. Louisiana Med. Soc. 115: 374-378, 1963.
30. *Caffey, E. M., Jones, R. D., Diamond, L. S., Burton, E.,* and *Bowen, W. T.:* Brief hospital treatment of schizophrenia— early results of a multiple-hospital study. Hospital and Community Psychiat. 19, 9, 282, 1968.
31. *Cameron, W. R.:* How to set up a county psychiatric emergency service. Amer. J. Pub. Health. 52: (Supplement to September, 1962).
32. *Campbell, J. P.,* and *Dunnette, M. D.:* Effectiveness of t-group experiences in managerial training and development. Psychol. Bull. 70, 2, August, 1968.
33. *Caplan, G.:* Practical steps for the family physician in the prevention of emotional disorder. JAMA, 170: 1497, July 25, 1959.
34. *Carse, J., Panton, N.,* and *Watt, A.:* A district mental health service. Lancet, 39-41, January 4, 1958.
35. *Castelnuovo-Tedesco, P.:* Brief psychotherapeutic treatment of depressive reactions. *In* Wayne, G. J. and Koegler, R. R. (Eds.) : Emergency Psychiatry and Brief Therapy. Boston: Little, Brown, 1966.
36. *Cattell, J. P., MacKinnon, R. A.,* and *Forster, E.:* Limited goal therapy in a psychiatric clinic. Amer. J. Psychiat. 120, 255, 1963.
37. *Chafetz, M. E.:* The effect of a psychiatric emergency service on motivation for psychotherapy. J. Nerv. Ment. Dis. 140: 442-448, 1965.
38. *Chandler, H. M.:* As reported anon, in "Crisis intervention: plan for therapy and family follow-up." Frontiers of Hospital Psychiatry, Vol. 4, No. 15, September, 1969.
39. *Coddington, D. R.:* The use of brief psychotherapy in a pediatric practice. J. of Paed. 60, 259, 1962.
40. *Coghill, M. A.:* Sensitivity training: a review of the controversy. Key Issue Series No. 1, Ithaca, New York: Cornell University.
41. *Cohn, J. V.:* The psychiatric emergency. Southern Med. J. 52: 547-553, May, 1959.
42. *Coleman, J. V., Janowicz, R., Fleck, S.,* and *Norton, N.:* A comparative study of a psychiatric clinic and a family agency: parts I and II. Social Casework, 38: 3-8, 74-80, January and February 1957.
43. *Coleman, J. V.:* Banter as psychotherapeutic intervention. Amer. J. Psychoanal. 22: 69-74, 1962.
44. *Coleman, J. V.,* and *Errera, P.:* The general hospital emergency

room and its psychiatric problems. Amer. J. Pub. Health, 53: 1294-1301, August, 1963.

45. *Coleman, M. D.*, and *Zwerling, I.*: The psychiatric emergency clinic: a flexible way of meeting community mental health needs. Amer. J. Psychiat. 115: 980-984, May, 1959.

46. *Coleman, M. D.*: Problems in an emergency psychiatric clinic. Mental Hospitals. 11: 26-27, May, 1960.

47. *Coleman, M. D.*: Methods of psychotherapy: emergency psychotherapy. *In* Masserman, J. H. and Moreno, J. L. (Eds.): Progress in Psychotherapy. New York: Grune and Stratton, 5: 78-85, 1960.

48. *Conn, J. H.*: Brief psychotherapy of the sex offender: a report of a liaison service between a court and a private psychiatrist. J. Clin. Psychopath. 10: 347-372, 1949.

49. *Cook, E. L.*: Short-term group therapy. J. Med. Soc. New Jersey. 63: 83, 1966.

50. *Courtenay, M.*: Sexual Discord in Marriage. London: Tavistock, 1968.

51. *Crabtree, L. H.*, and *Graller, J. L.*: As reported anon, in "Improvised, short-term therapy in a military center." Frontiers of Hospital Psychiatry, Vol. 5, No. 11, June, 1968.

52. *Deutsch, F.*: Applied Psychoanalysis: Selected Lectures on Psychotherapy. New York: Grune and Stratton, 1949.

53. *Dreiblatt, I. S.*, and *Weatherly, D.*: An evaluation of the efficacy of brief contact therapy with hospitalized psychiatric patients. J. Consul. Psychol. 29, 6, 513-519, 1965.

54. *English, H. B.*, and *English, A. C.*: The Comprehensive Dictionary of Psychological and Psychoanalytic Terms. New York: Longmans, Green and Company, 1958.

55. *Erlich, R. E.*, and *Phillips, P. B.*: Short-term psychotherapy of the aviator. Aerospace Med., 34 (11): 1046-1047, November, 1963.

56. *Errera, P., McKee, B., Smith, D. C.*, and *Gruber, R.*: Length of psychotherapy. Arch. Gen. Psychiat. 17: 454-458, 1967.

57. *Faires, M.*: Short-term counseling at the college level. J. Consul. Psychol. 2, 182-184, 1955.

58. *Farberow, N. L.*: As reported anon, in "Greater preventive role seen for suicide centers of future." Frontiers of Hospital Psychiatry, Vol. 5, No. 18, November, 1968.

59. *Fast, I.*: The process of vocational choice as a precipitant of personality change. Psychotherapy: Theory, Research and Practice. 5, 4, 1968.

60. *Fenichel, O.*: Brief psychotherapy. *In* Fenichel, H., and Rapaport, D. (Eds.): The Collected Papers of Otto Fenichel. New York: Norton, 1954.

61. *Ferenczi, S.:* The further development of an active therapy in psychoanalysis. *In* Further Contributions to The Theory and Techniques of Psychoanalysis. New York: Basic Books, 1951.
62. *Ferenczi, S.:* Contra-indications to the active psychoanalytic technique. *In* Further Contributions to The Theory and Techniques of Psychoanalysis. New York: Basic Books, 1951.
63. First Aid for Psychological Reactions in Disasters. Washington, D.C.: American Psychiatric Association, 1964.
64. *Forer, B. R.:* The therapeutic value of crisis. LASCP News. 5, 8, December, 1963.
65. *Frank, J. D.:* The role of hope in psychotherapy. Int. J. Psychiat. 5, 383-395, 1968.
66. *Freud, S.:* Turnings in the Ways of Psycho-analytic Therapy. Collected Papers, Vol. II, London: Hogarth, 1948.
67. *Freud, S.:* Group Psychology and The Analysis of The Ego. London: Hogarth, 1948.
68. *Friedman, H. J.:* Patient expectancy and symptom reduction. Arch. Gen. Psychiat. 8: 61-67, 1963.
69. *Friedman, T. T., Rolfe, P.,* and *Perry, S.:* Home treatment of psychiatric patients. Amer. J. of Psychiat. 116: 807-809, March, 1960.
70. *Frohman, B. S.:* Brief Psychotherapy. Philadelphia: Lea and Febiger, 1948.
71. *Fuerst, R. A.:* Problems of short time psychotherapy. Amer. J. Orthopsychiat. 8, 260, 1938.
72. *Gardner, E. A.:* Psychological care for the poor: the need for new service patterns with a proposal for meeting this need. *In* Cowen, E. L., Gardner, E. A., and Zax, M. (Eds.): Emergent Approaches to Mental Health Problems. New York: Appleton-Century-Crofts, 1967.
73. *Garetz, F.:* The psychiatric emergency. Medical Times. 88: 3, September, 1960.
74. *Garner, H. H.:* Brief psychotherapy. Int. J. Neuropsychiat. 1: 616, 1965.
75. *Gelb, L. A.,* and *Ullman, M.:* As reported anon, in "Instant psychotherapy offered at an outpatient psychiatric clinic." Frontiers of Hospital Psychiatry, Vol. 4, No. 14, August, 1967.
76. *Gillman, R. D.:* Brief psychotherapy: a psychoanalytic view. Amer. J. Psychiat. 122, 601, 1965.
77. *Glascote, R. M., Cumming, E., Hammersley, D. W., Ozarin, L. O.,* and *Smith, L. H.:* The Psychiatric Emergency. The Joint Information Service of the American Psychiatric Association and the National Association for Mental Health. 1966.
78. *Glover, E.:* The therapeutic effect of inexact interpretation: a contribution to the theory of suggestion. J. Psychoanal. 12, 37, 1931.

79. *Goldfarb, A. I.,* and *Turner, H.:* Psychotherapy of aged persons. II. utilization and effectiveness of "brief" therapy. Amer. J. Psychiat. 109, 916-921. 1953.
80. *Goldstein, A. P.:* Therapist-Patient Expectancies in Psychotherapy. New York: Macmillan, 1962.
81. *Goolishian, H. A.:* A brief psychotherapy program for disturbed adolescents. Am. J. Orthopsychiat. 32: 142-148, 1962.
82. *Gottschalk, L. A., Mayerson, P.,* and *Gottlieb, A. A.:* Prediction and evaluation of outcome in an emergency brief psychotherapy clinic. J. Nerv. Ment. Dis. 144, 2, 1967.
83. *Gould, R. I.:* Emergencies in the outpatient department. *In* Wayne, G. J., and Koegler, R. R. (Eds.): Emergency Psychiatry and Brief Therapy. Boston: Little, Brown, 1966.
84. *Green, S. L.,* and *Rothenberg, A. B.:* A Manual of First Aid for Mental Health In Childhood and Adolescence. New York: Julian Press, 1953.
85. *Greenacre, P.:* General problems of acting out. Psychoanal. Quart. 19: 455, 1950.
86. *Greenblatt, M., Moore, R.,* and *Albert, R.:* The Prevention of Hospitalization, Report on the Community Extension Service of the Massachusetts Mental Health Center, Boston, Massachusetts. New York: Grune and Stratton, 1963.
87. *Greenson, R.:* The Technique and Practice of Psychoanalysis, I. New York: International Universities Press, 1967.
88. *Grinker, R. R.:* Brief psychotherapy in psychosomatic problems. Psychosom. Med. 9, 78-103, 1947.
89. *Gross, R. B.:* Supportive therapy for the depressed college student. Psychotherapy: Theory, Research and Practice. 5, 4, 262-267, December, 1968.
90. *Gutheil, E. A.:* Basic outline of the active psychoanalytic technique. Psychoanal. Rev. 20, 53, 1933.
91. *Gutheil, E. A.:* Psychoanalysis and brief psychotherapy. J. Clin. Psychopath. 6: 207-230, 1944.
92. *Gwartney, R., Auerback, A., Nelken, S.,* and *Goshen, C.:* Panel discussion on psychiatric emergencies in general practice. JAMA. 170: 1022-1030, 1959.
93. *Haley, J.:* Control in brief psychotherapy. A.M.A. Arch. Gen. Psychiat. 4: 139-153, February, 1961.
94. *Haley, J.,* and *Hoffman, L.:* Techniques of Family Therapy. New York: Basic Books, 1967.
95. *Hansen, D. D.:* Psychological aspects of medical emergencies: an internist's view. *In* Wayne, G. J. and Koegler, R. R. (Eds.): Emergency Psychiatry and Brief Therapy. Boston: Little Brown, 1966.
96. *Harris, M. R., Kalis, B. L.,* and *Freeman, E. H.:* Precipitating

stress: an approach to brief therapy. Am. J. Psychother. 17: 465-471, 1963.

97. *Harris, R. E.,* and *Christiansen, C.:* Predictions of response to brief psychotherapy. J. Psychol. 21: 269-284, 1946.

98. *Harrower, M.:* A clinical psychologist looks at short-term therapy. *In* Wolberg, L. R. (Ed.): Short-term Psychotherapy. New York: Grune and Stratton, 1965.

99. *Herliky, C. E.:* Recognition and management of psychiatric emergencies. U.S. Armed Forces Med. J. 7: 25-35, 1956.

100. *Hoch, P. H.:* Short-term versus long-term therapy. *In* Wolberg, L. R. (Ed.): Short-Term Psychotherapy. New York: Grune and Stratton, 1965.

101. *Holland, C. J.:* Elimination by the parents of fire-setting behavior in a 7 year old boy. Behav. Res. and Therapy. 7, 1969.

102. *Howard, H. S.:* Of "gimmicks and gadgets" in brief psychotherapy. Delaware Med. J. 37: 265, 1965.

103. *Jackson, B. T.:* A case of voyeurism treated by counter conditioning. Behav. Res. and Therapy. 7, 1969.

104. *Jacobs, M. A., Muller, J. J., Eisman, H. D., Knitzer, J.,* and *Spilkan, A.:* The assessment of change in distress level and styles of adaptation as a function of psychotherapy. J. Nerv. Ment. Dis. 145, 5, 392-404, 1968.

105. *Jacobson, G. F.:* Crisis theory and treatment strategy: some socio-cultural and psychodynamic considerations. J. Nerv. Ment. Dis. 141: 209-218, 1965.

106. *Jacobson, G. F., Wilner, D. M., Morley, W. E., Schneider, S., Strickler, M.,* and *Sommer, G. J.:* The scope and practice of an early-access brief treatment psychiatric center. Amer. J. Psychiat. 121, 1176-1182, 1965.

107. *Jacobson, G. F., Strickler, M.,* and *Morley, W. E.:* Generic and individual approaches to crisis intervention. Am. J. Pub. Health. 58, 2, February, 1968.

108. *Janis, I. L.:* Psychological Stress. New York: John Wiley and Sons, 1958.

109. *Johnson, A. J.,* and *Szurek, S. A.:* The genesis of antisocial acting-out in children and adults. Psychoanal. Quart. 21, 323-343, 1952.

110. *Jones, E.:* The Life and Work of Sigmund Freud. Vol. II. New York: Basic Books, 1957.

111. *Jones, M.:* Intra- and extra-mural community psychiatry, in the scientific papers of the one hundred and sixteenth annual meeting of the American Psychiatric Association in summary form. Paper Number 13. 22, May, 1960.

112. *Kaffman, M.:* Short-term family therapy. Family Process 2: 216-234, 1963.

113. *Kalinowsky, L. B.:* The use of somatic treatments in short-term therapy. *In* Wolberg, L. R. (Ed.) : Short-term Psychotherapy. New York: Grune and Stratton, 1965.
114. *Kardiner, A.:* The Traumatic Neuroses of War. New York: Hoeber, 1941.
115. *Keeler, M. H.:* Short-term group therapy with hospitalized non-psychotic patients. N. Carolina Med. J. 21: 228-231, June, 1960.
116. *Kennedy, A.:* Psychiatric emergencies. Practitioner. 182: 428-436, April, 1959.
117. *Kielholz, P.:* Diagnosis and therapy of the depressive states. Acta Psychosomatic Geigy, American Issue, No. 1, 1959.
118. *Klein, D.,* and *Lindemann, E.:* Preventive intervention in individual and family crisis situations. *In* Caplan, G. (Ed.) : Prevention of Mental Disorders in Children. New York: Basic Books, Inc., 1961.
119. *Knight, R. P.:* Application of psychoanalytic concepts in psychotherapy. Bull. Menninger Clinic. 1, 99, 1937.
120. *Koegler, R. R.:* Brief-contact therapy and drugs in outpatient treatment. *In* Wayne, G. J. and Koegler, R. R. (Eds.) : Emergency Psychiatry and Brief Therapy. Boston: Little, Brown, 1966.
121. *Koegler, R. R.:* Brief therapy with children. *In* Wayne, G. J. and Koegler, R. R. (Eds.) : Emergency Psychiatry and Brief Therapy. Boston: Little, Brown, 1966.
122. *Koegler, R. R.,* and *Cannon, J. A.:* Treatment for the many. *In* Wayne, G. J. and Koegler, R. R. (Eds.) : Emergency Psychiatry and Brief Therapy. Boston: Little, Brown, 1966.
123. *Koegler, R. R.,* and *Brill, N. Q.:* Treatment of Psychiatric Outpatients. New York: Appleton-Century-Crofts, 1967.
124. *Koge, I.:* A community agency experiment in short-term methods. Nerv. Child. 8, 360-374, 1949.
125. *Kris, E. B.:* Intensive short-term treatment in a day care facility for the prevention of rehospitalization of patients in the community showing recurrence of psychotic symptoms. Psychiat. Quart. 34: 83-88, 1960.
126. *Kritzer, H.,* and *Pittman, F. S.:* As reported anon, in "Brief emergency room stay found useful for psychiatric cases." Frontiers of Hospital Psychiatry, Vol. 4, No. 15, September, 1967.
127. *Laing, R. D.:* The Politics of Experience. New York: Pantheon Books, 1967.
128. *Lakin, M.:* Some ethical issues in sensitivity training. Amer. Psychologist. 24, 10, October, 1969.
129. *Lang, P. J., Lazovik, A. D.,* and *Reynolds, D.:* Desensitization,

suggestibility and pseudotherapy. J. Abnorm. Psychol. 70, 395, 1965.
130. *Langsley, D. G., Pittman, F. S.,* and *Swank, G. E.:* As reported anon, in "Family crises in schizophrenics, other mental patients compared." Frontiers of Hospital Psychiatry, Vol. 5, No. 15, September, 1968.
131. *Lazarus, A. A.:* Group therapy of phobic disorders by systematic desensitization. J. Abnorm. and Soc. Psychol. 63, 504, 1961.
132. *Lemkau, P.,* and *Crocetti, G.:* The Amsterdam municipal psychiatric service. Amer. J. Psychiat. 117: 779-783, March, 1961.
133. *Lester, E. P.:* Brief psychotherapies in child psychiatry. Canad. Psychiat. Assoc. J. 13, 301-309, 1968.
134. *Levy, R. A.:* As reported anon, in "How to conduct 6-session crisis-oriented psychotherapy." Frontiers of Hospital Psychiatry, Vol. 4, No. 9, May, 1967.
135. *Lewin, K. K.:* A brief psychotherapy method. Penn. Med. J. 68: 43, 1965.
136. *Lichtenstein, E.,* and *Keutzer, C. S.:* Experimental investigation of diverse techniques to modify smoking: a follow-up report. Behav. Res. and Therapy. 7, 1969.
137. *Lindemann, E.:* Symptomatology and management of acute grief. Amer. J. Psychiat. 101, 141-148, 1944.
138. *Lindemann, E.,* and *Dawes, L. G.:* The use of psychoanalytic constructs in preventive psychiatry. *In* The Psychoanalytic Study of the Child. Vol. VII, New York: International Universities Press, 1952.
139. *Lindemann, E.:* Symptomatology and management of acute grief. *In* Parad, H. J. (Ed.): Crisis Intervention. New York: Family Service Association of America, 1965.
140. *Lord, E.:* Two sets of Rorschach records obtained before and after brief psychotherapy. J. Consult. Psychol. 14: 134-139, 1950.
141. *Mackey, R. A.:* Crisis theory: its development and relevance to social casework practice. Family Life Coordinator, 17, 3, 165-173, 1968.
142. *Maher, B. A.,* and *Katkovsky, W.:* The efficacy of brief clinical procedures in alleviating children's problems. J. Indiv. Psychol. 17: 205-211, 1961.
143. *Malamud, W.:* Brief psychotherapy in medical practice. Med. Clin. N. Amer. 1195-1206, 1948.
144. *Malan, D. H.:* A Study of Brief Psychotherapy. London: Tavistock Publications, 1963.
145. *McGuire, M. T.:* The process of short-term insight psychotherapy, I: J. Nerv. Ment. Dis. 141: 83-94, 1965.
146. *McGuire, M. T.:* The process of short-term insight psychother-

apy, II: content, expectations, and structure. J. Nerv. Ment. Dis. 141: 219-230, 1965.

147. *Meerloo, J. A. M.:* Emergency psychotherapy and mental first aid. Internat. Rec. Med. 171: 101-110, 1958.
148. *Meerloo, J. A. M.:* Mental First Aid: Toward Balance in a Dizzy World. New York: Hawthorne Books, 1966.
149. *Menninger, K.:* The Vital Balance. New York: Viking Press, 1963.
150. *Miller, A.:* A report on psychiatric emergencies. Canad. Hosp. 36: 36-37, December, 1959.
151. *Miller, L. C.:* Short-term therapy with adolescents. Amer. J. Orthopsychiat. 29: 772-779, 1959.
152. *Miller, L. C.:* Short-term therapy with adolescents. *In* Parad, H. J. (Ed.): Crisis Intervention. New York: Family Service Association of America, 1965.
153. *Miller, W. B.:* A psychiatric emergency service and some treatment concepts. Amer. J. Psychiat. 124: 924-933, 1968.
154. *Mintz, R. S.:* Depression and suicide. *In* Wayne, G. J. and Koegler, R. R. (Eds.): Emergency Psychiatry and Brief Therapy. Boston: Little, Brown, 1966.
155. *Mitchell, C.:* The uses and abuses of co-therapy as a technique in family unit therapy. Bull. of the Family Mental Health Clinic of Jewish Family Service. 1, 8-10, Spring, 1969.
156. *Morley, W. E.:* Treatment of the patient in crisis. Western Med. 3, 77, March, 1965.
157. *Morley, W. E., Messick, J. M.,* and *Aguilera, D. C.:* Crisis: paradigms of intervention. J. Psychiat. Nursing, November-December 1967.
158. *Morley, W. E.,* and *Brown, U. B.:* The crisis-intervention group: a natural mating or a marriage of convenience? Psychotherapy, Theory, Research and Practice, 6, 1, Winter, 1969.
159. *Morton, R. B.:* An experiment in brief psychotherapy. Psychol. Monogr. 69: 1, 1955.
160. *Muench, G. A.:* An investigation of time-limited psychotherapy. Amer. Psychologist. 19, 1964. (Abstract)
161. *Nehemkis, A. M.,* and *Lichtenstein, E.:* Conjoint social reinforcement in the treatment of smoking. Mimeo
162. *Normand, W. C., Fensterheim, H., Tannenbaum, G.,* and *Sager, C. J.:* The acceptance of the psychiatric walk-in clinic in a highly deprived community. Amer. J. Psychiat. 120, 533-539, December, 1963.
163. *Normand, W. C., Fensterheim, H.,* and *Schremzel, S.:* A systematic approach to brief therapy for patients from a low socioeconomic community. Comm. Mental Health J. 3: 349-354, 1967.

164. *Ostow, M.:* The consequences of ambivalence. Psychosomatics, IX. September-October 1968.
165. *Paidoussi, E. R.:* Some comparisons between family therapy and individual therapy. Bull. of the Family Mental Health Clinic of Jewish Family Service. 1, 11-12, Spring, 1969.
166. *Parad, H. J. (Ed.):* Crisis Intervention: Selected Readings. New York: Family Service Association of America. 1965.
167. *Park, L. C., and Covi, L.:* Non-blind placebo trial: an exploration of neurotic patients responses to placebo when its inert content is disclosed. Arch. Gen. Psychiat. 12: 336-345, 1965.
168. *Patterson, C. H.:* Divergence and convergence in psychotherapy. Amer. J. Psychotherapy, XXI, 1, 4-17, 1967.
169. *Paul, G. L.:* Insight Versus Desensitization in Psychotherapy. Stanford: Stanford University Press, 1966.
170. *Paul, L.:* Crisis intervention. Ment. Hyg. 50: 141-145, 1966.
171. *Phillips, E. L., and Johnston, M. H. S.:* Theoretical and clinical aspects of short-term, parent-child psychotherapy. Psychiatry. 7, 267-275, 1954.
172. *Phillips, E. L., and Wiener, D. N.:* Short-term Psychotherapy and Structural Behavior Change. New York: McGraw-Hill, 1966.
173. *Pinkerton, S.:* Mental first aid. The Wall Street J., CLXX, 103, November 27, 1967.
174. Proceedings of the Brief Psychotherapy Council. Chicago: Institute for Psychoanalysis, 1942, 1944, 1946.
175. *Prugh, D. G., and Brody, B.:* Brief relationship therapy in the military setting. Amer. J. Orthopsychiat. 16, 707-721, 1946.
176. *Pumpian-Mindlin, E.:* Consideration in the selection of patients for short-term therapy. Amer. J. Psychother. 7, 641, 1953.
177. *Quaytman, W.:* The Esalen (Schutz) phenomenon. J. Contemporary Psychotherapy. 2, 1, Summer, 1969.
178. *Querido, A.:* Early diagnosis and treatment services. *In* Elements of a Community Health Program. New York: Milbank Memorial Fund, 1956.
179. *Rado, S.:* Relationship of short-term psychotherapy to developmental stages of maturation and stages of treatment behavior. *In* Wolberg, L. R. (Ed.): Short-term Psychotherapy. New York: Grune and Stratton, 1965.
180. *Rapoport, L.:* The state of crisis: some theoretical considerations. *In* Parad, H. J. (Ed.): Crisis Intervention. New York: Family Service Association, 1965.
181. *Regan, P. F.:* Brief psychotherapy of depression. Amer. J. Psychiat. 122: 28-32, 1965.
182. *Resnick, H. L. P.:* As reported anon, in "Home treatment of families referred to emergency service." Frontiers of Hospital Psychiatry, Vol. 6, No. 19, November, 1969.

183. *Richardson, T. A.:* Hypnotherapy in frigidity. Med. Times. May, 1964.
184. *Richardson, T. A.:* Hypnotherapy in frigidity and parafrigidity problems. J. Amer. Soc. Psychosomatic Dentistry and Med. 15, 3, July, 1968.
185. *Ripley, H., Wolf, S.,* and *Wolff, H.:* Treatment in a psychosomatic clinic. J.A.M.A. 138, 949, 1948.
186. *Ritchie, A.:* Multiple impact therapy: an experiment. *In* Parad, H. J. (Ed.): Crisis Intervention: Selected Readings. New York: Family Service Association of America, 1965.
187. *Rogers, C.:* The group comes of age. Psychol. Today. 3, 7, December, 1969.
188. *Rosenbaum, C. P.:* Events of early therapy and brief therapy. Arch. Gen. Psychiat. 10: 506-512, 1964.
189. *Rosenbaum, M., Friedlander, J.,* and *Kaplan, S. M.:* Evaluation of the results of psychotherapy. Psychosom. Med. 18, 113, 1956.
190. *Rosenthal, H. M.:* Drug therapy in breaks and breakdowns. Treatment Monographs on Analytic Psychotherapy. 2, Fall, 1968.
191. *Rosenthal, H. R.:* Emergency psychotherapy: a crucial need. Psychoanal. Rev. 52: 446, 1965.
192. *Ross, M.:* Holland's social psychiatry service. Mental Hospitals. 14: 375-376, July, 1963.
193. *Rothenberg, S.:* Brief psycho-dynamically oriented therapy. Psychosom. Med. 17, 455-457, 1955.
194. *Sabin, J.:* Case reports of the Massachusetts mental health center. VI—short-term therapy of impotence and anxiety. Psychiat. Opinion. 5, 1, January, 1968.
195. *Saul, L. J.:* On the value of one or two interviews. Psychoanalytic Quart. 20: 613-615, 1951.
196. *Saul, L. J.:* Brief therapy in a case of torticollis. Samiska. 7: 139-141, 1953.
197. *Schmideberg, M.:* Short-analytic therapy. Nerv. Child. 8: 281-290, 1950.
198. *Schoenberg, B.,* and *Carr, A. C.:* An investigation of criteria for brief psychotherapy of neurodermatitis. Psychosom. Med. 25: 253-263, 1963.
199. *Schutz, W.:* Joy. New York: Grove Press, 1967.
200. *Schwartz, D. A.,* and *Doran, S. M.:* The no-patient hour. *In* Wayne, G. J. and Koegler, R. R. (Eds.): Emergency Psychiatry and Brief Therapy. Boston: Little, Brown, 1966.
201. *Seitz, P. F. D.:* Dynamically oriented brief psychotherapy: psychocutaneous excoriation syndromes. Psychosom. Med. 15: 200, 1953.

202. *Semrad, E. V., Binstock, W. A.,* and *White, B.:* Brief psychotherapy. Amer. J. Psychother. 20: 576, 1966.

203. *Shlien, J. M., Mosak, H. H.,* and *Dreikiers, R.:* Effects of time limits: a comparison of two psychotherapies. J. Counsel. Psychol. 9, 31-34, 1962.

204. *Sifneos, P. E.:* A concept of "emotional crisis." Mental Hygiene. 144, 2, 169-176, 1960.

205. *Sifneos, P. E.:* Seven-year's experience with short-term dynamic psychotherapy. *In* 6th Int. Congress of Psychotherapy; Selected Lectures. New York: S. Karger, 1965.

206. *Sifneos, P. E.:* Crisis psychotherapy. *In* Current Psychiatric Therapies, Vol. VI. New York: Grune and Stratton, 1966.

207. *Sifneos, P. E.:* Two different kinds of psychotherapy of short duration. Amer. J. Psychiat. 123, 1069, 1967.

208. *Sifneos, P. E.:* Learning to solve emotional problems: a controlled study of short-term anxiety-provoking psychotherapy. *In* Porter, R. (Ed.): The Role of Learning In Psychotherapy. London: J & A Churchill, 1968.

209. *Small, L.:* Crisis therapy: theory and method. *In* Goldman, G. G. and Milman, D. S. (Eds.): Innovations in Psychotherapy. Charles C Thomas, in press.

210. *Small, L.:* The Psychodiagnostic Formulation. A Guide to Therapeutic Intention. In progress.

211. *Socarides, C. W.:* On the usefulness of extremely brief psychoanalytic contacts. Psychoanal. Rev. 41: 340-346, 1954.

212. *Speers, R. W.:* Brief psychotherapy with college women: technique and criteria for selection. Amer. J. Orthopsychiat. 32: 434-444, 1962.

213. *Stein, H., Murdaugh, J. M.,* and *MacLeod, J. A.:* As reported anon, in "Emotional reaction to illness responds to brief psychotherapy." Frontiers of Hospital Psychiatry, Vol. 4, No. 15, September, 1967.

214. *Stekel, W.:* Technique of Analytical Psychotherapy. London: Bodley Head, 1950.

215. *Stern, M. D.:* The recognition and management of psychiatric emergencies. Med. Clinics of North America. 41, 817-829, May, 1957.

216. *Stierlin, H.:* Short-term vs long-term psychotherapy in the light of a general theory of human relationships. British J. Med. Psychology. 41, 357, December, 1968.

217. *Stone, L.:* Psychoanalysis and brief psychotherapy. Psychoanal. Quart. 20: 215-236, 1951.

218. *Strachey, J.:* The nature of the therapeutic action of psychoanalysis. Int. J. Psychoanal. 15, 127-159, 1934. Reprinted: Int. J. Psychoanal. 50, 275-292, 1969.

219. *Straker, M.:* Brief psychotherapy: a technique for general hospital outpatient psychiatry. Comprehensive Psychiat. 7: 39, 1966.
220. *Strean, H. S.,* and *Blatt, A.:* Long or short term therapy: some selected issues. J. Contemporary Psychotherapy. 1, 2, 115-122, 1969.
221. *Strickler, M.,* and *Allgeyer, J.:* The crisis group: a new application of crisis theory. Social Work. 12, 3, July, 1967.
222. *Sullivan, P. L., Miller, C.,* and *Smelser, W.:* Factors in length of stay and progress in psychotherapy. J. Cons. Psychol. 22, 1, 1958.
223. *Tannenbaum, S. A.:* Three brief psychoanalyses. Amer. J. Urol. 15: 145-151, 1919.
224. *Terhune, W. B.:* Brief psychotherapy with executives in industry. Progr. Psychother. 5: 132-139, 1960.
225. *Tompkins, H. J.:* Short-term therapy of the neuroses. Psychosom, VI 5, September-October 1965.
226. *Ungerleider, T.:* The psychiatric emergency—analysis of six months experience of a university hospital's consultation service. Arch. Gen. Psychiat. 3, 593-601, 1960.
227. *Visher, J. S.:* Brief psychotherapy in a mental hygiene clinic. Amer. J. Psychother. 13: 331-342, 1959.
228. *Wagner, M. K.:* Parent therapists: an operant conditioning method. Mental Hygiene, 52, 3, July, 1968.
229. *Wagner, M. K.:* A case of public masturbation, treated by operant conditioning. J. Child Psychol. Psychiat. 9, 1968.
230. *Wahl, C. W.:* The psychosomatic emergency. *In* Wayne, G. J. and Koegler, R. R. (Eds.) : Emergency Psychiatry and Brief Therapy. Boston: Little, Brown, 1966.
231. *Waldfogel, S.,* and *Gardner, G. E.:* Intervention in crises as a method of primary prevention. *In* Caplan, G. (Ed.) : Prevention of Mental Disorders in Children. New York: Basic Books, 1961.
232. *Walker, R. G.,* and *Kelley, F. E.:* Short-term psychotherapy with hospitalized schizophrenic patients. Acta Psychiat. Scand. 35: 34-56, 1960.
233. *Wallerstein, R. S.:* Introduction to the panel on psychoanalysis and psychotherapy. The relationship of psychoanalysis to psychotherapy—current issues. Int. J. Psychoanal. 50, 117, 1969.
234. *Walter, B.:* Theme and Variation. New York: Knopf, 1946.
235. *Waltzer, H., Hankoff, L. D., Engelhardt, D. M.,* and *Kaufman, I. C.:* Emergency psychiatric treatment in a receiving hospital. Mental Hospitals, November, 1963.
236. *Wayne, G. J.:* How long?—an approach to reducing the duration of inpatient treatment. *In* Wayne, G. J. and Koegler, R. R.

(Eds.): Emergency Psychiatry and Brief Therapy. Boston: Little, Brown, 1966.

237. *Wayne, G. J.,* and *Koegler, R. R.:* Emergency Psychiatry and Brief Therapy. Boston: Little, Brown, 1966.

238. *Whitehorn, J. C.,* and *Betz, B. J.:* A study of psychotherapeutic relationships between physicians and schizophrenic patients. Amer. J. Psychiat. 111, 321-331, 1954.

239. *Whittington, H. C.:* Transference in brief psychotherapy: experience in a college psychiatric clinic. Psychiatric Quart. 26: 503-518, 1962.

240. *Wilson, A.,* and *Smith, F. J.:* Counterconditioning therapy using free association: a pilot study. J. Abnormal Psychol. 73, 5, October, 1968.

241. *Winnicott, D. W.:* As reported anon, in "First interview supplies key to resumption of normal maturation." Frontiers of Hospital Psychiatry, Vol. 6, No. 15, September, 1969.

242. *Wolberg, A.:* The contribution of social casework to short-term psychotherapy. *In* Wolberg, L. R. (Ed.): Short-term Psychotherapy. New York: Grune and Stratton, 1965.

243. *Wolberg, L. R.:* Short-term Psychotherapy. New York: Grune and Stratton, 1965.

244. *Wolberg, L. R.:* Hypnosis in short-term therapy. *In* Wolberg, L. R. (Ed.): Short-term Psychotherapy. New York: Grune and Stratton, 1965.

245. *Wolberg, L. R.:* The technique of short-term psychotherapy. *In* Wolberg, L. R. (Ed.): Short-term Psychotherapy. New York: Grune and Stratton, 1965.

246. *Wolberg, L. R.:* The Technique of Psychotherapy, 2nd Edition. New York: Grune and Stratton, 1967.

247. *Wolf, A.:* Short-term group psychotherapy. *In* Wolberg, L. R. (Ed.): Short-term Psychotherapy. New York: Grune and Stratton, 1965.

248. *Wolk, R. L.:* The kernel interview. J. Long Island Consul. Center 5, 1, 1967.

249. *Wolpe, J.,* and *Lazarus, A. A.:* Behavior Therapy Techniques. Oxford: Pergamon Press, 1966.

250. *Yamamoto, J., Roath, M.,* and *Litman, R.:* As reported anon, in "Hospitalization not the answer to suicidal urge." Frontiers of Hospital Psychiatry, Vol. 6, No. 17, October, 1969.

Index

Abreaction technique, 89
Acting-out patients, treatment of, 68-69
Action syndromes, 31-32
Activity, therapist, 89-92
Adolescents: brief psychotherapy and, 20, 22, 51, 115, 149; models for brief psychotherapy involving, 70-71
Adsett, C. A., 220, 235
Advice-giving technique, 92
Advocate Approach, 151
Aguilera, D. C., 244
Aims, *see* Goals
Albert, R., 240
Aldrich, C. K., 37-38, 39, 79, 235; on termination of treatment, 161
Alexander, F., 4, 23, 27, 28, 33, 74, 88, 123, 133, 138, 235; on management of transference, 154; on support technique, 150; on termination of treatment, 162
Allgeyer, Jean, 127, 214, 248
Ambivalence, 108
American Psychiatric Association, 13
Anxiety, treatment of, 95

Anxiety arousal or provocation technique, 92
Anxiety-management therapies: outcome studies, 204-205; prognosis, 190
Anxiety-provoking therapy, 190
Anxiety-suppression technique, 92, 190
"Arousal" theory, 34-35
Assertive training technique, 92-93
Augenbraun, B., 48, 224, 235
Authoritarianism, brief psychotherapy and, 48 8
Autonomous drive for health theory, 36
Availability of therapist (technique), 92-94
Avnet, H. H., 6, 91, 184, 235; on prognosis, 188; outcome study of brief psychotherapy under prepaid health insurance plan, 208-209
Avoidance technique, 35-36, 94

Background, of brief psychotherapy, 1-53
Baker, E., 133, 137, 138, 236; model of brief psychotherapy, 61; on manage-